Patriot Fires

American Political Thought

EDITED BY

Wilson Carey McWilliams and Lance Banning

Melinda Lawson

Patriot Fires

Forging a

New American Nationalism

in the

Civil War North

 University Press of Kansas

Published by the University Press of Kansas (Lawrence, Kansas 66049), which was organized by the Kansas Board of Regents and is operated and funded by Emporia State University, Fort Hays State University, Kansas State University, Pittsburg State University, the University of Kansas, and Wichita State University

Library of Congress Cataloging-in-Publication Data

Lawson, Melinda, 1954–

Patriot fires : forging a new American nationalism in the Civil War North / Melinda Lawson.

p. cm. — (American political thought)

Includes bibliographical references and index.

ISBN 0-7006-1207-6 (cloth : alk. paper)

1. United States —History —Civil War, 1861–1865 —Social aspects. 2. Nationalism —United States —History —19th century. 3. Patriotism —United States —History —19th century. 4. National characteristics, American. 5. United States — Politics and government —1861–1865. 6. Northeastern States —Social conditions —19th century. 7. Northeastern States —Politics and government —19th century. 8. Political culture —United States — History —19th century. 9. Political culture —Northeastern States — History —19th century. I. Title II. Series.

E468.9 .L39 2002

973.7'1— dc21   2002006392

British Library Cataloguing in Publication Data is available.

Printed in the United States of America

10 9 8 7 6 5 4 3 2 1

The paper used in this publication meets the minimum requirements of the American National Standard for Permanence of Paper for Printed Library Materials Z39.48-1984.

Anthem of Liberty, solemn and grand,

Wake in thy loftiness, sweep through the land!

Light in each breast anew patriot fires

Pledge the old flag again—flag of our sires.

—Song written for the Northwestern Soldiers' Fair,

October 1863

Rekindle throughout all the States such a patriotic

fire as will consume all who strike at the Union of

our fathers, and all who sympathize with treason

or palliate their guilt.

—*Philadelphia North American and United States*

Gazette, July 16, 1862

Contents

Illustrations

Preface

In 1861, the United States was a nation ill prepared for civil war. Attacked at Fort Sumter, the federal government fought back in the name of the Union, but it was a loosely jointed Union, lacking in political, economic, or social cohesion. As the North became immersed in Civil War—a war that would require the massive mobilization of human and financial resources—the need for widespread, protracted support and sacrifice presented the country with a novel challenge.

This book studies the Union's cultural and ideological response to that challenge. I began my research for this project in 1989 for a dissertation at Columbia University under Professor Eric Foner. Through an examination of the speeches, pamphlets, pageants, sermons, and assemblies that supported and gave meaning to the war effort, I set out to uncover both the process of constructing patriotism in the Civil War North and the struggle over the meaning of national loyalty.

As my research progressed, I began to confront some of the larger issues suggested by the North's experience. The Civil War is considered to have given birth to the modern American nation-state. Wartime exigencies gave rise to the centralization of business and industry and to an unprecedented expansion of national power. But the process of nation-building was cultural and ideological as well as economic and political. How did the wartime construction of patriotism redefine the relationship of the individual to the national state? What was the impact of this process on American nationalism?

The construction of Civil War patriotism was suggestive in a second sense. The United States was the modern world's first democracy. How would it mobilize its populace for war? What would be the impact on democracy? During the Civil War, the tension between the claims of democratic liberty and the demands of patriotic loyalty were manifest.

In 1991, as the United States went to war in the Persian Gulf, the issues I was studying assumed an unexpected immediacy. Questions I found Civil War nation-builders addressing were the same ones being discussed on op-ed pages and talk shows. What are the rules for being a patriot in a democracy at war? What is the role of self-sacrifice? Of self-interest? What are the limits of dissent? Did the founders leave any instructions for Americans to follow?

A decade later, as I prepare my book to go to press, I find the nation immersed in these same issues in the war against terrorism. As we search for a balance between liberty and security, democracy and power, the meaning of patriotism—and of our identity as a nation—continues to be contested.

In the years that it has taken me to write this book, I have incurred many debts. I am grateful for the aid and encouragement of fellow graduate students and friends Mark Higbee, Elizabeth Hovey, Michael Kushner, Leah Murphy, Manisha Sinha, Craig Thurtell, and Penny Von Eschen. I also wish to thank several individuals who read portions of the book and provided valuable comments: Jeanie Attie, Ben Barker-Benfield, Sven Beckert, Elizabeth Griffin, Anne Hildreth, Amy Lawson-Ring, Mark E. Neely, Jr., and Patricia West. Participants at both the Dissertation Workshop at Columbia University and the Civil War Era Center Workshop at Penn State read papers drawn from the manuscript and offered incisive critical commentary.

The staffs at the following libraries graciously guided me through their archival collections: Baker Library at Harvard University, Boston Public Library, the Historical Society of Pennsylvania, Houghton Library at Harvard University, the Huntington Library, New York Public Library, New York State Library, and the Union League of Philadelphia. The New York Historical Society, The Historical Society of Pennsylvania, New York State Library, and the Illinois State Library were instrumental in providing illustrations. The MacArthur Committee on Peace and International Security provided funding for the early stages of my research, while the Humanities Faculty Development Fund at Union College helped defray expenses in the later stages of the book. My colleagues at Union College offered support, encouragement, and a stimulating environment in which to finish this project. Thanks also to Jane Earley, who rescued the manuscript from a last-minute computer crisis.

I am very grateful to Fred Woodward, director of the University Press of Kansas, whose unfailing enthusiasm, patience, and good humor made the process of turning a manuscript into a book almost fun. Susan Schott, Melinda Wirkus, and Joan Torkildson provided gracious assistance in guiding the book through the publication process. My thanks also to the anonymous reader for the press and to Iver Bernstein for their astute comments and assistance in giving the book more coherence. Thanks to Fordham University Press for allowing me to use material previously published as "Let the Nation Be Your

Bank: Jay Cooke and the Civil War Bond Drives," in Paul A. Cimbala and Randall Miller, editors, *An Uncommon Time: The Civil War and the Northern Homefront* (New York: Fordham University Press, 2002).

Over the years I have been fortunate to study under a number of outstanding historians: G. J. Barker-Benfield, Joshua Freeman, Gerald Leonard, Warren Roberts, and Lawrence Wittner. Members of my defense committee offered numerous insightful suggestions for turning the dissertation into a book: my thanks to Elizabeth Blackmar, Richard Bushman, Andrew Delbanco, and Charles Tilly. Professor Blackmar had a special impact on me as a graduate student—in her seminars she demonstrated the ever-questioning spirit essential to the historian's art.

I am deeply indebted to my adviser, Eric Foner. As a teacher and as a scholar, Professor Foner tackles broad historical questions and transcends standard historical categories without sacrificing rigor and precision. I have been consistently inspired by his example. My work has benefited enormously from his critical acumen and keen editorial eye. Most of all, I am grateful for his unwavering support and his faith in this project.

My parents, Jack and Marti Lawson, taught me early on the importance of pursuing intellectual passions. I am deeply saddened by the fact that my mother did not live to see the publication of this book. I am grateful to my siblings, Amy Lawson-Ring, Holly Wahlers, James Lawson, and Tom Lawson, for their warm encouragement and support. Thanks also to Nick Miroff, who was willing to listen to me explain my work long before he understood what it meant; he is one of my most ardent supporters. Anna Miroff's entrance into the world extended this study but greatly enriched the life of its author. Her admonishment, "Mom, I told everyone you're an author, and you haven't even published one book" provided me with the stamina I needed as I approached the final stretch.

Lastly, I would like to thank my husband, Bruce Miroff. My debt to him is enormous: he has graciously assumed far more than his share of household duties and child care, offered intellectual support and companionship, and contributed his superb editorial skills. Over the years I have been sustained by his love, and by his faith in me and in this book.

Introduction

In December 1863, the *Atlantic Monthly* carried an unusual and striking narrative. The anonymous article told of the life and recent death of Philip Nolan, a young officer in the Western Division of the early-nineteenth-century army. An accomplice in the schemes of Aaron Burr, Nolan was convicted of playing a minor role in a treasonous plot. At his sentencing he was asked if he had anything to say that might suggest his abiding loyalty to the United States. But the young officer was tired of the service; he was tired of orders; he was tired of the trial which seemed to drag on and on. In a "fit of frenzy," Nolan cried out, "Damn the United States! I wish I may never hear of the United States again!"[1]

The presiding colonel was terribly shocked. He withdrew from the room and, returning minutes later "with a face like a sheet," granted Nolan's wish. He would never, by the authority of the court, hear the name of the United States again. Nolan spent the next fifty-five years on a series of naval vessels. The crews on those ships were forbidden to speak to him of the United States; the ships never docked at home until he was transferred to a new vessel. Deprived of a homeland, Nolan slowly and painfully learned the true worth of his country. He missed her more than his friends or family, more than art or music or love or nature. Without her, he was nothing.[2]

On his deathbed in 1863, Nolan was visited in his cabin by an officer on board the vessel. As the officer later reported, the cabin had been transformed into "a little shrine." The Stars and Stripes were draped around a picture of Washington. Over his bed Nolan had painted an eagle, with lightning "blazing from his beak" and his claw grasping the globe. At the foot of his bed was a dated map of the old territories. Turning to his visitor, Nolan smiled. "Here, you see, I have a country!"[3]

Thus Philip Nolan became "the man without a country," and Civil War Americans learned a new way to envision their relationship with the nation: only through a collective national identity could one realize "self and freedom." Or, as the Reverend Joseph Fransioli argued in an 1863 sermon that later became a widely circulated pamphlet, "Deny the duty of loving your country, and you deny your own feelings; you deny mankind itself."[4]

As some but not all readers later discovered, there was no Philip Nolan. The article was in reality a short story, written by Edward Everett Hale, Unitarian minister, member of the Boston Union Club, and executive board member of the New England Loyal Publication Society. Distressed by the war weariness and defeatism that had descended upon the North, Hale had written the story to teach his readers the importance of loyalty to country. He intended that the story be read as fact and was upset when, by an editorial oversight, his name appeared in the index. But fiction or nonfiction, Hale's message struck a chord for a people struggling to understand the place of the nation in their lives. Within a year of its original publication, reprinted editions of "The Man Without a Country" sold half a million copies, and the story quickly earned a reputation as a minor classic.[5]

Although Hale was the sole author of this patriotic parable, his story was only one part of a much larger effort to cultivate loyalty and national identity throughout the Civil War North. Americans were a young people when the war began. They held powerful loyalties to their towns, their states, and their regions; their loyalty to nation was as yet untested. The Civil War called on Northerners for unprecedented support and sacrifice. With no official public relations office to rally the people behind the war—equivalent, for example, to World War I's Committee on Public Information—the job of defining the war in patriotic terms fell largely to private individuals or associations, each with their own motives and methods.

Thus, throughout the war, across the North, Americans produced and distributed diverse and at times contradictory ideas about the meaning of patriotism and of the American nation. As the Union's self-elected apostles lectured in lyceums; as they sent pamphlets to thousands of regional churches, schools, and gentlemen's clubs; as they marketed war bonds and hosted soldiers' fairs—in all cases, they told Northerners that the American nation-state was a source not only of self-realization and freedom, but also of cultural identity, history and tradition, economic well-being, and egalitarian millennialism. They set forth definitions of loyalty ranging from a liberal understanding of patriotism as the exercise of self-interest, to a Christian understanding of patriotism as sacrifice; from an unquestioning obedience to the national state, to a vigilant patriotism, rooted in conscience and tolerant of dissent. Together, these ideas about the nation and loyalty laid the groundwork for the cultural and ideological American nation-state.

That a new national identity and patriotism had emerged from the war was recognized almost immediately. "Before the war," wrote Ralph Waldo Emerson in the fall of 1864, "our patriotism was a firework, a salute, a serenade, for holidays and summer evenings, but the reality was cotton thread and complaisance." Now, with "the deaths of thousands and the determination of millions of men and women," American patriotism was, at long last, "real." New England theologian Horace Bushnell concurred: "We had not bled enough," he argued, "to . . . make us a proper nation. . . . We have now a new and stupendous chapter of national history."[6]

Most historians of the Civil War agree: the war, they argue, fostered a metamorphosis in American national identity. A restless, individualistic, acquisitive people, divided in their loyalties, suspicious of federal power, and tentative in their commitment to the nation, learned through the crucible of war the importance of organized, united action, a patriotism of sacrifice, and national as opposed to state loyalties. By war's end, a "Union" of states had become a "nation" of Americans.[7]

Both Emerson and Bushnell found the root of that change in the blood sacrifice of the soldiers. Over six hundred thousand men died in the Civil War. Surely their deaths, as well as the suffering of nearly half a million wounded, provided an organic element that the nation had heretofore lacked—a cement to the unity of the nation. Indeed, the cataclysm of this war has so overwhelmed the American imagination that the accompanying transformation in national identity has not appeared to require systematic investigation.[8]

But blood sacrifice alone cannot explain this transformation. The forging of enduring bonds of patriotism and the construction of a cohesive national identity can take place only if a people's wartime experiences are interpreted—if they are given public meaning. Abraham Lincoln's Gettysburg Address is a prime example of the translation of sacrifice into political conviction. "From these honored dead," Lincoln told his audience, Americans must take "increased devotion" to their nation's "new birth of freedom" and the perpetuation of "government of the people, by the people, for the people."[9]

This book sets out to explore the process by which Americans like Edward Everett Hale, Abraham Lincoln, and numerous other "interpreters" of the Civil War helped shape the cultural and ideological American nation-state. Who were the men and women who stepped forward to offer their definition of American nationality and patriotism? What stake did they have in the outcome? What ideas about the nation-state and its role in the life of its citizens did they present? How was loyalty to that state defined? Given the rural nature of the country and the relatively primitive state of communication, how did these agents disseminate their notions? If, as Heinrich von Treitschke, the nineteenth-century German historian and political theorist wrote, "It is war which turns a people into a nation," how did this happen in the case of the American Civil War?[10]

My approach to these questions has been influenced by the works of Benedict Anderson and Eric Hobsbawm. Anderson defines a nation as an "imagined political community." It is imagined, he argues, because "the members of even the smallest nation will never know most of their fellow members"; it is a community because "regardless of the actual inequality and exploitation that may prevail in each, the nation is always conceived as a deep, horizontal comradeship." Nationalism for Anderson is a "cultural artifact" whose construction demands investigation. Hobsbawm holds that nationalism is chiefly a principle asserting that the national unit and political unit should be congruent, and that the duty of national citizens to their national polity "overrides all other public obligations, and in extreme cases (such as wars) all other obligations of whatever kind." In addition, Hobsbawm and Terence Ranger have introduced the notion of "invented traditions"—myths, beliefs, or customs that appear to be rooted in a nation's earliest history, but which are in fact invented to help establish social cohesion and political legitimacy.[11]

Anderson and Hobsbawm study Asian and European nationalisms, but their approach is well suited to the American case. The United States has generally been neglected by historians of nationalism, in part because the standard building blocks—language, ethnicity, religion, territory, or culture— do not appear to have been the basis of its foundation. Instead, American nationalism is said to be rooted in an idea.[12]

But ideology alone cannot explain the richness and power of American national identity and loyalty. Indeed, as we will see, the Civil War exposed the fragility of the American idea as a basis of national unity. Thus, agents of Civil War nation-building brought more European-style tools to their task, depicting the nation in more traditional, historical, and cultural terms. These depictions, along with a renewed commitment to a revitalized American ideology, helped forge a new American national identity and patriotism.

ANTEBELLUM AMERICAN NATIONALISM

The challenges that faced Civil War nation-builders stemmed from the peculiar nature of antebellum national identity and loyalty. On the eve of the war, American nationalism was a unique amalgam: a product of the young country's English heritage, its New World environment, and its short but eventful history.[13]

The American Revolution crystallized the idea of the new nation as a rejection of European monarchy, aristocracy, and class divisions. Here was a chance, as Thomas Paine so optimistically asserted, to "begin the world over again"—to build a new society unburdened by tradition or history. The social cement that bound Old World societies—"kinship, patriarchy, and patronage"—would dissolve; in its place would arise bonds of "love, respect, and consent." These bonds would form the basis of a new nation. With representative government as its cornerstone, that nation would be dedicated to the protection of individual freedom and equality.[14]

The form that antebellum American national identity and patriotism assumed reflected the ideas of the Revolution as well as its unintended consequences. Notions of rights and consent laid the groundwork for a patriotism historians have labeled "contractual." Americans believed that the national state was formed by a contract that guaranteed them a body of rights and bound their country to an ideal. If the state violated those rights, or failed in its continuing representation of that ideal, the contract could be broken. This notion stood in sharp contrast to an Old World loyalty to country, in which attachment to a monarch or land was preeminent.[15]

American suspicions of concentrated power contributed to the formation of a weak national government, one that left domestic governance almost entirely to the states. Ambivalence about the national state became a mainstay of antebellum political culture. Democrats fought to reduce the federal government's role in economic and internal development, and some Northern Whigs labeled the national government as controlled by Democrats an instrument of the "Slave Power." Though most Whigs and many Republicans hoped to expand federal power and resources to promote the Market Revolution, this vision had not, on the eve of the war, been realized: the federal government exercised little control over the states and had little visible presence in its citizens' lives. With the exception of national elections and trips to the post office, most Americans had almost no contact or interaction with their national government.[16]

A society held together by kinship, patriarchy, and patronage gave way to one defined by space, opportunity, shared democratic institutions, and ambition. It was not "love, respect, consent, virtue, and disinterested leadership" that formed the ties and ligaments of this society, but the pursuit of self-interest in a popular democracy. As historian Harry Watson writes, "The Jacksonians' celebration of the rights of the common man . . . encouraged the belief that individual self-improvement was the supreme goal of American society." Although this ethic of ambition and progress took root in the North and was in many ways at odds with Southern life, Northerners inscribed it in the national narrative and Southerners were left to lay claim to a peculiar regionalism.[17]

It is not that Americans, both North and South, did not entertain a genuine, even ardent affection for the Union. This affection had been nurtured over the years by formal instruction in American history, geography, and spelling; by the growth of private corporate institutions that encouraged Americans from different regions to unite in the pursuit of a common goal; and by the proliferation of holidays, symbols, and myths that celebrated the revolutionary ideals of liberty and equality. By the eve of the war, Americans described an attachment to Union that historians have labeled mystical or spiritual.[18]

At the core of such sentiment lay a long-standing tradition of nationalistic millennialism. Since the mid–seventeenth century, Americans had embraced the idea of an elect nation: God had chosen America, with its unique origins, commitment to liberty, and material prosperity, to usher in a New World, creating "greater perfection and happiness than mankind has yet seen." Over time, the blending of the secular and the sacred in religious and political tracts became commonplace.[19]

During the 1840s, a new version of the American mission emerged. Founded in 1839, "Young America" began as a literary movement dedicated to the creation of a distinctly American culture. Young America's adherents, among whom could be found such writers as Nathaniel Hawthorne and Herman Melville, sought to "carry republican progressiveness into Literature as well as into Life." In the late 1840s, a political version of the Young America movement developed. John L. O'Sullivan declared it the nation's "manifest destiny" to "overspread and possess the whole of the continent which Providence had given us for the development of the great experiment of liberty." Tapping into both land hunger and cultural aspirations, Manifest Destiny became one of the most popular slogans of the era. Americans by the hundreds of thousands streamed across the West, displacing the land's native inhabitants in the name of the Anglo-Saxon American commitment to liberty and individual opportunity. Invoking this expansionist enthusiasm, members of the Democratic Party formed a political faction also called "Young

America." These men sympathized with the liberal revolutions in Europe, called for aggressive westward expansion, and hoped to promote American commerce in the Pacific.[20]

Young America and Manifest Destiny were hopeful, even exuberant expressions of American nationalism. But just as they reflected the nation's democratic energies, they drew on a more troubling feature of political culture in the United States: racial exclusion. As political theorist Rogers M. Smith points out, though American national identity is rooted in traditions of liberal individualism and republican virtue, it is equally informed by notions of ascription. From the Revolution to the eve of the Civil War, American citizens—with the exception of a small abolitionist minority—imagined themselves as a uniquely democratic and exclusively white community.[21]

Thus mid-nineteenth-century Americans understood their nation in republican, liberal, providential, cultural, and ascriptive terms. This multifaceted nationalism carried the nation through both the War of 1812—before universal white male suffrage placed more importance on citizens' attitudes toward the state—and the Mexican War, a small-scale war that neither threatened the existence of the Union nor demanded much from the average citizen. For a time, it appeared that American nationalism might be sufficient to rally the North behind the war for the Union. Northerners responded to the attack on Fort Sumter with an eruption of enthusiastic patriotism.[22]

But popular enthusiasm soon subsided, and as the war progressed American national identity encountered a major challenge. Mobilization for warfare is a remarkable state-building activity. As the state expands, so too does the need to increase the loyalty and commitment of the people. In the North, a rapidly expanding national state taxed and drafted its people, suspended the writ of habeas corpus, and moved to abolish slavery. For the first time, the federal government confronted the need for widespread, protracted support and sacrifice from a voting citizenry—a citizenry whose loyalty, as the grim realities of war took their toll, had other suitors.[23]

By 1862, battlefield defeats and mounting casualties had begun to dampen Northern morale. Economic hardship fueled wartime discontent: an agricultural depression gripped the Mississippi Valley from 1861 to 1862. In the East, wartime inflation produced an upward redistribution of income and denied workers the prosperity Northern farmers and businessmen seemed to be enjoying. Sectional strife and class resentments combined with suspicion of centralized government and antiabolitionist sentiment to inform the widespread defeat of the Republican Party at the polls in the 1862 election. The Emancipation Proclamation served to crystallize antiwar sentiment. On January 14, 1863, Clement Vallandigham, avowed sectionalist, states'-rights advocate, and antiabolitionist, issued a resounding call for an end to the war. "If, today, we secure peace," he told a rapt House of Representatives, "and begin the work of reunion, we shall yet escape; if not, I see nothing before us but universal political and social revolution, anarchy, and bloodshed, compared with which the reign of terror in France was a merciful visitation."[24]

In July 1863, wartime tensions came to a head in New York City's three-day draft riot. The riot was triggered by the Conscription Act, which, with its clause allowing draftees to hire a substitute or pay three hundred dollars in lieu of service, underscored class differences in wartime sacrifice. Violent protest in lesser forms marked the draft's reception in Pennsylvania, New Hampshire, New York, Ohio, much of the Midwest, and in the border states. Northern defeatism peaked in the spring and summer of 1863, but maintained a hold on parts of the North through the summer of 1864. In August of that year, President Lincoln drafted his now famous memo predicting as "extremely probable" the November defeat of his administration.[25]

Lincoln, of course, was wrong. Aided by victories on the battlefront, his administration was reelected. And, in the face of all its difficulties, the North prevailed. It managed to recruit enough troops, raise enough money, generate enough support, and evoke enough sacrifice to win the war. Many aspects of antebellum American nationalism worked to this end. Ideas of liberty, individual rights, and equality, a belief in the North as a stronghold of individual opportunity, and the deep conviction that the Union was, as Abraham Lincoln said, "the last best hope of earth" fueled the efforts of Northerners who sacrificed for their country. As James McPherson argues, the "glorious cause" of Union, defined in patriotic and ideological terms, sustained many of the soldiers who fought and died for the Union.[26]

But if American notions of liberty and rights moved Union soldiers to fight the Northern battle, interpreted differently, these same ideas moved others to rail against that fight. As Southerners were eager to point out, Revolutionary ideas of rights and consent had universal application, at least among whites: if the people of the South no longer consented to rule by the Union, surely they were entitled to change their form of government. Having "severed the bonds of oppression once," argued a young Confederate recruit, "now [we] for the second time throw off the yoke and be freemen still." This logic was not confined to the Confederacy: many Northern opponents of the war agreed that the South's claim to sovereignty was legitimately rooted in the tenets of the American Revolution.[27]

Notions of rights and government by compact generated further problems for the North. Northerners did not all understand their contract with the government in precisely the same terms. For Democrats, it was the constitutional guarantees to the states that bound them to the nation; for abolitionists, the promise of equality and liberty contained within the Declaration of Independence. During the course of the war, factions in both parties made it clear that their loyalty to the Union was contingent upon its continued embodiment of the principles they held most dear. "I am for the Constitution first, at all hazards; for whatever can be saved of the Union next," proclaimed Peace Democrat Clement L. Vallandigham. "If I am to love my country," prominent abolitionist Wendell Phillips told a crowd in December 1861, "it must be loveable; if I am to honor it, it must be worthy of respect."[28]

The ethic of individual interest also posed problems for a nation at war. Americans looked to the Union for freedom and prosperity; that the nation would provide both and ask little in return was taken for granted. In this atmosphere, patriotism could ring astonishingly hollow: "I had hoped my boy was going to make a smart, intelligent business man and was not such a goose as to be seduced from duty by the declamations of buncombe speeches," Judge Mellon of Pittsburgh admonished his newly enlisted son. "It is only greenhorns who enlist. You can learn nothing in the army. . . . In time you will come to understand and believe that a man may be a patriot without risking his own life or sacrificing his health." The notion that loyalty to country entailed sacrifice did not always come easily to Americans.[29]

The ideals of Manifest Destiny and racialism were equally limited in their usefulness as Northern rallying cries. Both had historically been tenets of the Democratic—not the Whig or the Republican—Party, and had been profoundly divisive, not only between North and South, but within the North as well. Providentialism would prove more useful to Northern war advocates. But even providential nationalism had limits, limits it shared with notions of Manifest Destiny and racialism. To the extent these ideals helped Americans feel themselves a nation, it was the people—not the national state—who were considered to embody the virtues, ideology, and destiny of America.[30]

If American ideas could not be relied upon to sustain the level of sacrifice required for civil war, there was little in the American nationalist repertoire to replace them. True to its promise, the Revolution had dismantled the more traditional sources of social cohesion. American patriotism was not, as Alexis de Tocqueville testified in 1835, that "instinctive, disinterested, and undefinable feeling," rooted in customs and traditions, which characterized European nations—a feeling, Tocqueville continued, that was "capable of making the most prodigious efforts" to save the state in times of crisis. Moreover, the nation's youth determined little in the way of shared history: "We have not," New York lawyer George Templeton Strong wrote in 1854, "like England or France, centuries of achievements or calamities to look back on . . . we have no 'record' of Americanism." Celebrated by some and bemoaned by others, the absence of that record clearly worked to the detriment of a nation in the midst of a Civil War.[31]

So too did strong sectional, state, and local loyalties. It was, after all, because he was forced to "side . . . with or against my section or my country" that Robert E. Lee chose to fight for the Confederacy. His dilemma was writ large across the South; on a smaller scale, the tug of section, state, or even locality was felt throughout the North as well. For though a multitude of identities might coexist peaceably in ordinary times, this was no ordinary time. The war pitted the interests of towns, states, or regions against that of the Union. Northerners with family or business ties to the South were encouraged to overlook them; northeastern cities whose ports depended on the Southern market were to endure its loss; and midwestern farm towns whose residents relied on the Mississippi were to face its closing in silence; for though their region might suffer, the nation came first.[32]

Yet, as historian Robert Wiebe argues, in antebellum America the "soft glow of the Union" could not compete with "hard local attachments" to villages, towns, cities, and states. Most Americans remained concerned to protect the rights of the states against those of the Union and located their primary identities in Massachusetts and Virginia, not in "these United States." Thus in 1861, Democrat and historian George Bancroft entreated an assembly of men to stop thinking of themselves as citizens of Massachusetts, or New England, or even the North, and begin to think of themselves as Americans. Clearly, Northerners did not yet subscribe to Hobsbawm's nationalist principle: that, particularly in wartime, the duty of national members to their national polity overrides all other duties. Americans' primary loyalty lay with their states; their relationship to their national polity was characterized by distance and distrust.[33]

In fact, the relationship of individual Americans to the national state would become one of the dominant themes of Civil War nation-building. Americans had grappled with this relationship since the founding: though the

Constitution sought to establish the supremacy of the national government, in 1791 the states had ratified a Bill of Rights which protected the rights of individuals against the national state. Nearly eighty years later, in the wake of the war, the Fourteenth Amendment would elaborate a historic shift in that relationship—the national government would come to possess the power to prevent the states from abridging individual rights. The amendment fulfilled constitutionally a shift that the war itself set in motion. Painting the nation and the federal government which claimed to speak for it in a more positive light was an important task of Civil War nation-builders.

THE CIVIL WAR AND A TRANSCENDENT AMERICAN NATIONALISM

This book describes the construction of a new American nationalism—one that more closely resembled the European patriotism Tocqueville described as "instinctive," "disinterested," and "capable of making the most prodigious efforts" to save the state in times of crisis. Although most scholars today agree that patriotism is not, in reality, "instinctive," but is constructed, and although European nationalism in truth had a number of variants, Tocqueville's definition is nonetheless apt. It is this distinction—that between a national identity rooted in history and tradition and producing "an undefinable feeling" and a more rational, contractual national identity, rooted in an idea—which informs my argument. During the Civil War, a nationalism that met Tocqueville's criteria did emerge in the North and proved itself capable of saving the state in its time of crisis.

There were three dimensions to this transformation. First, Civil War nation-builders *cultivated a preeminent national loyalty* rooted in existing religious, political, and cultural values and identities: a loyalty that would prove more durable than that rooted in the subjective national idea. Second, Civil War nation-builders *redefined the relationship between the individual and the national state,* presenting the state as benefactor, not threat, to individual Americans. Third, these men and women *enveloped the nation-state in a mystical aura.* This last process consisted of several elements, including the sanctification of the nation-state through sacrifice, the establishment of the "roots" that Civil War nation-builders felt Americans lacked, and the creation of an ideology that proclaimed this aura.

This book will refer to the nationalism that resulted as "transcendent." I intend this term as a broad rubric, encompassing several meanings. First, the nationalism that was forged during the war incorporated and then transcended many of the characteristics of American political culture which had heretofore presented as obstacles to a preeminent national identity. State and local identities, individual self-interest, and partisan loyalties all became *vehicles* for the construction of a paramount sense of nationhood. Moreover, this new nationalism transcended both the abstract and increasingly divisive "idea" of America and the contractual basis of American patriotism. It acknowledged the ideological roots of American national identity, but located new underpinnings in history, tradition, and culture. Finally, transcendent nationalism assigned a spiritual meaning not just to the nation, but to the newly empowered nation-state.

The chapters that follow examine six agents of this transcendent nationalism. My focus in these chapters is on self-conscious nation-builders. The men and women whose work I explore initiated national "projects" designed to mobilize the population in support of particular visions of the nation-state or of patriotism. Chapter 1 examines the efforts of the women who organized the Sanitary Fairs—large-scale, sentimental exhibitions held across the North for the benefit of the Union's sick and wounded troops. Chapter 2 studies the contributions of the ambitious Philadelphia financier Jay Cooke, whose war bond drives supplied the Union with millions of much-needed capital. Chapter 3 explores the heated battles between Republicans and Democrats as each party strove to define the nation and patriotism in terms consistent with its party's values and commitments. Chapter 4 examines the urban "Union Leagues," upper-class gentlemen's clubs that brought together an embattled intellectual and professional elite with powerful business interests in a coalition designed to rally support for the national state. Chapter 5 examines the egalitarian visions of the abolitionist movement's foremost wartime lyceum orators, Wendell Phillips, Frederick Douglass, and Anna Dickinson.

Civil War ideas of patriotism and nation were diverse and at times contradictory. It was the extraordinary accomplishment of Abraham Lincoln to construct a composite national loyalty—one that drew from nearly all the elements in the Union's patriotic repertoire. Chapter 6 examines Lincoln's contribution to the construction of patriotism and nation, a contribution that went beyond recapitulation, as Lincoln skillfully infused his synthesis with a profound ideological significance. Ironically, though Lincoln set out to restore the notion of American identity as rooted in an idea, his death provided the nation with an organic element it had previously lacked.

There are limits to this study. No doubt numerous individual "agents" without conscious nation-building agendas also lent their voices to the construction of national identity. Union soldiers, for example, expressed their beliefs about the war and the nation they hoped it would create in their letters home. Those letters have been explored in James McPherson's *For Cause and Comrades* and will not be examined here. I have also chosen to limit this study to the home front. Though battlefield activities regularly informed wartime patriotism, the battles themselves, as well as the soldiers who fought them, are addressed chiefly as they figured in the nationalist projects of others.[34]

Finally, it is important to note that this is not a study of the "hearts and minds" of the people. As Eric Hobsbawm has pointed out, "Official ideologies of states and movements are not guides to what is in the minds of even the most loyal citizens and supporters." Though wherever possible I have noted reactions as described by newspapers or observers, I do not claim to speak for the masses. Rather, this is a study of how people who were in a position to speak and be heard defined national identity and patriotism.[35]

Together, the efforts of these agents constituted a process by which the Civil War produced a transcendent American nationalism. This process included ideology: struggling to control the direction and purpose of the war, Radical Republicans, Democrats, abolitionists, and Abraham Lincoln set forth conflicting definitions of the nation and patriotism, raising debates over the meaning of the American idea and how best to fulfill its promise to profound heights. But Civil War nation-builders also worked to effect a change in the very character of American national identity. If, as Tocqueville lamented, the individualism that pervaded an American's nationality hid "his descendants and separate[d] his contemporaries from him," leaving him "confine[d] . . . entirely within the solitude of his own heart," the Civil War began a process whereby Americans could lay claim to a more European-style national identity and patriotism. Depictions of the nation as an entity existing independent of the idea of America helped lay the groundwork for a loyalty to nation— as opposed to locality, state, or party—which could become the primary civic, and at times private, duty. These depictions shaped a more complex but ultimately more dependable national identity than the antebellum version. It was this new version of American national identity, incorporating—and sometimes diminishing—commitments to liberty and equality, that made room for the South and the rebellious portion of the North after the war.[36]

"A Union Love Feast"

The Sanitary Fairs,
Civil War Patriotism, and
National Identity

At dawn on the opening day of the Northwestern Soldiers' Fair, the streets of Chicago bustled with activity. Flags, banners, and bunting decorated the city's homes and storefronts; businesses, schools, and courts closed so that all might attend. Men and women dressed in holiday attire and draped their wagons with flags and banners. As the morning progressed, the crowd grew festive in anticipation of the fair's opening: bands played patriotic music, youths sang patriotic songs, and a brilliant sun attested to the glory of the day.[1]

At ten o'clock the procession for the fair—a large-scale exhibition and bazaar designed to raise money for the care of the Union's sick and wounded—began. With the Chicago police at its head, a six-mile-long stream of carriages and wagons, marching bands, and militia wound through the streets of downtown Chicago. Local, state, and national leaders joined the Northwest's lodges, benevolent associations, churches, firemen, Sunday schools, and "all manner of societies in all manner of insignia" in the procession. A four-horse car carried the female employees of a local manufacturing company: seated at sewing machines, they were engaged in making overcoats for the soldiers. Wagons filled with singing children were followed by those carrying butchers and horseshoers. Bringing up the rear, nearly one hundred carts driven by regional farmers overflowed with potatoes, onions, squash, beets, turnips, cabbages, apples, and cider; field-workers rode atop the produce. Tumultuous applause and cheers greeted the farmers as they

unloaded their gifts; a round of speeches and a thirty-four-gun salute officially opened the fair.[2]

Six large halls, each festooned with flags, bunting, evergreen, and eagles,
housed the fair. Fair workers, Chicago's most prominent women among them,
wore uniforms of red, white, and blue. Visitors moved from hall to hall. They
purchased clothing, toys, perfume, glassware, paintings, statues, pianos, and
cabinets. Historic and patriotic memorabilia, for viewing or for sale, abounded:
guns and rifles, blood-stained Union or Confederate flags, photos of various
national leaders, and a tobacco box belonging to the "immortal Puritan," John
Alden, who arrived aboard the *Mayflower* in 1620. By far the most prized
object the fair offered for sale was the original manuscript of the Emancipation Proclamation, donated by President Lincoln, who acknowledged that he
had "some desire to retain the paper," but felt it better to surrender it if it
might "contribute to the relief or comfort of the soldiers."[3]

A "Manufacturers Hall" housed contributions from the area's mechanics: reapers, mowers, and threshing machines joined "every conceivable style
of washing and wringing machines, . . . carriage springs, axles, . . . and buggy
spokes" in a grand exhibition of manufacturing talent and skill. Many of the
items donated were prizewinners from recent state fairs, prime specimens
of the nation's industrial progress.[4]

In the fair's National Art Gallery, hundreds of works of art were on view,
borrowed from the nation's elite or painted for the occasion by contemporary
artists. Works by European masters such as Rembrandt, Sassaferato, and
Tintoretto were arranged side by side with those by American artists; emphasis was placed on American landscapes and portraits of American leaders. Twenty-five thousand people visited the gallery. Deemed by many the
"finest Art Exhibit ever seen in the Western States," it remained open for
two weeks following the closing of the fair itself.[5]

In the dining hall fourteen tables served three hundred patrons, five times
a day; each table was presided over by a "matron" from the city's elite families, who supplied the linen and silver for that table. Younger women from
the same class, "accustomed to being served in their own homes," waited
the tables, serving donated oysters, turkey, duck, roast, chicken, puddings,
and pies to thousands of men and women from all walks of life.[6]

At night the crowds flocked to Chicago's Metropolitan Hall, where fair
organizers had arranged entertainment every evening of the fair. The walls of
the theater were decorated with flags; pillars were draped in red, white, and
blue; and banners scattered throughout proclaimed mottoes "expressive of faith

in God, devotion to the country, and undying interest in her brave defenders."
Busts of Lincoln and Daniel Webster flanked the stage, while an eagle grasping the Stars and Stripes in one claw and lightning in the other was suspended
above it. Two hundred children dressed in white and crowned with flowers
sang patriotic songs the first night of the fair; at the end they waved flags and
blew kisses. Tableaux—classical, historical, allegorical, and patriotic—were
welcomed by enthusiastic audiences: at the conclusion of one entitled "Goddess of Liberty," the Goddess herself burst into song, in hopes that her anthem
would "light in each breast anew patriot fires!" Following cheers and applause,
the company, "as if inspired anew with patriotic fervor," was joined by the
audience in a rousing rendition of "The Star Spangled Banner."[7]

The Northwestern Soldiers' Fair ran from October 27 to November 7,
1863. By all accounts it was a smashing success, both as a fund-raiser—it
netted nearly one hundred thousand dollars, well over the twenty-five thousand dollars for which its organizers had hoped—and as a patriotic spectacle.
Indeed, the opening day alone would "never be forgotten," proclaimed the
Chicago Tribune, "either in the City of Chicago or in the West. Memorable
it will remain both as history and as patriotism. Such a sight was never before seen in the West upon any occasion; and we doubt whether a more
magnificent spectacle was ever presented in the streets of the Empire City
itself." For a short while, the *Tribune* asserted, Chicago had been transformed, "converted . . . into a vast theater of wonders."[8]

The Northwestern Fair was only the first of a wave of "Sanitary Fairs"
that swept across the nation between the fall of 1863 and the summer of 1865.
Nearly every major city in the North was home to one, raising from $216.69
in Damariscotta, Maine, to over $1,000,000.00 in Manhattan. Like their
institutional affiliate, the Union-wide philanthropic United States Sanitary
Commission (USSC), fair organizers hoped the exhibitions would aid not just
the Union's ailing troops, but its ailing spirit as well: that it would unite organizers and visitors alike in a "grateful demonstration" of loyalty and devotion to the nation. Their intense patriotic nature led one observer to label
the St. Louis Fair a "Union Love Feast."[9]

But the significance of the Sanitary Fairs transcends overt patriotic spectacle. The fairs set forth distinctive ideas about the newly centralizing nation
and the meaning of patriotism. Though organizers recognized institutional and
ideological debts to the Sanitary Commission, their approach to cultivating
a national identity differed markedly from that of the discipline-minded commission. The popular success of the fairs owed much to those differences.

Fair organizers spread word of the fairs through the use of long-standing church and philanthropic networks, networks which the Sanitary Commission marshaled in its campaign to centralize relief efforts. But where commission leaders encouraged national identity by challenging persistent local and state identities, organizers of the Sanitary Fairs converted localism into a *vehicle* for the construction of a preeminent national identity. Inspired by a mid-nineteenth-century wave of civic boosterism, cities and towns across the country sought to outdo one another in what became a series of tributes to the nation.[10]

The task of constructing these tributes consumed entire communities. The collective labor of organizers and participants produced more than a fair: it created an arena for national civic action, a chance for American men, women, and children to "see themselves" acting as national citizens. Weeks or months of preparation for the event, as well as the experience of the fair itself, suggested that large and distant though it might at times seem, the nation-state could delineate a meaningful political community—"imagined" though that community might be.[11]

If the fairs' methods of cultivating a national mind-set among a diverse and conflicted people differed from that of the commission, so too did the content of their message. Against the trend toward legislative and institutional notions of benevolence and social change—a trend exemplified by the Sanitary Commission—they appealed to more traditional ideas about moral suasion, the superior virtue of women, and Christian sacrifice. Informed by these tenets, fair literature and rhetoric set forth an understanding of patriotism grounded not in notions of consent or contract, but in mid-nineteenth-century ideas of Christian charity. Participants portrayed their nation as holy, or Godlike, and themselves as Christ figures, nobly laying their offerings upon the altar of their country so that others might continue to live in freedom. Americans were charged with a "sacred duty" to sacrifice for this "Holy mission" on which the nation had embarked.[12]

Rarely, however, did the fairs discuss the exact nature of that "Holy mission." Indeed, the success of the fairs both as fund-raisers and as national patriotic spectacle lay in part in their ability to offer a meaning of the nation and patriotism that avoided discussions of the war itself or the direction that war was taking. Soldiers were suffering, in fact they were dying, and in light of their sacrifice, support for the war and a small contribution to the fair was the least that a civilian might do. Framing the war in these terms, the fairs removed from discussion such central issues as free labor, slavery, and emancipation. Focusing on the soldiers' suffering, they found a least common denominator around which all Americans could unite.

Finally, the fairs offered Americans the nation as a source of cultural identity. In an age intrigued by the promise of the nation-state, the fairs brought concrete, vivid images to an all too often abstract, theoretical discourse. If, as George Templeton Strong claimed, nineteenth-century Americans "crave[d] a history, instinctively," yet were "without the eras that belong to older nationalities," Sanitary Fairs offered Americans a sacred historical past: they gathered the nation's arms and trophies, its art and artifacts, and displayed them together under a single roof for the first time. Many of the fairs offered period rooms, unprecedented recreations of the lifestyles of colonial or Revolutionary America. Considered as the material culture of a nation, the fairs' scale, comprehensiveness, and accessibility were unprecedented.[13]

ROOTS OF THE SANITARY FAIRS

The Northwestern Soldiers' Fair was the first of the wartime Sanitary Fairs, but its organizers, Mary A. Livermore and Jane C. Hoge, did not act without precedent. Such large-scale bazaars had been used by English philanthropists since the early nineteenth century; Americans had imported the idea and adapted it to their own purposes. At times such fairs were held for political causes: abolitionist women in Rochester, New York, organized a large-scale antislavery fair in 1851.[14]

Like their predecessors, Livermore and Hoge—along with the organizers of Sanitary Fairs across the country—brought both philanthropic and political hopes to the fairs. They aimed to raise money to care for the soldiers; they also hoped to bring attention to and favor upon the United States Sanitary Commission, the organization that lent its name—if not always its wholehearted support—to the fairs. Finally, it was their intent that the fairs rally residents of sponsoring cities, as well as surrounding towns and villages, in support of the Union.[15]

The yearning for a clearer and more reliable national identity was prevalent among much of the Northern upper class and its intellectuals. It was in large part this motive that lay behind the creation of the United States Sanitary Commission. Founded in June of 1861, the USSC was, on the surface, a humanitarian organization; one of its historians has called it the "largest, most powerful, and most highly organized philanthropic activity that had ever been seen in America." Its members sought to bring modern health care methods to relief efforts: they introduced to the battlefield such medical developments as open-air hospitals and on-site ambulance services. Working through the Women's Central Relief Association (WCRA), they created a national network for the channeling of the products of soldiers' aid societies—bandages, clothing, and food—to a central clearinghouse, from which the supplies were distributed across the North.[16]

But, as Henry Bellows, the commission's president, acknowledged some years later, the USSC "was not from its inception a merely humanitarian or beneficent association. It necessarily took on that appearance. . . . But its projectors were men with strong political purpose . . . induced to take this means of giving expression to their solicitude for the national life." Along with fellow commission officers George Templeton Strong and Frederick Law Olmsted, Bellows saw in the war an opportunity to cultivate a new national political culture: to teach Americans the dangers of unharnessed philanthropy and the democratic individualism it represented, to introduce them to the virtues of order, discipline, and strong national institutions. In addition, they hoped that the war would lead to "a time of personal sacrifices," so that the Americans might be "gradually schooled to endure hardship."[17]

As part of their experiment in nationalism, commission leaders sought to provide Americans with the experience of participation in "the national life." Directing the energies of women and men across the country away from the philanthropic needs of their locales and toward those of the nation instead, the commission offered Northerners, who, with the exception of post offices and national elections, had markedly little contact with the federal government, a chance to act as national citizens. As Henry Bellows explained, Americans' national patriotism needed to be "reinvigorated" through a "fellowship in humanity." Bellows believed that "a great scheme of practical service, which united men and women, cities and villages, distant States and Territories, in one protracted, systematic, laborious, and costly work—a work of an impersonal character—animated by love for the national cause, the national soldier, and not merely by personal affection or solicitude for their own particular flesh and blood, would develop, purify, and strengthen the imperiled sentiment of nationality." If words like "systematic," "laborious," and "impersonal" rendered Bellows's national life a fairly grim prospect, it was the almost clinical sense of duty, discipline, and sacrifice they bespoke that lay at the heart of the commission's notion of the ideal American character. Indeed, the commission underscored its disdain of emotion in its *State-*

ment of Objects and Methods, announcing its refusal to appeal to constituents on humanitarian grounds, to "dwell . . . on the pathetic and touching incidents of its work." It urged members instead to address "the practical good sense of the community," pointing out that every life saved through the work of the commission translated into a monetary savings of at least one thousand dollars.[18]

The desire to create a form of national life that would offer Americans a chance to act as national citizens and thereby nourish their national identity was expressed by other Sanitary leaders, who managed to imbue the concept with a bit more warmth. Describing the parade of the Seventh Regiment through the streets of New York, Strong happily noted the "new thrill of national life . . . that stirred all the throng." Hoping for something less ephemeral than a parade, Olmsted suggested that the very purpose of the soldiers' aid societies was to keep "love of the Union alive through healthy, social contact, expression, and labor." As historian Jeanie Attie explains, the items these women's labor produced were far less important to the Sanitary elite than the "*process* of their participation in the national life," a process designed to teach Americans the importance of hard work and suffering, instill them with a sense of duty and rigor, and cultivate attachments to the nation.[19]

The Sanitary Commission met with relative success in its efforts to modernize health care for the Union's sick and wounded. But historians have suggested that, to the extent that the goal of the commission was the nationalization of local relief efforts and, by implication, of the loyalties of American citizens, the commission failed. Attie has pointed to the marked resistance that the commission encountered as it worked to centralize relief efforts: though commission leaders successfully encouraged many local aid societies to affiliate with the national association—almost fifteen hundred aid societies had affiliated by late 1862—they were mistaken in their assumption that the women of the North would be willing or able to provide the commission with a continuous stream of relief supplies. Complaining of financial hardship, familial obligations, preexisting benevolent commitments, and an "aversion to systemized action," women in aid societies organized with less regularity and donated fewer supplies than the commission had hoped. Commissioners were also wrong in thinking that these women would willingly transfer their benevolence—and with it, their loyalties—from a local to a national venue.[20]

As members of the commission, it was the hope of the women who organized the first Sanitary Fair that it might succeed where the commission's impersonal rhetoric and organizational centralization had failed—that it would not only "replenish the treasury of the Commission," but "develop a grateful demonstration of the loyalty of the Northwest to our beloved but struggling country." And in fact, the fairs did engage the attention, energies, and enthusiasm of Northerners much more successfully than did the commission. Though some disdained the sudden flurry of patriotic benevolence, with one contemptuous New Yorker labeling the fairs "the apotheosis of fashionable and cheap patriotism," most Northerners embraced the fairs. As commission official Alfred J. Bloor said, "One might as well try to dam up the Niagara as to stem the succession of 'Fairs' which, gathering their impulse at Chicago, will now sweep over the country, carrying city, town, and village in the current." Numerous Sanitary Fairs followed the first; though each had its own characteristics, most shared the broad outlines of that first fair in Chicago.[21]

THE SANITARY FAIR PHENOMENON

By October of 1863, when the Chicago fair debuted, nearly every city and town across the North had staged some sort of fund-raiser for its soldiers, including picnics, concerts, parties, festivals, and bazaars. But the Northwestern Soldiers' Fair was different. Its scale, its inclusiveness, and its financial goals were unprecedented; so was its Union-wide focus. Aiming expressly to stimulate a national patriotism among its participants and its visitors, it was a consciously political fair, with consciously national content.[22]

In the immediate wake of the Northwestern Fair, cities, towns, and villages across the North began planning their own "Sanitary Fairs," modeling them after the Chicago exhibition. We will never know precisely how many Sanitary Fairs were held: as William Y. Thompson, the fairs' first modern historian, explains, fairs were held "throughout the country," but in many cases left no official records, and were thus "'born to blush unseen' except in their immediate localities."[23]

Like the first Chicago fair, many of these fairs were the project of the upper-class women who resided in the hosting towns and villages. But if the Northwestern Soldiers' Fair was, in the words of Mary Livermore, "preeminently an enterprise of women," the gender division in the fairs that followed was more complex. In Manhattan, male commission leaders persuaded prominent upper-class women to undertake the project, then struggled with those same women for control of the fair's direction. Most fairs included men on their committees, though at times, as in the case of the Poughkeepsie fair,

all *officers* were women. Many fairs boasted not one but two sets of committees: for every female committee, there was a male counterpart. In some
instances—Philadelphia and Cincinnati, for example—the male committees
officially assumed responsibility. But in many cases—Philadelphia among
them—male leadership was illusory, as women defined the direction of the
fairs and performed the majority of the labor.[24]

Contemporary limits on female public behavior, particularly among the
upper-class Northerners who organized the fairs, further confuse the question of who controlled these exhibitions. Upper-class women did not speak
in public: even in Chicago, men delivered the opening addresses, publicly
defining the fair and its goals. Yet most fairs appear to have been informed
primarily by women, and even where men did control the fairs, they remained
largely true to the model defined by Hoge and Livermore.[25]

In planning and organizing the fairs, fair leaders relied heavily on a preexisting network of women in charitable societies. Beginning as early as the
1790s, American women had been forming charitable societies and auxiliaries
to male societies as a means of combating the poverty and vice they saw around
them. With the firing on Fort Sumter on April 12, 1861, these women's organizations—as well as female sewing circles and church auxiliaries across the
country—voluntarily reconfigured themselves as soldiers' aid societies. By
the end of April, a formal effort to organize and direct the charitable efforts
of these societies was under way: the Women's Central Relief Association
aimed to "consecrate scattered efforts by a large and formal organization."
Five months later, the WCRA was subsumed under the authority of the
United States Sanitary Commission.[26]

By the time Sanitary Fair planners found cause to employ this network,
it was both vast and well organized. Hundreds of aid societies had affiliated
with the commission; many of those that remained outside the commission's
purview were nonetheless accessible through older, informal philanthropic
networks. Most of these societies operated on a district system: members were
assigned to specific geographic areas, then canvassed for donations within
those areas. This system took aid society members into urban spaces and
remote rural districts. Fair organizers used these channels to disseminate
word of the fair, ask for cooperation and support, and distribute instructions.[27]

Though the fairs themselves varied from town to town, most drew heavily
on the Chicago model, adding or altering attractions as they saw fit. A grand
procession generally opened the fairs, with inaugural speakers including
mayors and governors, and, on at least two occasions, President Lincoln. Each

fair had a "great hall," or bazaar room, where from dozens to hundreds of tables displayed the donated items for sale. Offerings ranged from handmade blouses and candles to an eagle resting on a wreath woven from the hair of Lincoln, Seward, Chase, and twenty-two other prominent national leaders. Standard departments included arms and trophies rooms, "curiosity shops," industrial and agricultural rooms, and nightly entertainment. Many fairs also offered period rooms, post offices, and horticultural rooms.[28]

Most fairs were designed to appeal to Northerners from all walks of life: ticket prices varied from twenty-five cents for a single admission to five dollars for a "season" ticket. On average, admission for a single day cost fifty cents. Fairs ran from three days in Stamford, Connecticut, to four weeks in

One of the chief features of Philadelphia's Sanitary Fair was the floral department or horticultural room. This sketch illustrates the enormous scale and elegance of many of these fairs. Published in the fair newspaper during the run of the fair itself, its depiction of wounded soldiers (foreground) reinforced the fair's theme of sacrifice for the nation. (The Floral Department of the Great Central Fair, Philadelphia. *Our Daily Fare*. Courtesy New York State Library.)

St. Louis. As a rule the fairs were well attended: over 250,000 people purchased tickets to the Philadelphia fair alone. All told, it is likely that millions of Northerners worked on or attended Civil War Sanitary Fairs, which together raised almost $4.5 million, almost $3 million of which went to the central treasury of the Sanitary Commission.[29]

Commission leaders were less grateful than might have been expected. The fairs, they complained, gave the Northern public the impression that the commission was much better off financially than it in fact was. As a result, donations following a fair declined. Moreover, the fairs constituted a "diverting influence," tapping into energies commissioners wished reserved for the work of the commission itself. The commission pleaded with the women contributing to the fairs to make this a "pastime" only, presumably one that could be pursued in addition to—not instead of—the work they did for the commission.[30]

Such appeals met limited success. Work on the Sanitary Fairs offered women—and men as well—a host of benefits that work for the Sanitary Commission did not; one of the most important of these was the ability to work for the nation without setting aside local or state loyalties.

LOCALISM, CIVIC BOOSTERISM, AND THE SANITARY FAIRS

Within days of the opening of the Northwestern Soldiers' Fair in Chicago, a letter from "A Lady" appeared in the *Cincinnati Times,* urging the women of that city to undertake a similar endeavor. "We should not let Chicago, or any other place, be in advance of us in our efforts," the letter proclaimed. Indeed, the success of the Chicago Fair—both as fund-raiser and as patriotic spectacle—inspired a host of imitators, initially driven at least in part by a competitive civic boosterism. "Sanitary Fair," as William Thompson testifies, became "a patriotic byword," and few major cities were willing to be outdone by their neighbors. "The city of Philadelphia has never been behind any of her sisters in devotion to the soldier," proclaimed the resolution announcing that city's plans for a Sanitary Fair. For Brooklyn, an ongoing competition with Manhattan provided incentive. "Overshadowed by her mighty neighbor" for years, Brooklyn felt "put upon her mettle to show a proud record." And in the center of the Brooklyn Fair's Mechanics Hall a large broom sent by the managers of the Cincinnati fair bore the words "We have swept up 240,000; Brooklyn, beat this if you can"; an addendum read, "Brooklyn sees the 240,000, and goes $150,000 better."[31]

"'Strong' Teamster—Bully for both of you! But look out, New York, no crowding! That Brooklyn feller's got as big a sack as your'n and it's fuller up top!"

Hosting cities of the Sanitary Fairs sought to outdo one another in their devotion to the nation. This cartoon depicts the rivalry between Manhattan and Brooklyn, as representatives from these fairs rush to place their earnings in the U.S. Sanitary Commission's Treasury. (Cartoon from *Drum Beat*, the Brooklyn and Long Island Sanitary Fair newspaper. Courtesy New York State Library.)

Such competition clearly worked to motivate fair organizers and participants: inspired to protect or enhance the reputations of their cities, states, or regions, they worked to construct grander and more lucrative tributes to the nation. Though no doubt the highest honor accorded a fair was to exceed all others in strictly financial terms, fair organizers also competed for alternative honors: Philadelphia and New York each laid claim to the creation of the largest and most complete art gallery, offering, as the editor of the *Metropolitan Fair* asserted, an unprecedented opportunity for "studying American art in its present condition, in its advance upon its past efforts, and in its relation to modern European work." Attempts were made to "establish an order of precedence in beauty" among the various patriotic exhibitions, and smaller cities such as Albany and Poughkeepsie, whose fairs were unable to compete with the larger exhibitions, pointed proudly to their respective historic roles as "the birthplace of our Union" and "the seat of colonial wisdom during the revolutionary struggle."[32]

If competition between cities informed both the pervasiveness and the extravagance of these celebrations of nation, within each individual fair more particular identities were both respected and rewarded. Most fairs encouraged participants to organize, report, and display by society or locale. Records of contributions were kept and often published, and proud society members or county residents managed bazaar tables overflowing with national patriotic offerings, clearly labeled by local affiliation. Though counties predominated, groups represented by booths at the fair in Albany included Gypsies, Shakers, and Yankees, while the second Chicago Fair boasted Universalist, Unitarian, and Roman Catholic tables.[33]

Unlike the commission elite, then, which appeared to view existing local, state, regional, religious, and ethnic identities as obstacles to the construction of a preeminent national identity, Sanitary Fair organizers viewed these same identities as mechanisms for that construction. Organizers called on Americans, not as atomized individuals but as legitimate members of preexisting groups, to join in a tribute to the nation. Though commission leaders worried that this recognition of local identities constituted their celebration, rivalries between and within fairs focused to a significant degree on great shows of commitment to the *nation*. Fair planners aimed to construct the most elaborate national exhibition or contribute the most money to a national cause; hosting cities vied to place themselves securely within national history. Where such grand hopes were not viable, planners aimed, as a reviewer of a fair concert held in Jefferson County, Missouri, explained, to show their efforts "worthy of the name the good people of that county have ever sustained for liberality and patriotism." As fair mania swept the North, America's large cities and small villages alike strove to establish their place within and commitment to the nation.[34]

THE SANITARY FAIRS AND THE NATIONAL LIFE

The construction of these tributes to nation was a monumental task, one that required the efforts and energies of thousands of individuals and organizations. Northerners were usually eager to cooperate. Though commission leaders objected, participants paid little heed. For the fairs offered a much more appealing version of the "national life" than that which the commissioners themselves proposed. Unlike the commissioners' projects, they accommodated local or regional identities. Moreover, they provided a welcome break from the grim realities of life on the home front: they were exciting, dramatic, and immensely rewarding. Through the months of preparations that preceded the fairs and through the experience of the fairs themselves, they provided an arena for meaningful national civic action, thereby helping to redefine the relationship between the individual and the American nation-state.[35]

When plans for a fair were initiated in any given town, women and men eagerly rushed to participate. Months before the actual event, committees were formed, meetings were arranged, rallies were held. "Come one, come all" cried a Missouri paper advertising a grand gathering of fair committees; and they did—merchants, lawyers, artisans, homemakers, newspapermen, and farmers crowded into the halls for the "rousing" meetings that laid the groundwork for the cities' fairs.[36]

Participation in the fairs' planning took numerous forms. Residents of the host city and of surrounding towns and villages planned and rehearsed for concerts, soirees, poetry readings, and tableaux to be held as benefits weeks before the fairs' grand openings.[37] Fair workers canvassed cities, towns, and villages for donations. Women weary of sewing shirts and socks for the commission designed "useful and ornamental articles in wax, leather, shell, bead, hair seed and cone work." Men "clubbed together" to work after hours to build threshing machines, corn planters, pumps, and drills for the fair. Artists painted and sculpted for the fair; the wealthy lent the valuable works of art already in their possession. In Philadelphia, a Committee on Labor, Income, and Revenue asked every Philadelphian to donate one day's wages or profits to the fair. A surprise response came from six "ladies of the night" who, in a broadside announcing their participation in this "Christian duty to humanity," offered to donate a day's income and called on the men of the city to "come forward and spend a day's labor for suffering humanity, and show themselves to be men, not deadheads, as the whole receipts will be devoted to the worthy purpose . . . providing there is anything left after treating the party."[38]

On opening day of the fair, thousands of the men, women, and children who had worked to make the fair a reality flocked to the site to celebrate. The inaugural procession offered a continuation of the opportunity to participate in this tribute to country: marching, riding, or watching the parade, fair-goers partook in the palpable energy and excitement of the day. Speeches by prominent officials—Lincoln himself spoke at the inaugural of the Baltimore fair—were followed by patriotic performances. In Philadelphia thousands of onlookers joined the official fair chorus in singing "The Star Spangled Banner." Many fairs staged "a farmers' procession" similar to that which marked Chicago's fair inaugural. A dramatic and moving ritual, this procession enabled farmers whose age or health forbade military service to act out their role as vital national citizens.[39]

Inside the fair buildings, traditional country fair activities—country dances, quilting bees, apple-paring contests—served the cause of the nation, as did an elaborate sword contest wherein voters chose their favorite general. Period kitchens also invited viewer participation: entering the world of their ancestors, visitors sat side by side and ate old-fashioned food in an atmosphere rich with their shared national history.[40]

Not all Northerners embraced the fairs. Personal rivalries within and between committees at times undermined fair solidarity; the lotteries held at some fairs sparked heated debate over morality; and contributions were not always forthcoming. Moreover, though fair organizers in most towns set out to attract Northerners from all walks of life—the Metropolitan fair journal "Rough Hints" proposed that the fair should be "universal; enlisting all sympathies from the highest to the lowest—democratic, without being vulgar; elegant, without being exclusive; fashionable, without being frivolous, popular, without being mediocre . . . with something for everybody to do, something for everybody to buy"—those that violated the fairs' genteel protocol were harshly dealt with. Metropolitan fair managers placed placards around the necks of three women found picking pockets and marched them throughout the fair to the tune of "The Rogues' March."[41]

Still, most Northerners appeared eager to leave their normal occupations to engage in this meaningful and fulfilling work for the soldiers and the nation. Those who did not help plan the fair rushed to attend it: in many cases crowds gathered hours before the fairs opened, packed the halls of the fairs day and night, and clamored for closing dates to be postponed. As J. Matthew Gallman notes in his history of the Philadelphia fair, according to contemporary diaries in that region, "nearly every Philadelphian was aware of the fair, . . . most visited it, and . . . almost all were strongly enthusiastic."[42]

As these thousands—and at times tens of thousands—of Americans gathered together in the name of the soldiers and the nation for which they fought, the fair that had brought them together became, as Sarah Edwards Henshaw noted of the Chicago fair, not merely an "exhibition of taste," but "an affirmation of principle." As the *Chicago Tribune* reported, the people "seemed to overflow with loyalty, and could not contain themselves. For a long time they had been silent . . . but there, in all those thousands of men, they saw themselves multiplied . . . and felt that their hour of triumphant speech had finally come."[43]

Offering Northerners the opportunity to act out their roles as national citizens in an important and rewarding manner, the Sanitary Fairs suggested that the nation could serve as a source of meaningful political community. If, as historian Benedict Anderson argues, that community was by definition an "imagined community"—one in which members could never know one another, but would live instead in "the image of their communion"—the Sanitary Fairs provided a local forum for that communion. They offered in essence a microcosm of the nation: a temporary arena within which scattered Americans could experience a sense of shared national life.[44]

As contemporary descriptions of fair events suggest, that shared life could be fun—even exhilarating. But for fair organizers, its meaning ran deeper. Faced with the needs of hundreds of thousands of sick and wounded Union soldiers, the fairs carried a message about the meaning of nationality that contemporaries fervently believed Americans needed to hear: that at its heart, membership in a nation meant a willingness to sacrifice.

SACRIFICE AND BENEVOLENCE IN ANTEBELLUM AMERICA

Sanitary Commission leaders were among the most vocal proponents of a new sense of sacrificial duty to nation. Distressed by both the impact of prosperity on the American character and the tentative and self-interested nature of American loyalty, they called for the cultivation of a national loyalty that placed nation above other civic—and at times personal—obligations. Sanitary leaders were not alone in their concerns: as the patriotic outbursts that followed the attack on Fort Sumter faded, complaints about the weakness of American loyalty appeared in articles, sermons, and speeches. Many focused on Americans' unwillingness to accept material sacrifice: "Making haste to be rich has been the universal mania of our people," exclaimed a New York orator in 1861, "when the warning voice of patriotism came down from Pisgah Heights of thought into the busy haunts of commerce, . . . we have dubbed it an idiotic ebullition of fanaticism." Republicanism, the chief civic tradition which might in the past have tempered such reluctance to subordinate self to polity, was on the wane, and a willingness to sacrifice for the public good was by 1860 simply not a prominent element of popular political culture. Americans looked to the Union to provide freedom and the conditions for economic advantage; they were willing to give little in return.[45]

But with the war came hopes that all this might change. As Henry Bellows explained to a friend, "Our people . . . are not really suffering anything as other peoples know suffering. That they may be gradually schooled to endure hardship like soldiers is my most solicitous and constant prayer." George Templeton Strong echoed Bellows's hopes, adding, "Without the shedding of blood there is no remission of sins."[46]

As Strong's religious metaphor suggests, the problem was not that Americans were unfamiliar with the notions of suffering and sacrifice, for these concepts underlay most Americans' understanding of Christianity. Indeed, as Lewis P. Saum has shown, popular antebellum references to Providence suggest less a sense of national destiny and hope—a meaning suggested by contemporary leaders and accepted as widespread by historians—than a resignation to suffering. Though evangelical religion and revivalism held out the possibility of agency and the hope of redemption, they also stressed submission and sacrifice. Still, to the extent Americans accepted suffering or volunteered sacrifice, for the most part it was in a religious—not a civic—context.[47]

The closest thing to a civic culture of sacrifice that did exist in pre–Civil War America was to be found in the social reform movement, and, most significantly for our purposes, in the female branch of that movement. Grounded in an ideology of female benevolence and Christian charity, the tenets of the female reform movement underlay the Sanitary Fair movement as well. Women, according to this ideology, were characterized by "humility, modesty, submission, [and] piety"; they were thus "God's appointed agent[s] of morality." They were under a special obligation to ease the hardships of others and help achieve social redemption; personal sacrifice was a routine element of such work.[48]

Most Americans viewed these traits as distinctly feminine; indeed, they lay at the heart of the culture of separate spheres. But in light of women's special virtues, it was their obligation to promote their superior morality. Such notions of women as uniquely virtuous provided an understanding for the role and value of women in a republican polity. But like religious ideas of sacrifice and suffering, the female ideology of Christian charity and benevolent obligation did not extend to male conceptions of citizenship or to antebellum understandings of national patriotism.[49]

By the immediate prewar period, a shift was under way in Northern attitudes toward benevolence. A new approach drew less on sentiment, moral suasion, and a belief in the superiority of women, turning instead to scientific principle, legislative reform, and institution building. The commission exemplified this trend: though in the end it did not abide by its stated eschewal of sentiment, at times indulging in descriptions of the "pathetic and touching incidents" of its work, it emphasized efficiency, discipline, and order.[50]

But if the Sanitary Commission was a part of this trend, the Sanitary Fairs were not. Many of the women who organized the Sanitary Fairs represented an "older generation of benevolent workers," committed still to the principles of moral suasion and the moral superiority of women.[51] They used sentiment freely, and, in a war whose casualties would reach hundreds of thousands in the North alone, such appeals were not without impact. Indeed, the Sanitary Fair's presentation of the suffering and deaths of Union soldiers helped to form a bridge between a female culture of Christian sacrifice and benevolence and American notions of patriotism.

SUFFERING SOLDIERS AND BENEVOLENT WOMEN: THE SANITARY FAIRS AND THE NOTION OF SACRIFICE

Northerners were no doubt all too familiar with the notion that Union soldiers were suffering, if only on a personal level: most had lost someone they knew, whether family, friend, or neighbor. The Sanitary Fairs cast that suffering in broad civic, yet markedly sentimental relief. Circulars entreating donations of time, goods, or money appealed overtly to the emotions of participants and visitors: "Let each one open his heart and his storehouses to this appeal" urged a Northern Ohio circular, "and we should have a mighty flood of harvest wealth that would sweep in a resistless tide down to the very borders of the far-off land where our soldiers are watching, waiting, suffering for us, fighting our battles and standing between these Northern homes of plenty and war's destruction." Fair literature appealed to Northerners to remember the "brave, noble, scar-worn soldiers," "the unfainting energies and heroism of our noble brothers in the tented field," and "our noble heroes, white and black, who are offering their breasts as a rampart to check the steps of those who would destroy our constitution, and trample the banner of beauty and glory in the dust."[52]

The theme of the soldiers' sacrifices and suffering continued within the fairs themselves. A walk through the bazaar alone, noted one observer of the

Great Western Fair, was "the most eloquent appeal ever made to the human heart." Bloodstained flags and flowers were frequently set out for display or sale: one fair offered a gilded frame enclosing a blood-encrusted leaf from Gettysburg.[53]

Most fairs held soldiers' dinners, elaborate events to which soldiers housed at nearby camps, hospitals, or convalescent homes were invited. As Mary Livermore later remembered, the dinner at the Northwestern Fair greeted "a bronzed, scarred, emaciated, halt, blind, deaf, crippled, skeleton corps, some without arms, some without legs, some swinging painfully on crutches, some leaning feebly on those stronger than themselves, all bearing evidence in their persons that they had suffered for their country." This powerful sight brought most in the hall to tears, and emotions ran high throughout the patriotic songs, cheers, and battle cries that punctuated the meal.[54]

This focus on the soldiers and their suffering served several purposes. First, it provided a rallying point for a North still divided over such issues as civil liberties, the fate of slavery, and the meaning of freedom. Because the goal of the fairs was to raise money for the soldiers, and because the fairs placed sentiment at the center of their appeals, they managed to engage Northerners in a statement of support for both the war and the nation, re-moving controversial questions from discussion. In fact, the rhetoric and symbols that helped give meaning to the Sanitary Fairs almost never made reference to these issues at all. Focusing on the soldiers' needs, the Sanitary Fairs defined the war in terms to which all Americans could relate, inde-pendent of their political or ideological leanings. Speaking at the opening ceremonies of the Philadelphia Fair, Pennsylvania governor Andrew Curtin called on Northerners to set aside their differences and unite for the soldiers:

> My friends, if there is one man more than another whom you can admit to your sincere reverence and respect, it is the private soldier. He is the true, noble man of this land. He falls with unrecorded name; he serves in the army for no small pay; no pageant marks his funeral . . . let us forget all differences in opinion in politics, in sects and in religion, and declare, with one voice, for our bleeding and distracted country.[55]

The centrality of the soldiers served a second purpose: focusing on the soldiers and their suffering, removing political and ideological issues from discussion, the fairs set forth the idea that patriotism was defined by sacri-fice for nation in its time of war, independent of one's ideological or political commitments. In the course of paying tribute to the Union's wounded and fallen soldiers, Sanitary Fair literature urged patriotic civilians to view their own contributions in comparison. In Maryland, Governor Augustus W. Bradford addressed the Baltimore fair's inaugural, urging those who had assumed they had "fully discharged all their public obligations when they have promptly paid all their Government taxes" to "think of the sacrifices of the soldiers . . . who have given so much more." Measuring patriotism in terms of comparative sacrifice, the fairs called on Americans to give of themselves for the war effort—to sacrifice for the good of their nation.[56]

For those Americans who needed guidance in their roles as sacrificing civilian patriots, the fairs set forth the women who labored on the fairs as models. Though the role of men varied from fair to fair, organizers, participants, and observers alike acknowledged that the impulse, labor, and message of the Sanitary Fairs were rooted in a distinctly female culture of Christian charity. The fairs were the "gentle voice of woman's charity"; a "gigantic work . . . ordained by sovereign female will." Like the soldiers, the women of the fairs could be looked to for inspiration, for a lesson in patriotism defined by sacrifice. They were, wrote the historian of one fair, "leading the people, by the sweet spell of [their] own example, in the work of patriotism and the ministrations of Christian love."[57]

The sacrifices made by the women who planned and worked at the fairs were widely noted. "Many thousands of women labored with that patient toil women only know how to endure," commented one observer, "a heart-offering involving no ordinary effort and self-sacrifice." The labors of the fairs sent women to their sickbeds and even to their deaths. "Indeed," remarked one observer of the New York Fair, "in the month of March, each day saw some lady drop from her place, until it was remarked that the fair had become a monster living upon the human flesh." Those women who did not actually plan the fairs made sacrifices of different sorts. Tales abounded of female servants donating a week's pay and of poor widows laying their "last mite" upon the altar of their country.[58]

But perhaps the most colorful example of the use of the fairs' women as models of Christian charity was the description of the scene in the dining room of the Great Western Fair, where upper-class women waited tables as their service to God and country—a sacrifice worthy, according to one observer, of Christ himself:

> It was quite natural that there should be shrinking from the public performance of such menial labor, . . . especially when it was known that the tables

were to be opened freely . . . to all comers, and that the city would be filled with strangers. . . . It reminded one of the scene when Christ washed the disciples' feet—an act by which he intended to teach that true greatness shows itself by stooping to the necessities of the lowest, and that no work, however humble, degrades the loftiest, when performed for a noble purpose and in the spirit of Christian love. . . . Thousands learned there and in the bazaar a lesson in patriotism, in self-denial, and Christian benevolence which they will never forget. . . . Thousands felt that it was a noble exemplification of real patriotism and of the spirit of the gospel.[59]

Framed in these terms, the sacrifice of the women of the fair, as well as that of the soldiers, served a third purpose. Comparisons to Christ and a rhetoric of suffering for country in the spirit of the gospel worked to sanctify the war and bathe the nation-state in a religious glow.

Thus, through the medium of the Sanitary Fairs, female notions of Christian charity and sacrifice formed the roots of a civic definition of American patriotism that transcended antebellum precepts of contract and consent. Inspired by both the example of the soldiers and that of the country's women, Northerners were called on to sacrifice as an indication of their patriotic devotion. "We give our wealth for those who give their health for us," proclaimed a commemorative medal at the Philadelphia fair, while a banner at the Cincinnati fair read, "Let Your Patriotism Reach Your Pocket." Even President Lincoln commented on the benevolence the fairs had inspired, recognizing it as a measurement of the people's patriotism. These "voluntary contributions," he noted, "given freely, zealously, and earnestly, on top of all the disturbances of business, the taxation and burdens that the war has imposed upon us," gave "proof that the national resources are not at all exhausted; that the national spirit of patriotism is even stronger than at the commencement of the rebellion." Or, as the editor of the history of the Great Central Fair observed, "in this war, patriotism and holy charity are twin sisters."[60]

THE SANITARY FAIRS AND THE CELEBRATION OF THE NATION

Though Americans brought local identities and pride to the fairs; though they were moved by notions of morality and Christian sacrifice, in the end the focus of the fairs was the nation. At the behest of the women and men who organized the fairs, cities and towns, farmers and merchants, adults and children competed to create the most spectacular and lucrative tribute to their country. The result was a celebration of nation unlike anything nineteenth-century Americans had ever seen: one that offered Americans rich, vivid, concrete images of their nation, its accomplishments, and its history.

Such images were invaluable to the Union war effort. For this was an age that celebrated the nation-state, which, as the German philosopher Georg Wilhelm Friedrich Hegel suggested, saw the nation as the culmination of all of civilization, the logical and inevitable end for which all of history had been but a prelude. In speeches and in pamphlets, Northern intellectuals pointed to this inevitability, or called on Americans to look to the examples of the Old World, of England, or of France, and to draw from those examples lessons in how a patriotic people behave in times of war.

But Americans did not have the history, customs, or traditions of the Old World; they did not have the foundations of the sort of loyalty to nation for which the pamphlets called. If for some this absence served as the hallmark of American democracy, for others, it represented a void. Again it is George T. Strong who expressed this void in his fellow Americans' lives: "We are so young a people," he wrote in his diary in 1854, "that we feel the want of nationality, and delight in whatever asserts our 'national' existence. We have not, like England or France, centuries of achievements or calamities to look back on; we have no 'record' of Americanism and we feel its want." Intellectual treatises on the logic of the nation-state would not produce that record.[61]

Nor could the museums, historical societies, libraries, and art galleries that were scattered across the North. For up until the late nineteenth century, few institutions in the United States combined high culture or serious history with any sort of popular educational purpose. Indeed, early attempts at the democratization of knowledge through public access to museums had given way to the "vulgarization" of those institutions: in the late eighteenth and early nineteenth centuries, both Charles Peale and John Pintard saw their efforts at creating places of "scholarship and rational instruction" give way to "mere places of popular amusement" featuring rare birds and tattooed heads; ultimately, P. T. Barnum purchased both their collections for his amusement center. Though historical societies and college museums maintained collections of records and artifacts, most had no public function, serving largely as repositories or for the educational benefit of private students.[62]

Art fared little better. Though in the forty years preceding the Civil War American artists had managed to establish a presence in the larger cities—founding professional associations, running artists' academies, and showing in numerous personal galleries—*public* art museums were essentially nonexistent. The public institutions that did exist—the Boston Atheneum, for example—offered occasional exhibitions, but for the most part Americans did not have access to major works of American or international art.[63]

But what intellectual treatises and antebellum museums and galleries could not produce, Sanitary Fairs did. Visitors to the fairs entered a world where the nation's accomplishments and its history were available to all—where exhibits of plows and steam engines created a record of the nation's agricultural and industrial progress, while artifacts, arms, furniture, and art were displayed for the masses by virtue of their association with American heroes or history.

Most fairs housed industrial or agricultural rooms, where collections of the North's technological accomplishments—past and present—produced a celebration of the nation's role in "this wonderful mechanical age." Displays of such industrial wonders as steamboats and washing machines inspired pride not only in what one observer labeled "American ingenuity, science, and skill," but in the democratic direction such ingenuity was taking. Comparisons to Europe, where "nearly the whole energy of mind is devoted to increase the power and splendor of governments, and to multiply luxuries for the aristocracies and the wealthy," were inevitable. "Here," noted the superintendent of the produce hall at the Great Western Fair, "science becomes the willing handmaid of the workers. . . . American genius has led the way, under the inspiration of free institutions, in the introduction of agricultural machinery . . . the influence which it is destined to exert upon (other) nations is entirely beyond our present power to measure."[64]

In the larger cities—New York, Boston, Philadelphia, Baltimore, Chicago, Brooklyn, and Cincinnati among them—the fairs boasted art galleries as well. These galleries offered impressive collections of American art, juxtaposed with that of the European masters. The Metropolitan Fair collection, which included Frederic Church's *Heart of the Andes* and Emanuel Leutze's *Washington Crossing the Delaware,* was valued at $420,000; when it opened in early April 1864, the *New York Herald* noted, "No collection of pictures equal to that in the Fine Art Gallery . . . has ever been opened to the public on this continent." Two months later, Philadelphia opened its fair gallery, which surpassed the New York collection, offering "beyond question the largest, the most valuable, the most complete collection of paintings ever known in America."[65]

Never before had there been such an opportunity for Americans to study American art, particularly in juxtaposition with that of the European masters. Visitors to the fairs were well pleased: commenting on the collection in Cincinnati, a reviewer noted that "we have already the germs of an American school of art . . . the American mind will not always confine itself to the copying of European models. . . . We have the beginnings of an American literature; we shall have American art." At the New York fair, one visitor found "the most hopeful auguries respecting our artistic future, and the assertion often made before, now came to be commonly believed, that in landscape painting, at least, our National Academicians were in advance of all Europe, to say nothing of the rest of the world." Not just the art, but the galleries themselves were compared to those in Europe. Philadelphians claimed that although wanting the "fretted ceiling and architectural proportions of the time-honored galleries of Europe," their collection compared favorably with the best collections ever presented on the continent.[66]

The galleries were among the most popular of the fairs' attractions. Attendance at the Philadelphia gallery reached seven thousand in a single day, excluding season-ticket holders. In Chicago the gallery remained open weeks after the fair itself had closed. Visitors at all galleries expressed regret that the exhibitions were ephemeral: "Must this thing of beauty be dispersed, and no more seen? Can it not remain to be a joy forever?" Numerous calls were heard for the creation of a permanent national museum of art.[67]

Industrial rooms and art galleries offered records of the nation's past accomplishments even as they looked eagerly to the promise of the future. In the context of a society enamored with the notion of progress, they assured insecure Americans that their nation held a place at the forefront of that inevitable march toward a brighter tomorrow. But not all Americans embraced this celebration of progress. As historian Michael Kammen has noted, beginning in the 1850s, expressions of ambivalence about progress were increasingly common, serving as a "nascent basis" for the nostalgia and tradition that characterized the last third of the nineteenth century.[68]

It was to this ambivalence—as well as to the yearning for "assertions of our national existence"—that the fairs' curiosity shops, relic rooms, and period rooms appealed. "Curiosity Shops" displayed such historical items as Indian costumes, a tablecloth from the *Mayflower,* a piece of Plymouth Rock, fabric from George Washington's clothes, and autographs of the country's past and present leaders. "Arms and Trophies" rooms featured guns, knives, swords, and bloodstained, shrapnel-rent flags from all four of the nation's wars.[69]

But the most original contribution of the Sanitary Fairs to the material culture of the nation was the period room: collections of the furniture, paintings, knickknacks, and clothing of a particular time, brought together for display in a room designed solely for their viewing. Philadelphia offered a Pennsylvania kitchen and a William Penn parlor, Baltimore and Brooklyn displayed New England kitchens, Poughkeepsie created an Old Dutchess County room, New York boasted a Knickerbocker kitchen, and the second Chicago fair offered a New England farmhouse.[70]

Though these rooms varied in specific content, they held in common what one historian has called an attempt to "reinforce the fileopietism of the day" and to create "an aura of charm and romance, a snug haven from the forces of modernism that lived outside." The Knickerbocker kitchen of the Metropolitan fair, for instance, was described as a "broad, low room, with overhead ponderous beams garnished with festoons of dried apples, rows of dip-candles, seed-corn, and bright red peppers, etc." Old crockery, iron candlesticks on the mantle, and an antique bed furnished this room designed to remind spectators of the time when the Knickerbockers governed the island of Manhattan. As represented in the Metropolitan fair, this was a time when all classes and races worked together for the common good: here the city's elite women dressed in robes of great-grandmothers and served ham and head cheese, spiced veal and beef, waffles, mince and apple pies. On the corner of the hearth sat "Chloe" and "Caesar," described by the fair's contemporary historian as "respectable people of color, the one busy with knitting, the other 'on hospitable cares intent,' scraped his fiddle for the beguilement of visitors. Sometimes, for more boisterous amusement, there came in a real Virginia Darky, all ebony and ivory, who could dance a 'breakdown' with all the vigor and splendor of embellishment of an age that is passing away."[71]

Such was the mood of most of the Sanitary Fair period rooms: spinning wheels, antique furniture, and fireplaces, elite women dressed in period costume and serving the masses, and caricatured servile African-Americans presented a comforting—if markedly inaccurate—picture of the past. As a historian of the Brooklyn fair explained, "The idea was to live in the Past, and the Present was ignominiously banished. Many, before leaving the New England Kitchen, howsoever well satisfied with the new ways about us, were fain to conclude, 'the old is better.'"[72]

Or, at least that the old was worthy of memory: that America had a meaningful history, a sacred past. For between them, the industrial and agricultural rooms, curiosity shops, arms and trophies rooms, art museums, and period rooms of the Sanitary Fairs constituted the closest thing to a national museum that Civil War Americans had ever seen. This collection of the nation's material culture, available to any Northerner who could purchase a ticket to the fair, offered the very "record of . . . Americanism" for which Strong had called. The fairs invented a traditional America whose romance enveloped the endangered nation-state.

The Civil War Sanitary Fairs constructed a version of national identity and patriotism which, in direct contrast to that posited by the Sanitary Commission, drew on existing values and beliefs. Utilizing such long-standing cultural forms as localism, domestic feminism, and Christian charity, they incorporated and at times transcended these notions, molding them into new understandings of identity and duty.

At the heart of those new understandings lay a sense of the nation as a source of cultural pride and patriotism as Christian sacrifice. The fairs' approach to cultural nation-building was Janus-faced: it offered Northerners confidence in the nation's future as well as comforting, nostalgic images of the nation's past. Its notion of patriotism, though lacking in significant ideological content, served nonetheless as a tocsin for a nation inclined too much toward the pursuit of individual happiness, too little toward sacrifice for the good of the whole.

Let the Nation Be Your Bank

Jay Cooke and
the War Bond Drives

In July 1894, Jay Cooke, prominent Philadelphia banker and Civil War financier, reflected on his services to the Union: "Like Moses and Washington and Lincoln and Grant," he wrote, "I have been—I firmly believe—God's chosen instrument, especially in the financial work of saving the Union during the greatest war that has ever been fought in the history of Man." Cooke detailed the bond drives he had engineered during the course of the war, then concluded: "I absolutely by my own faith and energy and means saved the nation financially and did not realize any profit therefrom . . . the public should know even at this late period the unselfishness and sacrifices made by myself and [my] firm."[1]

Written nearly thirty years after the close of the war, Cooke's reminiscences evoke images of civic duty and Christian sacrifice, much like the ideas of patriotism that emerged from the Sanitary Fairs. Cooke spoke of volunteerism and obligation, of unheralded patriotic service without expectation of reward. Contemplating his own role as well as that of the masses of wartime bondholders, he described how his efforts had rallied Americans behind the war, how that patriotic uprising had saved the nation. But time had colored Cooke's memories of the war: the bond drives themselves tell a different story.[2]

Jay Cooke was indeed the preeminent financier of the Civil War. His services to the North were invaluable: granted nearly exclusive rights to market the nation's first genuinely popular war loans, he raised over $1 billion for the Union cause. Beginning in the fall of 1862, Cooke developed a far-reaching network through which he advertised and distributed the national loans. He sold bonds through his own banking house and contracted with numerous banks around the country. He hired traveling agents to take the offer of the loan into "every nook and corner" of the North, and, as Union troops advanced, into the South as well. In less than three years he rose from relative obscurity to become a national legend: marveling at his accomplishments, contemporaries labeled him "the Napoleon of Finance," "Our Modern Midas," and, after the great financier of the American Revolution, the "Robert Morris of the Civil War."[3]

But as Cooke's agents carried the national debt into the farthest reaches of the Union, they brought with them notions of patriotism and nation markedly different from those set forth by the Sanitary Fairs. Cooke taught Americans that patriotism was less about civic duty than it was about opportunity; less a mandate for self-sacrifice than a matter of self-interest. If the Sanitary Fairs offered the nation as a source of cultural identity, Cooke offered it as a source of economic well-being. He crafted a classical liberal understanding of patriotism, one in which the appetitive actions of self-serving individuals would combine to produce the greatest public good. In doing so, Cooke upended conventional wisdom about the threat that self-interest posed to the American state: in his hands, self-interest became a vehicle for the construction of a preeminent national loyalty. Cooke's own role in the bond drives suggests that he exemplified the very notions of patriotism that he promulgated.[4]

THE FINANCIAL CRISIS OF WAR

At a special session of Congress convening on July 4, 1861, President Abraham Lincoln estimated that the government would require $400 million for the fiscal year beginning July 1 to conduct a "short and decisive" war. Salmon P. Chase, Ohio lawyer and ex-governor, and the newly appointed secretary of the treasury, asked Congress for only $320 million.[5]

The projections of the president and the secretary did not seem unreasonable: less than twenty years earlier, the Mexican War had cost the federal government just over $63 million. But the United States had never fought a war on the scale to which the Civil War eventually progressed: By the time the South surrendered, the war had cost the United States federal government $3.2 billion (1865 dollars).[6]

Had the daunting task of financing this war been at all evident, Salmon Chase would not have appeared the man for the job. The secretary himself acknowledged how "imperfectly" he was qualified "by experience, by talents, or by special acquirements for such a charge." Indeed, Chase had little knowledge and almost no experience in economics, which, like many others of his time, he understood primarily in moral and constitutional terms. A strict hard-money man, Chase rejected most of the advice offered him by the banking community.[7]

The secretary instead chose to follow an outdated precedent established fifty years earlier by Albert Gallatin, Thomas Jefferson's secretary of the treasury. He would rely on revenue to continue the federal government's normal operations, turning to loans to finance the actual war effort. Chase's approach was based on the assumption that, historically, tariffs on imported goods exceeded the modest, normal expenses of the federal government. Repayment of wartime debt would be secured from the government surplus over a period of years following the war.[8]

But the federal government had in fact run a deficit for the four years preceding Fort Sumter. It had suffered a loss of revenue as a result of both the reduced tariff of 1857 and the Panic of the same year. Though by the summer of 1860 the nation had for the most part recovered from the Panic, the probability of Lincoln's election and fears of Southern reaction sent another shock through the business world. The import duties, which in years past had supplied 90 percent of the federal government's revenue, fell to one half of what they had been, in part because Southern ports were not forwarding the duties they received.[9]

The nation's incipient financial woes before them, the North's bankers responded with restraint when asked to furnish the government with money: in 1860 Treasury Secretary Cobb asked the banking community for $10 million in loans and received $7 million; in February 1861, Secretary Dix asked for $8 million and received $7 million; in April and May requests had not been fulfilled, and the most recent request for $14 million had returned nothing.

Undeterred by the dramatic decline in revenue and the financial community's lukewarm response to past requests, Chase pursued his plan to finance the war through loans. In July and August of 1861, Congress authorized $250 million in loans to meet the North's military expenses. Chase did propose that $100 million of the loan be made a popular loan, thus relieving the bankers of a portion of their burden. The nation's preeminent bankers would purchase the bonds from the government but only temporarily; they would in turn market the loan to the people of the North.[10]

The bankers who agreed to undertake this loan assumed many risks. With its reduced revenues and the volatile political situation, the federal government brought a questionable fiscal capacity to the negotiating table. In addition, it placed unreasonable demands on its business partners: in a world where merchants and manufacturers, businesses and banks conducted transactions in checks or bank notes, the national government demanded that all payments to itself be made only in gold. This "specie requirement," a part of the Independent Treasury Act of 1846, imposed a particularly onerous burden on those banks required by state law (or mutual agreement) to maintain gold reserves in proportion to their deposits and notes. Were the bankers to lend money to Chase, they would have to surrender a significant portion of their gold reserves. Though many in the business community pleaded with Chase to suspend the requirement, Chase refused.[11]

But perhaps the greatest risk the bankers faced lay in the fact that in the mid–nineteenth century, ordinary Americans did not invest in securities. Indeed, this was a people so suspicious of the financial community that the dominant party of the last generation had demanded that its government keep its money in non-interest-producing treasuries and conduct its business in gold. Most Americans knew almost nothing about securities: in a country where only 20 percent of the population lived in urban areas, and 55 percent of the inhabitants still lived off the land, money was saved at home or in local banks, or was reinvested in the family farm. Even those Americans who did think in terms of outside investment were unfamiliar with the notion of investing in the federal government. As the *Boston Daily Adviser* explained, "A United States Loan has never hitherto been heard of far outside of the larger cities." Not surprisingly, Chase's loan failed to raise the needed funds.[12]

With declining revenues from tariffs its only other source of income, the government had, by the end of 1861, reached a crisis point. Its loan was failing, its troops were going unpaid, its wartime suppliers were nearly insolvent. On December 30, 1861, the North's banks, their resources strained to the breaking point—in part by Chase's intransigence on the specie requirement—stopped specie payments. The Union's finances looked grim.[13]

By January of 1862, the Ways and Means Committee of the Thirty-seventh Congress had devised a three-step plan to bring money into the government's empty coffers. The plan included a proposal for legal tender notes, taxation, and a national bank system. These proposals were not designed to replace but to supplement the national loans. In fact, their supporters hoped that each would boost the sales of bonds in its own way: the wide distribution of legal tender would supply potential purchasers of bonds with the means to invest; taxes would provide the government's creditors with a much-needed show of faith, and the national bank system would create new markets for the bonds as well as help to stabilize the currency.[14]

It was the first element of the plan that received immediate attention. In February 1862 Congress passed and the president approved the Legal Tender Act. The bill authorized the issue of $150 million in United States notes and made these notes lawful money. The second section of this bill authorized the sale of $500 million worth of government bonds bearing 6 percent interest. The bonds, which matured in twenty years but were payable in five, came to be known as "five-twenties." Though legal tender might be used in their purchase, interest on the bonds was to be payable in gold.[15]

But still the bonds did not sell. Few banks were willing to buy large numbers of the bonds except with an eye toward resale: As Chase himself explained, "It is too plain for comment that where the government is always in the market offering her bonds at par for her own notes, subscribers to these bonds in large amounts cannot expect to make profits if they take them at par." By late 1862, the hurdles the government loan faced proved insurmountable, and the five-twenty loan was, as Chase's assistant George Harrington explained, "peremptorily refused in the market."[16]

Finally, in October 1862, with the expenses of the war burgeoning and his own loan campaign on the verge of collapse, Chase turned in desperation to Jay Cooke. In an unprecedented move, he offered the private banker sole agency of the government loan.[17]

JAY COOKE, GOVERNMENT BANKER

In his first nineteen months as the secretary of the U.S. Treasury, Salmon Chase had worked with numerous private bankers, but it is doubtful that any of them had courted him quite so assiduously as had Jay Cooke. On March 1, 1861, three days before Abraham Lincoln's inauguration and six weeks before the attack at Fort Sumter, Cooke had written to his brother Henry David Cooke, a personal friend of the secretary of the treasury and the editor of the *Ohio State Journal,* a Republican organ which had supported Chase in his campaign for reelection as Governor of Ohio. "I see Chase is in the Treasury," Cooke observed; "—now what is to be done?—can't you inaugurate something whereby we can all safely make some cash?" Three weeks later Cooke's father, Eleutheros, wrote his son Jay along similar lines: "H. D.'s plan of getting Chase into the Cabinet and Sherman into the Senate is accomplished, and . . . now is the time for making money by

Cooke's bond drives raised over $1 billion for the Union cause.
(Jay Cooke, Civil War financier. Courtesy of Historical Society of
Pennsylvania.)

honest contracts out of the government . . . the door is open to make up all
your losses."[18]

Cooke began his campaign to acquire the business of the government.
From the beginning, Jay Cooke and Company—a relatively small firm es-
tablished in January of 1861—was active in war finance. Cooke was one
of numerous bankers to handle government loans in April and again in
September. Though the latter, Chase's National Loan, fared quite poorly,
Cooke's agency proved a success. Employing methods similar to those he

would use in his own drive a year later, Cooke sold over $5 million of the National Loan.[19]

But Cooke aspired to more. With each task he undertook, he laid the groundwork for the assumption of greater responsibility: to his brother Henry, his Washington representative, he wrote, "We must all study by our watchful care of the interests confided to us to justify this confidence and to show [Chase] that the treasury is a gainer by our confidential connection with it. . . . I want the Governor to trust to our good management, integrity and skill." Cooke continually urged Chase to consider a more active role for his firm in the government's finances, promising strict confidentiality and caution, and assured him that "our movements will be . . . for the best interest of the government." The secretary, whose inexperience and stubbornness had alienated many of the nation's largest bankers, appeared to welcome the association, and in time Cooke came to act as Chase's financial adviser, making recommendations concerning government loans, taxation, specie, banking, and legal tender.[20]

In his suggestions to Chase, Cooke prefigured the views of government and private enterprise which would later inform the bond drives. Impatient with the way the government conducted its affairs, he envisioned a variety of roles for private bankers—preferably his own firm—in the government economy. In July 1861 Cooke offered to move to Washington, where, in partnership with another prominent firm, he would open a "first class banking establishment" and "give personal attention" to the business of the government, including management of the nation's wartime loans. Cooke qualified his offer: "We could not be expected to leave our comfortable homes and positions here without some great inducement and we state frankly that we would if we succeeded expect a fair commission from the treasury." Though this particular offer was not accepted, in February 1862 Cooke did establish a Washington branch of Cooke and Company.[21]

In January 1862 Cooke made a striking suggestion, one that spoke to his apparently strong belief in the privatization of government finance. He proposed the issue of "circulation" based on a United States loan and "15 or 20 percent of private capital." In his view,

> private parties (banks and associations) and not the government—should manage the details of circulation—and that their fifteen or twenty percent of actual capital should be guaranteed against an irredeemable currency. I wished also that some great inducement could be offered to meet the present emergency . . . my plan would give individual enterprise the care of distrib-

uting this uniform currency and with the aid of government keep it always on a sound basis.

Later that same month, Cooke suggested that Chase allow him to serve as a mediator between the Treasury and the banks of Philadelphia, New York, and Boston.[22]

Cooke's campaign to win Chase's business did not end with his offers to facilitate government finance. Cooke also cultivated a personal relationship with Chase: the two families were frequent visitors at one another's homes, and Cooke eventually persuaded Chase to accept personal loans. "I am gratified that you thus allow me to oblige you," Cooke enthused as he sent Chase a check for two thousand dollars. "As I can do so without the slightest inconvenience, command me at all times in any matter for your own or the public good." Cooke also served as Chase's personal investment broker, and regularly sent him checks for the proceeds of private stock transactions.[23]

By June of 1862, Henry Cooke was able to tell his brother of the secretary's plans to allow their firm a significant role in the handling of the five-twenty loan. "He has had enough of outside parties," he wrote. Jay Cooke had at last succeeded: his firm was not an outside party; he was, in effect, the government's banker.[24]

THE WAR BOND CAMPAIGN

On October 23, 1862, the secretary of the treasury officially granted Cooke exclusive private agency for the federal government's $500 million "five-twenty" loan. (This was the first of two popular war loans which Cooke was to handle: in January 1865, he contracted with William Fessenden, Chase's successor, for the sale and distribution of the "seven-thirty" war loan.) The five-twenty bonds were to be available in denominations as low as fifty dollars, so that "every Capitalist, be he large or small, or Merchant, Mechanic, Farmer, . . . should invest at once his spare funds." Maturing in twenty years but redeemable in five, they would earn 6 percent interest and could be purchased with the newly issued, controversial legal tender.[25]

To market the loan, Cooke was allowed one-half of 1 percent of the proceeds for the first $10 million, and three-eighths percent thereafter. With this commission, he was to pay all expenses, including advertising, transportation, distribution, and commission for his agents and subagents. The banker enthusiastically accepted the appointment, promising to "work night and day at it."[26]

Drawing on his experience in the marketing of the national loan, Cooke developed an impressive and far-reaching network for the advertisement and distribution of the five-twenties and their successors, the seven-thirties. He sold bonds through his own banking house and contracted with the nation's most prominent bankers and stockbrokers. In the East, Cooke appointed six leading financial men to organize marketing and sales by region; they in turn arranged with local bankers to act as subagents. In the West, where banking was less well organized, Cooke hired hundreds of traveling agents to recruit and train bankers, first in the larger cities, and then, as the campaign progressed, in smaller towns and villages. If no bank was available, Cooke instructed his agents to secure the services of one "competent" person who could give the matter "complete attention": real estate officers, insurance men, or community leaders. In time over twenty-five hundred local and traveling agents and subagents for the five-twenty loan canvassed the nation; for the seven-thirty loan that number increased to between four and five thousand. These agents visited every northern and western state and territory, and, as the Union troops moved into Confederate regions, Southern states as well: bonds were sold in West Virginia, Virginia, Louisiana, Tennessee, Kentucky, and Missouri. As the Northern press noted, "The old saying was that 'wherever the Union Army went, the printing press accompanied it.' The new saying will be, 'Wherever Rebel territory is conquered, JAY COOKE'S agents will appear.'"[27]

Within this broad network of banks and agents, the men who contracted to sell the loan constructed their own intricate networks. To reach their potential customers, Cooke's agents visited local newspaper offices, banks, hotels, post offices, courthouses, reading rooms, factories, and railroad stations, courting the cashiers, clerks, and officials they encountered. They left behind circulars, pamphlets, and handbills, posted signs on walls, tree trunks, and telegraph poles. They urged postmasters to mail handbills to town residents; they urged clergymen to recruit their parishioners. During the seven-thirty campaign, agents set up night offices, replete with coffee and doughnuts, so that working women and men could invest their savings. In larger cities, such offices were established in the factory districts or along the waterfront; in smaller towns they required only "the counter in a corner drug or grocery store." Near military training grounds, agents were instructed to sell bonds to soldiers on payday; once the war was over, they met the soldiers as they were discharged. In rural areas, agents traveled into the backwoods and sold the bonds door-to-door. Inspired in part by the promise of a generous commission, they carved out their territories and asked that Cooke keep other agents out, lest "we hit up against each other, and others get the benefit of my circulars."[28]

Cooke managed this sprawling network of agents and capital from his office in Philadelphia. As Harriet Larson notes in her biography of Cooke, at a time when no coordinating agency such as the Federal Reserve System existed, this was a monumental undertaking. In it, Cooke was the beneficiary of developments in transportation and communication. The telegraph industry offered almost instantaneous exchange of information; confined to the East for years, by 1860 it reached as far west as California. Moreover, though many early telegraph companies had been unreliable, consolidation, particularly of Western Union, had improved the telegraph system's efficiency. American railroads, which had expanded rapidly in the 1840s and 1850s, constituted a thirty-thousand-mile national network on the eve of the war, linking all major eastern cities and extending into the western territories. Through aggressive use of the telegraph, Cooke was able to keep in touch with his agents and stay abreast of the progress of the loan, receiving daily and at times even hourly updates. Cooke used the nation's railroads to carry agents and bonds across the nation, into the farthest reaches of the country.[29]

Developments in print technology and in mechanisms for the collection and distribution of news also eased Cooke's task. As the process of printing became less expensive, more periodicals appeared, as did advertising agencies. Such phenomena made advertising on a national level possible for the first time, and Cooke made the most of it. Indeed, his exhaustive use of the press to promote the government loan was unprecedented. Whether working through advertising agencies or dealing directly with editors or his own agents, he insisted at all times that the loan be kept before the public with liberal advertising in local papers, including those aimed at immigrant readers.[30]

But Cooke wanted more from the nation's newspapers than room in their advertising columns: he wanted frequent, lengthy, and enthusiastic endorsements as well. His agents paid generously for the advertisements that pervaded the Northern press, including foreign-language and religious journals; in return, they extracted promises of "favorable . . . notice" from grateful editors. "My advertising shall not discriminate," Cooke assured Chase, "but give to all parties who will speak a good word for the government and finances—the same patronage."[31]

Cooperative papers featured articles describing the government loans and extolling their virtues. Though the editors themselves were occasionally the authors, more often the articles were copies of editorials penned by Cooke, his brother, his agents, or "able and expert journalist[s]," appearing initially in the nation's more prominent journals and then syndicated to "lesser" papers. Agent John Wills, whose region featured numerous county papers, assured Cooke that local editors would allow him to write for any of them "at any time."[32]

Where advertising patronage was not sufficient, Cooke or his agents tried other tacks. Two prominent New York bankers who served as agents for the five-twenty loan wrote of efforts to coax endorsements—for the bond drive as well as for the fiscal policies of the Treasury—from reluctant editors. They found one local editor "rather opinionated on the subject of bullion and paper," but assured Cooke that "if rightly approached, (Mr. Tinney) can be induced to . . . write for the next number a very different article." During the campaign for the seven-thirty loan, Cooke offered those newspaper men who presented the loan or the nation's financial policies in a positive light options on fifty thousand dollars' worth of U.S. bonds for a specified period of time. The holder received the profit on the transaction minus 6 percent interest. In a testament to the success of this method, editors clipped their columns and sent them to Philadelphia to persuade Cooke of their loyalty.[33]

Cooke also asked that the papers print daily updates of the progress of the loan in the area. Some printed the names of subscribers in the previous twenty-four hours; others listed local or regional sales figures, hoping to prompt competition between towns, counties, or even states.[34]

Not all press for the loans was favorable. Agents sent into border states or recently reclaimed Southern states often encountered skepticism from the antiwar Copperhead press. But, as five-twenty agents Paul Jagode and F. L. Loes discovered when the loan received unfavorable notice in an extreme Copperhead newspaper in Milwaukee, any press was good press, and the overall effect of this approach remained the same: Americans across the country, opening newspapers in cities or towns, at home or in reading rooms, in county stores or in courthouses, could not escape notice of the five-twenty, and later the seven-thirty, loan. It is in these ads and editorials that so pervaded the Northern press that we can see the ideas about patriotism and the nation that Cooke and his bond campaign set before the American people.[35]

LET THE NATION BE YOUR BANK

As a seasoned businessman, Jay Cooke was somewhat cynical about questions of human motivation. His letters to his brother Henry and to Salmon

Chase emphasized the importance of "inducements" in financial operations, both for himself—"We ... must be careful not to work for honor
alone"— and for others: "No one here heartily loved their country better than
their pockets."[36]

So in his loan campaigns, Cooke wasted little time appealing to the "honor"
of his prospective buyers. Rarely did he speak of love of liberty, devotion to
country, or the moral obligations of the home front. Nor did he appeal to
Civil War Americans' republican heritage: Cooke's patriotism was defined
in terms of neither civic duty nor civic virtue. Particularly in the first campaign, when the war was young, its aim contested, its future unclear, Cooke's
main appeal to his customers was as rational, self-interested individuals. He
developed a market-model patriotism, wherein the Union faithful came together not as a moral or social whole, but as appetitive individuals acting in
their own interest, painlessly yet inexorably furthering the public good in the
process.[37]

Cooke's belief in the primacy of self-interest and its role in the public good
had roots in a debate of two centuries' standing. Joyce Appleby has traced
the outlines of this debate to seventeenth-century England, where a group
of economists challenged the dominant notion of a managed economy,
suggesting instead that the economy be viewed as "an aggregation of self-
interested individual producer-consumers." By the late eighteenth century,
when Adam Smith's *Wealth of Nations* was published, the tenets it pro-
pounded were familiar discourse to intellectuals, merchants, and manufacturers in England as well as in the United States.[38]

For Smith, human society consisted of a series of market relations between self-interested individuals: each went about the business of pursuing
his or her own good, and from the competition inherent in this pursuit
emerged the greatest public good. As Smith explained, "It is not from the
benevolence of the butcher, the brewer, or the baker that we expect our dinner, but from their regard to their own interest." Though ever in contention
with older republican notions of society, by the Civil War, Smith's beliefs had
entered the mainstream of American thought. They informed ideas about
the relationship both between the government and the economy and between
a people and their state.[39]

Such liberal tenets did not, however, easily lend themselves to the language of patriotism, particularly a wartime patriotism. Notions of Christian
sacrifice, of moral obligation, obedience, and republican civic duty seemed
far better suited to the demands on a wartime citizenry than did the idea of

self-interest. Cooke's accomplishment was the creation of an alternative definition of loyalty—one that mobilized self-interest in the service of the nation-state. Cooke set forth an accessible and profitable version of national patriotism, rooted in a liberal understanding of citizenship as the pursuit of self-interest, even in times of war.

Cooke laid the groundwork for this appeal by suggesting that the government had chosen to offer the loan to common Americans not as a response to wartime exigencies, but as a democratization of the privilege of investment. Though the decision to appeal to the masses was in fact rooted in the belief that, by themselves, the nation's bankers and capitalists could not or would not finance the war, the bond literature stood this convention on its head. As an article heralding the democratic nature of the five-twenty loan asserted, "The Government with impartial wisdom has not left this loan to rich speculators alone, who would gladly buy up the bonds in vast amounts, but, by taking subscriptions in small sums, has put the permanent advantage of the Loan within the reach of the people." Ads and editorials emphasized that while the loan offered "great advantages" to "large capitalists," it held out "special inducements" to "those who wish to make a safe and profitable investment of small savings."[40]

An obstacle to the success of such an appeal lay in the average American's ignorance of small-scale securities. Agents would have to educate their customers: fortunately, Cooke had developed a model for such an education while marketing the national loan. Selling bonds in the front office of his banking house, he had spent hours explaining the "whys and wherefores" of investment. Describing a day in which 142 subscribers had purchased $121,000 worth of bonds, Cooke wrote to Chase of the "pains" he and his agents had taken "to explain to each person . . . fully, so that they understand." Cooke's approach had proven immensely successful in 1861, and he enacted a similar system for the sale of the five-twenties and the seven-thirties. In his own office in Philadelphia and across the North in banks or storefronts, agents patiently explained investment securities to interested women and men.[41]

But clearly neither Cooke nor his agents could personally educate the hundreds of thousands of investors he hoped would fund the nation's war debt. Adapting his model to a larger scale, Cooke devised a series of flyers with a question and answer format. In one such circular, a fictional farmer wrote Cooke asking a number of questions concerning methods of payment, taxes, interest, and maturation. "I have no doubt that a good many of my neighbors would like to take these bonds," the farmer said, "and if you will answer my questions I will show the letter to them." The circular containing these questions along with Cooke's replies became one of the most widely circulated loan publications.[42]

In almost all the bond literature, Cooke emphasized the safety of the government loan. One of his greatest challenges was to convince Americans that the nation-state and its economy were, in spite of the crisis of war, sound investments offering ready return. Indeed, in accepting the agency of the five-twenties, Cooke had written to Chase that it was his intention "to enlighten the whole community fully and constantly on the subject of the nation's resources and finances."[43]

Thus, many of the circulars and editorials that described the government loans also detailed the "enormous strength and wealth of the loyal states." They compared the nation's current debt to those of various European countries and found it modest by comparison. They placed that modest debt in the context of the country's glorious future: its ever-increasing population, its flourishing home industries, its unappreciated resources: "We have vast territories untouched by the plow, mines of all precious metals of which we have hardly opened the doors, a population full of life, energy, enterprise and industry, and the accumulated wealth of money and labor of the old countries pouring into the lap of our giant and ever-to-be-united republic." The ads frequently urged readers to take note of the nation's past economic accomplishments, particularly in a comparative light. The nation's debts were smaller, its resources were greater, its credit unblemished. Americans could celebrate the "eminent financial prestige" their country had attained "before the world." Though such prosperity and prestige might inspire pride, more important, they underwrote the nation's popular loan, which could rightly be considered but a "FIRST MORTGAGE upon all Railroads, Canals, Bank Stocks, and Securities, and the immense products of all manufacturers, &c., &c., in the country."[44]

But the strength of the government bonds did not arise solely from their basis in a sound nation and flourishing economy. The bonds were also widely acclaimed for their profitability: "these Government securities are regarded by Capitalists as the very best in the market," a typical editorial proclaimed. Cooke's ads pointed to security, high rates of interest, legal tender convertibility, and, one of the most frequently heralded features of the loan, exemption from state and municipal taxes. An ad for the seven-thirties urged readers to invest their earnings "where they will be forever safe . . . where Cities, Counties, and States Can't Tax them—and where they will draw the BIGGEST INTEREST!"[45]

This resort to the prospective customer's business sense was particularly well illustrated by the ads that labeled the loan—in fact the federal government itself—a savings bank. Appealing in particular to the unseasoned investor, ads for the seven-thirties described the advantages of the government loan, then proclaimed it "a National Savings Bank." One urged readers to "fetch on your little sums of $50 and $100. MAKE THE U.S. GOVERNMENT YOUR SAVINGS BANK."[46]

Only rarely did the ads for government bonds mention the importance of patriotism, citizenship, the war, or even Union. Although such themes appeared more frequently in the seven-thirty campaign—when the mood of the country as a whole had shifted in support of the Republican war aims—Cooke's main appeal to his customers in both bond campaigns was to their self-interest. Thus in making the case for the war loans, a widely syndicated seven-thirty editorial asserted that "the chief arguments for inducing an investment in this loan are . . . (1) the high rate of interest allowed; (2) the convertibility of the notes, in 1867, into a gold interest and principal paying bond; (3) the release of the amount thus invested from state, county, or city tax." The fact that the bonds in question were war bonds was not even mentioned.[47]

When patriotism was invoked, it was often as an afterthought: A five-hundred-word article in the *Buffalo Express* described the loan's pecuniary

This advertisement for Night Offices for the seven-thirty loan illustrates the drive's appeal to ordinary people. It also highlights the depiction of the nation as both a source of economic well-being and a shield from the incursions of states and localities. (Advertisement for War Bonds, 1864)

advantages, then concluded: "Altogether, the loan offers the best of investments to capital, and provides the best of savings banks for people of small, accumulated means, besides appealing to the patriotism of every good citizen." The sole reference in an article in the *Galena Gazette* came at the end of a five-hundred-word discussion of the financial features of the loan, as the editor assured his readers that the bonds were a bargain "aside from all considerations of a patriotic nature."[48]

The most common—and striking—form in which patriotism appeared in the bond literature, however, was in direct conjunction with the idea of self-interest. Cooke's ads and editorials regularly linked the two notions: "Self-interest as well as patriotism make them popular," proclaimed a typical ad, while a second pointed out that while bondholders would "subserve their own interest, they will at the same time be patriotically placing at the disposal of the . . . government, money to carry on the war." A third explained:

> Patriotism alone, would not have made the Five-Twenty loan so popular. It is popular because people know it is the best, the safest investment they can find. A man not only lends the Government a thousand dollars from patriotism, but because he knows that it will pay him sure profit. . . . Let every one aid [the government], for in doing so, he helps to shorten the war, and build his own fortune.

A popular circular entitled "The Best Way to Put Out Money at Interest" described just such a man: a "hale old farmer from Berks county" who invested five thousand dollars "as he has concluded to put his money where he is not only sure of interest, but he is aiding the Government."[49]

One ad acknowledged that in theory, patriotism might require sacrifice, but offered the ordinary American, who might find it difficult to subordinate self to country, a more palatable version of civic duty: Boasting the headline "PATRIOTISM AND PROFIT," a column in the *Boston Traveler* read,

> Everyone should do all in his power to support the government in the present emergency, however his personal interests may be affected thereby. The truly patriotic will do so at the sacrifice of his own individual interests. But it is certainly more agreeable to aid the government and at the same time promote one's own advantage.[50]

In March of 1863, when it became clear that the bond drives were to be a smashing success, the bond literature began to employ patriotism in another guise. Still unwilling to rely on love of country to persuade Americans to buy the loan, the vast majority of bond advertisements continued to appeal almost solely to Americans' self-interest, but the editorials syndicated by Cooke and his agents began to attribute the popularity of the loan to the patriotism of the people. "Nothing could more forcibly illustrate the determined and unflinching spirit of the Loyal States than the noble subscription to the national 'five-twenty' loan," proclaimed one editorial. Another found that increasing sales evidenced "immovable confidence in the government,— and affords most unmistakable and overwhelming proof of the unabating zeal for the right, the sterling integrity, the undying devotion to the Union, the strong adherence to the Government, the immortal patriotism, and the illimitable resources of the American people."[51]

As Americans from all walks of life invested in government bonds, their collective action was proclaimed a patriotic uprising. Inspired perhaps by the hope that social pressure might serve as an effective rallying force, the literature described a community united in action. "The spectacle is really sublime," one article reflected:

> Men of all classes, all politics, all professions unite in the determination to make the Government strong with the wealth of a nation. The earnest, hard working Cabinet officer, the earnest, hard working mechanic, stand side-by-side in their devotion to the country. The millionaire invests his hundreds of thousands, the laboring man his fifty or hundred dollars.

Articles and editorials celebrated not just this perceived uprising, but its popular, democratic nature. In images evocative of Walt Whitman's America, they described the masses of diverse customers who daily thronged Cooke's agencies:

> Americans, Germans, Englishmen, Frenchmen, Spaniards, Irish, Dutch. . . . Soldiers and civilians, the merchant with his thousands, and the mechanic with only his few hundreds, . . . the lady with an annual income of ten thousand and the washer woman with only a few hundred, the farmer who had just sold his fat cattle, and his hired man who had just received his yearly wages . . . a little old Irish woman whose wrinkled face and whitened locks indicated some seventy winters.

All these stood side by side in the office where war bonds were sold.[52]

Particular pride was taken in the fact that Americans' "pecuniary patriotism" rendered European financial support unnecessary. Describing the bond drives as the second "grand uprising of the loyal people," the *Fitzgerald City*

Stern described how "we were told by European prophets that we could never carry on such a colossal war . . . [but] we don't want to be the debtor of the old world. Americans have money enough to pay American armies, and they have a Government which deserves their confidence, and which they will maintain with the dollar as well as the bayonet." Another editorial, pointing also to Europe's initial skepticism, proclaimed, "All the vast sums of money required by the government have been cheerfully furnished by the people, and far from exhausting our resources, we are but beginning to prove them."[53]

The women and men whose purchase of five-twenty and seven-thirty bonds had made this coup possible were publicly acknowledged for their patriotic deeds. The *Philadelphia Inquirer,* for example, listed the names of the day's subscribers in a testament to their devotion to country. Across the nation, other papers followed suit, paying tribute to the loyal by name, or, if space did not allow, by state, town, or neighborhood. "Well Done Ohio!" proclaimed a Pennsylvania editorial:

> The same electric impulse that swayed the popular heart as regiment after regiment filed past our doors, amid cheers and music, and the waving of banners, seems to have taken for itself a new direction, and is now manifesting itself by the lavish outpouring of money in exchange for bonds, with which to carry on the war against the Rebellion. A most healthy index of this loyal and generous confidence in the Government is afforded by the State of Ohio. . . . Her sons have fought on every battlefield under the inspiration of cheering assurances from their homes. And now Ohio seals her good works, and glorifies herself by the avidity with which her people subscribe to the Government Loan.[54]

THE IMPACT OF THE BOND DRIVES

Cooke's message seemed to find a receptive audience. The bond drives were remarkably successful: sales of the five-twenties soon exceeded even Cooke's expectations. On a single day in April 1863, the campaign brought in over $10 million; one day in October, sales reached $15 million. Though military triumphs no doubt encouraged prospective investors, battlefield defeats did not appear to deter them: sales continued, for instance, at the average of $2 million per day even through the gloom of Fredericksburg. Printers could not keep up with the orders, and bond certificates were soon in short supply. In July 1863 the convertibility feature expired, but the loan continued through Cooke's agency. When the five-twenty campaign ended in January

1864, the limit of $500 million had been exceeded: subscriptions totaled $510,776,450. Through his agency Cooke had sold almost $364 million of that amount. The seven-thirty loan was even more successful: Cooke sold $700 million of an $800 million loan.[55]

Though the bulk of these bonds were purchased in the Northeast, the loan was distributed in the border states and in the West as well. Contemporaries marveled at the demand for bonds in Maryland, West Virginia, Kentucky, Missouri, Indiana, and Illinois, both because some of this demand arose in sections where there had previously been "no call for this class of investment," and because many subscriptions came from areas that were openly secessionist. William T. Page, a bank agent from Evansville, Indiana, sold over ten thousand dollars' worth of five-twenties, reporting the entire amount from a "Copperhead neighborhood . . . I doubt if a single person who subscribes for the bonds ever had a real Union pulsation of the heart since the rebellion broke out."[56]

It is difficult to determine how many bonds were purchased by small subscribers as opposed to large investors. The bond literature itself points to the purchase of the loan by Americans from all walks of life; though its authors may have exaggerated the popular appeal of the drives, other evidence suggests that while the greater dollar amount belonged in the hands of large investors, a remarkable number of bonds were held by individuals of lesser means. Over five hundred thousand different parties subscribed to the loan. The proliferation of night offices during the seven-thirty campaign—Cooke instructed his brother to open thirty to forty in Washington and Georgetown, and the *New York Tribune* listed twelve in New York City—suggests that many of these subscribers were working- or middle-class men and women. Indeed, when the *Tribune* attempted to classify the roughly one hundred bond buyers who visited a night office on Bleecker Street one evening, it estimated that sixty were "mechanics or laborers," twenty were "saloon keepers, small dealers, and soldiers," and the reminder were working women, women in mourning, and "vendors, clerks, and even boys." In an article entitled "Who Are the Bondholders?" the *Nation* called the five-twenties and seven-thirties "a favorite investment of all the thriftiest . . . portion of the working classes." The loan was also taken in rural regions: an agent from Vermont wrote, "Farmers who live in little cabins, wear homespun clothes and ride to church and town in two-horse wagons without springs, have in many instances several thousand dollars loaned to the government."[57]

But, equally important for our purposes, for every American who purchased a bond, scores who did not heard about them. Cooke's agents traveled into every "nook and corner" of the Union; they carried with them not just bonds, but a vision of the government and of the nation. Across the country, in banks, libraries, hotels, reading rooms, and on their doorsteps, millions of Americans—most of whom had heretofore had little contact with the federal government—opened their doors or their papers and encountered Cooke's agents or advertisements.

Emphasizing the financial aspects of the bonds, Cooke's campaign worked to redefine the relationship between individual Americans and the national state. Cooke told his customers that the federal government could be a source of profit for them. He pointed to the exemptions from state and local taxes that the national loan provided, defining the federal government as protector—as a source of refuge from the financial incursions of states and municipalities. In Cooke's campaigns, the federal government overtly offered to serve its citizens as a savings bank. Cooke told them that the nation—in explicit contrast to the states and localities—could be a source of economic well-being.[58]

In defining the nation in these terms, Cooke was extending to middle- and working-class Americans the image of the nation which Alexander Hamilton had offered the financial and commercial classes seventy years earlier: that of directly serving their material interests. Though both Daniel Webster and Henry Carey had previously attempted to give a democratic base to Hamilton's economic nationalism, arguing in effect that the Whigs' protectionist and internal improvement policies would indirectly benefit the masses, never before had America's farmers and artisans, its mechanics and laborers, been offered so direct an economic stake in the welfare of the nation.[59]

The idea that the national loan might cultivate loyalty based on material interest did not go unrecognized. "Every dollar taken of this loan," wrote five-twenty agent S. Davis to Cooke, "is not only a blow against the rebellion, but is cementing the people by the tie of interest to the General Government." During the seven-thirty campaign, an editorial in the *Lane Express* noted that the taking of the loan by the masses "strengthens the Nation. These small subscribers . . . will pinch and save and work to buy more, and thus weave themselves into the very life and interests of the Government. . . . The distribution of SEVEN-THIRTYS among the people is a guarantee of permanent Union between the East and West, and the Centre and the Extremes." And at least one bondholder indicated that he now understood his connection to the Union in different terms: according to the *Philadelphia Press*, a soldier in the Army of the Potomac wrote Cooke that, having invested his surplus earnings in five-twenties, he felt newly inspired to win the war, for "if I fight hard enough, my bonds will be good."[60]

The idea of the national state as a source of economic well-being was furthered by the particular notion of loyalty that Cooke set forward. The United States was a newly centralizing nation; the obligations of its citizens were ill defined. Citizenship might be about asserting a principle, or participation in a polity, or even sacrifice. Appealing to Americans to fund the war debt, the bond literature acknowledged these more conventional forms of patriotism as legitimate. But they were not, Cooke suggested, for all, or even most Americans. He proposed an alternative form of service to country, in which the demands of citizenship could be met through the act of entering the market to purchase an interest-bearing, profit-producing bond. Linking patriotism and profit, he offered a notion of citizenship that, unlike that set forth by the Sanitary Fairs, did not require the subordination of private interest to the public good. Rather, he suggested, from the pursuit of private interest, public good would ensue.

In time self-interest came to not just serve, but to be equated with patriotism in the bond literature. Purchasing the loan with its promise of profit, bondholders were then regaled with stories of their patriotism, and their names were printed in lists of the loyal. Their acts of pragmatism were redefined: self-interest now equaled patriotism.

THE LIMITS OF SELF-INTERESTED PATRIOTISM

There were, of course, limits to the compatibility of self-interest and public good—limits that Cooke himself pushed up against regularly. Forced to choose between furthering the good of his country and that of his estate, Cooke repeatedly denied that such a choice existed, even as he plunged ahead with the pursuit of his own fortune.

Not surprisingly, the tremendous success of the bond drives meant success for Cooke as well. By most accounts, contemporary and historical, he was made rich by the war. Cooke netted at least $220,000 in the fifteen-month five-twenty campaign alone. Given the labor Cooke invested, the risks he undertook, and the amount of money he raised for the Union, many have viewed this sum as fair recompense. But it is not the amount Cooke earned that is disturbing. Rather, it is the fact that though he was clearly making a fortune from the drives, Cooke fought to do better, even when the good of the government and the nation were put at risk thereby.[61]

When Cooke agreed to undertake the agency for the government war loans, he foresaw many benefits. He was aware that a successful bond drive would bring him a substantial commission; he knew he stood to establish a national reputation as well. But the loans also offered another advantage: by keeping the millions collected for bonds on deposit in his own account or in the banks of his more trusted agents for only a short while, Cooke and his banking firm could make untold amounts in interest. This practice no doubt bolstered Cooke's profits significantly, if surreptitiously; more important for our purposes, it was a source of constant tension between Cooke, Chase, and their critics. The correspondence that reveals this tension also reveals a some-what incorrigible Cooke, driven to maximize his personal profit, seemingly incapable of restraint.[62]

Salmon Chase was not unaware of these tendencies in Cooke, having confronted them in his dealings with the banker during his agency for the National Loan in 1861. Shortly after his appointment as agent to that loan, Cooke asked to be allowed to keep a "good running balance," increasing his earnings by "letting the balance lay on deposit." Chase does not appear to have assented, for within days Cooke was being chastised for failing to de-posit loan proceeds with the government. He may have complied for a short while, but a remarkable incident the following spring illustrates his capacity for flouting the secretary's authority. On March 22, 1862, Chase authorized Cooke, as one of numerous national agents, to dispose of 750,000 seven-thirty bonds, in order to "make immediate provisions for payment of troops going into the fields." Chase asked that the money for the soldiers' paychecks be submitted to the government as soon as possible. Over a month later, though the assistant treasury in New York had sold and relinquished its $3 million in bonds within days of its authorization, Cooke had not yet transferred a significant portion of the loan proceeds in his account to the Treasury, hav-ing otherwise invested the funds. Though the government appears to have profited in the transaction, so does Cooke. In an uncharacteristically sharp reprimand, Chase reminded Cooke that the money had been intended to pay soldiers, and asked that in the future he be advised if Cooke found "this employment of your means unremunerative."[63]

If Chase thought that Cooke had learned his lesson, he was mistaken. Throughout the five-twenty campaign, Chase continually urged Cooke to deposit into the federal Treasury the large sums collected in the bond drives. He was joined in this quest by Cooke's brother and Washington liaison, Henry David Cooke, who had cautioned Jay before the five-twenty contract "not to show anxiety to keep the deposit." But less than three weeks following his appointment to the five-twenty loan, to the consternation of his brother and Chase, Cooke was holding $1.5 million of the government's money in his account. Henry Cooke pleaded with him to deposit the money: "It would look badly if it should get out . . . Governor C. has boundless confidence in you, . . . hence there seems to be a peculiar obligation, on our part, not to strain it too far." In December Henry David wrote Jay that Chase was again inquiring about Cooke's balance. Though he covered for his brother, suggesting that perhaps sales were slow, Henry urged Jay to "reduce the balance to the lowest possible point . . . it would hardly do for [Chase] to know that you have so large a balance in your hands."[64]

Forced to continually admonish the Philadelphia banker for failing to deliver government funds, both Chase and Henry David grew apologetic. At one point Chase asked that Jay Cooke not think him "parsimonious because I keep an eye on you"; in another letter he acknowledged that Cooke might think him "technical." Henry Cooke trod even more carefully: "We make these suggestions with diffidence, and hope you will not think the pupils are lecturing the teacher, to whom they look up with the sincerest reverence and respect."[65]

But if his close associates were loathe to condemn Cooke, the politicians and bankers who questioned his exclusive agency were not. Immediately following the appointment of Cooke to the five-twenty loan, jealous banking interests joined Chase's political enemies in questioning the exclusivity of the arrangement. Amid mounting charges of favoritism, suggestions of corruption emerged. On December 22, 1862, Massachusetts representative Charles A. Train proposed a congressional investigation of the Treasury to "inquire whether any officer or employee . . . is a partner, or interested directly or indirectly in any banking house . . . having contracts with the Government." Though this investigation did not materialize, the acrimony persisted. Cooke's reluctance to forward the proceeds of his sales came to the attention of Chase's correspondents, one remarking to the secretary that "somebody must be losing a pile of interest by these delays." Speculating on Cooke's profits, the *New York World* announced that the American people were being "humbugged" and "cheated"; in a later congressional debate a Congressman Hendricks charged that Cooke "has been made rich by the drippings of the Treasury."[66]

Such accusations haunted Chase, who pressed Cooke harder, if ineffectively, for compliance. Fearing for his reputation, in June 1863 Chase announced his intention to reduce Cooke's commission. Cooke protested vehemently and threatened to quit. Chase grew impatient. "I have," he pointed out, "a duty to the country to perform which forbids me to pay rates which will not be approved by all right-minded men; and I cannot think that now, when your past services have been fully compensated, and when the necessity for extensive advertising must be greatly reduced and the amount of subscriptions so largely increased that a very low rate will afford you a larger remuneration than a very high rate formerly, the original compensation should be continued." In the end it was left to Henry Cooke to remind his brother that there were more than profits at stake: "We must all make some sacrifices for our country."[67]

Cooke accepted the reduced commission reluctantly, and sales continued unabated. But the struggle had taken its toll on Chase. Though he continued to use the services of Cooke's firm once the five-twenty loan had closed, he did not suggest another exclusive agency. Neither, until the end of his brief tenure in office, did his successor, William P. Fessenden. Fearing a reprise of the charges and innuendos faced by Chase, when the need for a second national loan became clear, Fessenden turned to the National Banks to sell the second set of bonds, the seven-thirties. By January 1865, however, the National Banks had failed to sell a significant portion of the loan. Fessenden offered Cooke the agency, then left office. To Fessenden's successor, Hugh McCullough, was left the trial of coping with Cooke, his intransigence, and yet another round of charges and countercharges.[68]

JAY COOKE AND THE CONSTRUCTION OF PATRIOTISM

Jay Cooke's wartime rise to fame and fortune became legendary: "As rich as Jay Cooke" was for many years a popular expression. But if the image was enduring, the money was not. Cooke undertook the financing of the Northern Pacific Railroad and overextended his firm: in 1873, the United States District Court for eastern Pennsylvania declared Cooke and Company bankrupt. Though later in his life Cooke regained much of his personal fortune through private investments, by the estimation of one biographer, his banking career had ended in failure.[69]

Cooke spent the final years of his life living with his daughter. With her help, he began writing his memoirs, recalling his wartime contributions in terms reminiscent of the patriotism of the Sanitary Fairs. Thirty years after the fact, he recounted the sense of duty to country which led him to undertake the government loan "without any hope or expectation of commissions of any kind." But, as the story of the bond drives suggests, Cooke did not accurately depict the nature of his service to the Union.[70]

In fact, far from its alleged roots in civic duty and Christian sacrifice, Cooke's patriotism was grounded instead in classical liberalism. To the project of funding the war debt, he brought both a profound faith in the overriding human drive for economic self-improvement and the assumption that that drive would operate in service of the public good. Cooke's patriot was an economic—not a civic—man, even in the public realm. This belief informed his campaign to acquire the business of the government as well as the conceptualization and execution of the bond drives themselves. Thus Cooke's was a market-model patriotism: in the context of a fluid mid-nineteenth-century political culture—one informed by shifting notions of the relationship between the individual and society—it showed how patriotism in a society based not on republican civic duty, but on the pursuit of individual interest, could work.

Cooke's vision of the nation was perfectly suited to his self-interested citizen, for it offered the nation, first and foremost, as a source of economic well-being. Cooke detailed the strength and wealth of the Union. He presented the federal government which presided over that Union as one big savings bank, waiting to return high rates of interest, eager to protect its citizens' earnings from the taxes of states and municipalities. He argued that the popular nature of the loan was but an attempt to make the benefits of this nation and this government available to everyday Americans.

The idea that the nation might directly serve its citizens' material interests was not new; it had been the foundation of the Hamiltonian plan to bind the moneyed classes to the federal government. What was new was Cooke's democratization of this notion. Setting out to sell bonds to Americans "of all classes, all politics, all professions," through a labyrinthine network of agents and subagents, newspapers and flyers, Cooke brought this vision to America's cities and towns, through its villages and into its hinterlands.[71]

3

"From Democracy to Loyalty"

The Partisan Construction of National Identity

> The triumph of the Republican party in 1860 was the triumph of freedom over slavery. . . . Sir, Democratic policy not only gave birth to the rebellion, Democrats, and only Democrats, are in arms against their country. . . . Not only is it true that rebels are Democrats, but so are Rebel sympathizers, whether in the North or South. On the other hand, Loyalty and Republicanism go hand-in-hand throughout the Union, as perfectly as treason and slavery.
> —George Julian, Indiana Republican congressman, February 18, 1863

> It is true, sir, that in the madness of the hour, amid the bitter and relentless persecution of every man who would not bow the knee to the party in power, and confess unlimited confidence in it, and promise unhesitating support of all that it demanded, usurpations of power,

breaches of the Constitution, and all, . . . I was hunted and
hounded . . . as an enemy to my country.

—Clement L. Vallandigham, Ohio Democratic congressman,
January 7, 1862

In the destruction which this party policy has brought
upon this country, we have a sufficient lesson of the
danger of a party . . . that would light a conflagration of
the labor, wealth, and prosperity of the whole people, to
roast its paltry party potatoe.

—*Cincinnati Daily Gazette*, April 3, 1863

For the men and women who lived through the Civil War, political parties offered more than voting cues on election day. Distinctive party
ideologies and a contentious party culture infused Americans with passionate partisan identities—identities that profoundly informed contemporary
understandings of political events. Wartime policies representing the realization of a free labor ideal to a Republican might, for a Democrat, threaten
the violation of dearly held states'-rights tenets. Similarly, Republicans who
embraced the emerging nation-state as a guarantor of freedom for all men
were challenged by Democrats who feared that the growing power of that
same national state jeopardized liberty for white men.[1]

Party ideologies were imbued with a sense of immediacy by a spirited,
ubiquitous party culture. Indeed, in this society marked by its penchant for
association, party affiliation often served as the preeminent civic identity.
Americans formed fierce party attachments early in life, and the majority
remained true to those attachments. Disdain and even contempt for the
opposition was the concomitant to such loyalty: as contemporary observer
Jabez Hammond noted, "The contests between parties have been incessant,
fierce, and at times ferocious—each party charging the other with designs
fatal to the prosperity of the state and the rights of the people."[2]

Given the centrality of parties to nineteenth-century political culture, it is not surprising to find that, for many Americans, definitions of loyalty and national identity during the Civil War revolved around party. For Radical Republicans like Indiana congressman George Julian, the 1860 election meant that the antislavery principles of the Republican Party had become the principles of the nation. Resistance to those principles, or to the war being waged to secure them, was treason. Thus loyalty to country was only possible in the context of Republicanism. Julian opposed all efforts to appease the Democratic Party, labeling it "the great nursing mother that had fed and pampered [the rebellion]."[3]

Julian aimed his charges at all Democrats, but Democrats who actually opposed the war, labeled "Copperheads" by their Republican opponents, found themselves particularly vulnerable. Clement Vallandigham, avowed sectionalist, states'-rights advocate, and antiabolitionist congressman from Ohio, established himself as the spokesman for the peace movement in January 1863, when he delivered an hour-long oration calling for an end to the "experiment of war" before a spellbound Congress. But Vallandigham had been outspoken in his opposition to the war measures and aims of the Lincoln administration almost from the beginning, and his patriotism was frequently impugned as a result. In 1863, in defiance of a military edict which rendered criticism of the administration tantamount to treason, he issued a rousing speech in which he called on the people to "inform the minions of usurped power" that they would not tolerate "such restrictions upon their liberties." Vallandigham was arrested, convicted, and exiled to the Confederacy.[4]

Julian and Vallandigham represented the extremes of their respective parties. Moderate and conservative Republicans, at times concerned less with the principles that brought their party into being than with the need to maintain or further that party's hold on power, downplayed Republican Party ideology. They focused instead on the need for unity in times of war, independent of personal political preference. "The voice of party should be hushed," proclaimed Indiana governor Oliver P. Morton, a cry echoed by Republicans across the North. Many such Republicans sought to make room for Democrats in their wartime organization; indeed, the party temporarily merged its identity into a new, allegedly nonpartisan "Union Party," dedicated to preserving the nation in its time of crisis. Though critics pointed out that the Republican Party and the Union Party were one and the same, the new party appeared to give its members a moral authority traditional Democrats and Republicans lacked. Speaking from the platform of that authority, Union Party members argued that loyalty in wartime demanded the abandonment of party; anything less was treason.[5]

A minority of Democrats heeded the Republicans' call and assimilated themselves into the Republican or Union Party for the duration of the war. Another minority, led by Vallandigham, came to oppose the war and actively campaigned for peace. But the vast majority of Democrats chose a middle ground: supportive of a war for "the Constitution as it is, the Union as it was," they voted troops and money for the war effort, but they were increasingly critical of the evolving goals and tactics of the Republican administration. For refusing to abandon their party, these Democrats were accused of being slaves to party, of sacrificing the "prosperity of the whole people" to "roast [their] paltry party potatoe." For their criticism of the conduct of the war, they were accused of treason. Defined out of national loyalty and identity by Republicans, Democrats struggled to find a role for themselves as a loyal opposition party in a democracy at war.[6]

As the war progressed, this task became increasingly difficult. In response to the exigencies of war, Civil War Republicans set out to build a nation-state embodying the party's values and commitments. They posited the supremacy of the national government over its composite states and localities; they further proposed that the nation-state and the national administration were indistinguishable. Thus the emerging nation-state was effectively a party-state. For Republicans, the implications for national loyalty were clear. If a passionate party loyalty was the preeminent civic identity, that loyalty might be easily recast as national loyalty: it was but a short step from party member to loyal national citizen. For Democrats the process would prove more troublesome.

PARTY CULTURE IN THE ANTEBELLUM ERA

"The cares of political life engross a most prominent place in the occupation of a citizen of the United States," wrote Alexis de Tocqueville in 1835, "and almost the only pleasure of which an American has any idea, is to take a part in the Government, and to discuss the part he has taken." The average antebellum white male American was said to be consumed with a passion for politics.[7]

At the center of that passion and excitement stood political parties; and around those parties, a distinct culture had developed: a system of habits, forms, and rhetorical modes through which first Democrats and Whigs, then Democrats and Republicans contested for political power. During the war, this culture served as a resource for the construction of a national identity rooted in party loyalty. It helped define the terms of debate in a heated, protracted discourse on the meaning of patriotism.

One important feature of this partisan culture was the notion of party identification and fidelity. In the early summer of 1862, James Hughes, former Democrat and wartime Union Party leader, addressed an Indianapolis crowd: in the past, he argued, the prosperity of the nation had been such that "the claim of the government upon the loyalty of the citizen has never been felt." Americans' loyalty had instead been given "to parties, and to men. So long as the Constitution was not in danger, party leaders have had a monopoly on the loyalty of the people."[8]

Hughes was not alone in his observation: the devotion and ardor mid-nineteenth-century Americans bestowed on their political parties was widely noted. Such devotion was, to be sure, more common among Democrats; it was also subject to the ability of each party to speak to the shifting concerns and interests of its constituency—hence, in the fifteen years prior to the Civil War, a major third party rose and fell, one of the nation's two major parties dissolved, and a new party arose to take its place. Nevertheless, Americans were, by the time of the war, accustomed to identifying as loyal party citizens.[9]

If parties took the loyalty that some felt the nation deserved, in return they served as a nationalizing force. As the chief link between the politics of cities and towns and those of the nation, parties framed national issues in terms to which locally oriented citizens could relate, and they reinterpreted local issues along national party lines. They helped popularize America's symbols, myths, and institutions and provided ways in which Americans might express their devotion to country. Parties served as a vehicle for what Robert Wiebe has called a "lodge democracy": brotherhoods forming "widening circles of connection that linked citizens over vast differences." Finally, parties helped Americans understand their nation and clarify its principles.[10]

The national vision such efforts produced was, in turn, inextricably linked to party. For Democrats, America was a nation whose ideals included states' rights, political equality for white men, and limited, decentralized government. Whigs imagined a different America, one that gave power to the federal government to shape its conservative social and progressive economic future. Though most Republicans were ex-Whigs and therefore harbored

Whig hopes and visions, as a coalition party, Republicans promulgated anti-Southern, pro-Union free labor tenets. Each party believed fervently in the virtue of its vision and insisted that its vision alone embodied the real America.[11]

With each election, in the words of historian Joel Silbey, "a contest for the soul of America," antebellum political rhetoric was marked by hyperbole and vituperation. Only the "haunts of debauchery and vice" voted Democratic, warned Horace Greeley; while according to Democrats, Whigs were "our national evil genius" proclaiming "a foul morass of aristocratic heresies." Elections thus assumed a near-apocalyptic urgency, as the fate of the nation hung precariously, if incrementally, on every contest, no matter how small.[12]

Ironically, one feature of this contentious party culture was a lingering suspicion—real or rhetorical—of political parties themselves. A legacy of republicanism, antiparty ideology had declined dramatically by the 1830s and 1840s, but remnants of the discourse lingered—remnants that, paradoxically, Civil War leaders would refashion for partisan advantage.[13]

With the coming of the Civil War, the rhetoric of this spirited, contentious party culture acquired a new meaning. The presence of war meant that Republicans, who controlled the national administration, now defined the Union for which a war was being fought: conflicting visions were not an option. Devotion to party at the expense of nation was no longer merely troubling: it jeopardized the very existence of the Union. And the dire warnings that marked antebellum politics—the charges of corruption and "designs fatal to the prosperity of the state and the rights of the people"—gave way effortlessly to charges of outright treason. It was but a short step to the Republicans' next proposition, that loyalty to the nation entailed loyalty to the Republican Party—or at least to the Union Party, its wartime, nonpartisan embodiment.[14]

Between the party rivalry of the prewar years and that which informed notions of loyalty during the war, however, a brief recess interposed. With the attack on Fort Sumter, partisan wrangling came to a halt. Republicans and Democrats alike now urged Northerners to set party aside and rally behind their imperiled Union. Republicans, holding the presidency, Congress, and the majority of the governorships, rushed to assure Democrats of the nonpartisan nature of their intent. "We are no longer Republicans or Democrats," wrote the editor of the Republican *Indianapolis Daily Journal*. "In this hour of our country's trial, we know no party, but that which upholds the flag of our country." Democrats responded in kind. One of the most powerful calls for unity came from Illinois senator and Democratic idol Stephen Douglas. "There are only two sides to this question," he told a Chicago crowd. "Every man must be for the United States or against it. There can be no neutrals in this war, only patriots—or traitors." In what would become his last speech, he proclaimed, "Whoever is not prepared to sacrifice party organizations and platforms on the altar of his country, does not deserve the support or countenance of honest people."[15]

Douglas's death one month later lent his words more force and longevity than he himself might have wished. For as the war progressed, many Democrats began to question both the direction the war was taking and the nonpartisan claims of the Republicans. Indeed, Douglas's demise itself engendered controversy, as Illinois' Republican governor Richard Yates rejected calls to replace the deceased senator with a War Democrat, choosing an old-time Whig instead. Slowly, party politics began to reassert itself. And though this was true to some degree across the country, partisan strife appeared in its most bitter, vociferous form in the Midwest, especially Indiana, Illinois, and Ohio, where economic, demographic, and geopolitical factors produced a wide range of political opinion and the fate of the Republican Party often seemed precarious, and in New York, where party divisions were aggravated by class and racial tensions and one of the North's two wartime Democratic governors provided national leadership for a burgeoning opposition to centralization and the draft.

In these battles for control of state governments and the direction of the war, the partisan definition of loyalty became a major weapon. If antebellum Americans embraced contractual notions of patriotism—if they believed that loyalty to the nation was contingent on their approval of that nation's actions—wartime Americans were told that unquestioning support for the Republican Party (or its stand-in, the Union Party) was the mark of patriotic dedication to the nation.

THE MIDWEST AND THE REEMERGENCE OF PARTISAN CONFLICT

The wartime politics of the Midwest forms a remarkable tale. In Illinois, a constitutional convention dominated by Democrats tried to strip the Republican governor of any meaningful executive power; in Indiana, Republican legislators fled the capital to prevent a quorum, and constitutional government collapsed, not for a single legislative session, but for two entire years. In Ohio, Clement Vallandigham, convicted for treason and exiled to the Confederacy, ran as the Democratic candidate for governor, and the ensuing campaign witnessed brawls, assaults, and at least two murders. In all three states, reports of secret societies, midnight meetings, conspiracies, and infiltrations of government bodies became the stuff of everyday politics.[16]

The speed and vigor with which midwestern partisan conflict revived surprised few. Illinois, Indiana, and Ohio were, in a sense, microcosms of the nation. Migrants from abolitionist New England and the mid-Atlantic populated the northern parts of these states; the men and women residing in the southern portions hailed from the South. Much as it had within the Union itself, the war in these states cast into broad relief the tensions between a Southern slave agricultural society and a Northern, nascent industrial, free labor society. Though such tensions were clearly tempered by the fact that these were not, in fact, slave states, the business and familial ties that many midwesterners maintained with the South led them to question the wisdom of antislavery, even in its mildest forms. These southern midwesterners also shared the South's suspicion of New England Puritanism, as well as its racism.[17]

At the outbreak of the war, migration from the Northeast had come to exceed that from the South; as a result, the Republican Party had gained the upper hand in all three states. Republican governors stood poised to work with Republican legislatures. Though both parties initially rallied behind the war, once the impact of war began to be felt, bipartisan support quickly unraveled. The Mississippi River blockade deprived farmers of an outlet for their produce, creating a food glut. Manufacturing and commercial firms dependent on Southern markets floundered. Many midwestern banks held paper currency based in Southern bonds; some were forced to declare bankruptcy. Between 1861 and 1862, an economic depression engulfed the upper Mississippi Valley.[18]

For midwestern Republicans, economic hardship might be tolerated in the name of principle, or even party. But for Democrats, many of the war measures the Republican administration enacted threatened not just their pocketbooks, but their most dearly held partisan beliefs. Democrats watched nervously as Republicans began enacting policies that favored industrial interests over agricultural concerns, towns over rural areas. They shuddered at the prospect of emancipation, and as possibility became probability, began proposing new black codes to close their states to African-Americans.

Ultimately, they tried to wrest control of the state from Republicans. But Republicans fought back, using a weapon only the party in power could effectively wield: a narrowly defined understanding of loyalty, which conflated the Republican administration and the nation, attributed any criticism of the war or its measures to partyism, and labeled traitorous all Democrats who resisted this construction.

In Illinois, this struggle began in January 1862, as a state constitutional convention assembled. Delegates to the convention had been elected the previous fall and were disproportionately Democratic. Charged merely with rewriting several outdated provisions in the state's fourteen-year-old constitution, upon convening they revealed loftier ambitions. Many refused to take an oath prescribed by the legislative statute that had convened them. The convention embarked on a dramatic and visibly partisan course. It began an embarrassing investigation of state war expenditures, cut the governor's term in half, gerrymandered legislative and congressional districts, and proposed that it, not the legislature, had the authority to choose a replacement for the late Senator Douglas. For their part, Republicans complained early on that the convention was comprised of "partisan hacks . . . intent on securing partisan control of the state." In a statewide campaign aimed at discrediting the work of the convention, they attacked the loyalty not only of the convention delegates, but of the Democratic Party. In June the new constitution was overwhelmingly defeated at the polls.[19]

Partisan wrangling continued in Illinois, picking up speed when the fall 1862 elections ushered in a Democratic legislature. Representatives adopted a resolution that listed fifteen grievances against the governor and the president. They proposed the creation of a military council to appoint officers and approve spending, powers normally reserved to the governor, and gerrymandered congressional districts. Republicans responded once again with a full-fledged attack on the loyalty of the Democratic Party. But their real moment of triumph came in June 1863, when, taking full advantage of an absence of Democrats and a disagreement between the houses on an adjournment date, Governor Yates prorogued the legislature, freeing himself of Democratic challenges to his policies and authority.[20]

Indiana's experience closely resembled that of Illinois. Though no constitutional convention structured the bitter partisan struggles, by early 1862, all pretenses of bipartisanship had disappeared. In January a Democratic conference condemned the Republican administration's usurpation of power, abolitionism, suspension of habeas corpus, and "arbitrary" arrests. In October, seven of Indiana's eleven congressional districts went Democratic, as did the state legislature. Like Yates, in January 1863 Indiana governor Oliver P. Morton faced a hostile state legislature intent on redistricting and on stripping the governor of as much power and patronage as possible. And, like Yates, Morton managed to eliminate the threat. Following a campaign aimed at discrediting the loyalty of the Democratic legislature, Republican legislators bolted to avoid a quorum, first in January, and again in February. They did not return until January 1865.[21]

In Ohio, early attempts at a fusion, or Union, party brought many of the state's Democrats and Republicans together. But old party affiliations died hard, and by the fall of 1861, increasing dissent both within the party and between the legislature and Governor William Dennison laid bare the partisan outlines of the state. Increasingly, Democrats in Ohio rejected the notion of a Union party and expressed their vehement opposition to Republican war measures. In the fall of 1863, when Ohio was scheduled to hold her gubernatorial election, Democrats nominated exiled traitor Clement Vallandigham to face Union party candidate John Brough.[22]

NEW YORK AND THE REEMERGENCE OF PARTISAN CONFLICT

Though antiadministration sentiment flourished in the Midwest, it was New York that provided the Republican administration with perhaps its biggest challenge: the July 1863 New York City draft riots. A product of the political, class, and racial tensions which divided New York City at midcentury, the riots—examined later in some depth—were also the culmination of over two years of Democratic resistance to war measures and war aims.

Like Illinois, Indiana, and Ohio, New York's experience was informed by demographic, economic, and geopolitical factors. Migration from New England marked northern and western portions of the state; these areas became strongholds of abolitionism and Republicanism. In southern and eastern New York, descendants of Dutch settlers were joined by German and Irish immigrants. In the city itself, a thriving seaport produced both a merchant population dependent on trade with the South and a large Irish immigrant population. Two Republican and three Democratic factions competed for influence; one of these three, the Democratic Mozart Hall, served as a mouthpiece for the antiwar movement. Downstate New York generally voted Democratic.[23]

Racial tensions, no doubt common to all antebellum cities, ran particularly high in New York City. As Iver Bernstein explains, New York boasted an unusually fluid labor market, and the resident Irish population competed for the city's jobs with a "daily flood of new arrivals." The white labor force feared competition both from the city's resident blacks and from the influx of freed blacks that Democrats warned would be the inevitable result of abolition. Class tensions also ran high. New York was the home to many of the nation's wealthiest and most powerful men, yet boasted the highest crime and disease mortality rate of any city in the Western world.[24]

In view of the potential for Democratic resistance, politics in New York State was surprisingly stable early in the war. Republicans controlled both houses of the legislature as well as the state house. Though an active peace press joined a small contingent of Peace Democrats organized by Mozart Hall in denouncing the war and held meetings to agitate for compromise and though the state's leading Democrats regularly registered their unhappiness with the burgeoning role of the federal government and the threatened departure from a war aimed solely at restoring the Union, the Democratic party nonetheless proclaimed support for the war effort and voted for money and troops, and legislative sessions ran smoothly.[25]

But in the autumn 1862 elections, New York voters placed Horatio Seymour, a states'-rights advocate and opponent of both abolition and centralization, in the gubernatorial chair. As one of the North's two wartime Democratic state chief executives, and, more important, as the governor of the nation's most heavily populated state, Seymour was now in a position to offer leadership to the North's antiadministration forces. In his first Annual Message in January 1863, he declared that the constitutions of the nation and the state were equally sacred and pronounced it his sworn duty to defend that of the state. He urged the legislature to address the class inequalities inherent in the draft laws, and warned that war "builds up an active class who gain power and wealth by the taxation imposed upon the labor and property of the mass of citizens." He condemned arbitrary arrests and declared it a "high crime" for the federal government to abduct a citizen of New York State. And in his first official act as governor, he ordered the arrest of the metropolitan police commissioners who had cooperated, per the request of national authorities, in the arrest and detention of Southern sympathizers. New York Democrats who had silently opposed the war or the Republican party-state had found their champion.[26]

The legislative session of 1863 was, according to a historian of New York, "one of the most exciting and disgraceful" in the history of the state. Though Republicans had managed to hold on to the state Senate, Democrats had taken a majority in the assembly. But that majority was based in part on eight "Union Democrats" who were not guaranteed to the Democratic Party. Thus the election of a Speaker for the legislature became the focus of a four-week-long melee, during which crowds in the galleries cheered Democrats, hissed Republicans, and threw fruit; members threatened fistfights, and no legislation—with the exception of a bill for the construction of a hospital for disabled soldiers—was debated. It was, wrote the *New York Tribune,* a scene "which would have disgraced a barroom caucus." Partisanship in New York had revived.[27]

As these political battles played out in Illinois, Indiana, Ohio, and New York, it became clear that issues of economics and slavery, constitution and civil liberties were not the only factors driving political leaders to partisan hyperbole. Both the Democratic and the Republican parties confronted major wartime *institutional* challenges. As the opposition party during a civil war, the Democracy struggled to maintain both its essential character and its legitimacy. In its more optimistic moments, it also hoped to wrest control of state offices—and, eventually, the national government—from Republicans. If in New York the project was well under way, in the Midwest it seemed eminently feasible: Democrats had traditionally carried Illinois and Indiana, and Ohio had vacillated between the two parties for years. Though Republicans had captured all three states in 1860, that capture had been on a platform of free labor, not a war for emancipation, a Whig state, and, as many Midwesterners saw it, New England industrial interests.[28]

Republicans faced a different task. 1860 had delivered a clear victory, but the party was still young and undeveloped. Since decentralization was a hallmark of antebellum political parties, much of the work confronting Republicans would take place on a state, not a national, level. Yates and Morton were important party leaders and invaluable assets to the war effort. Republicans could ill afford a Democratic victory—electoral or strategic—in these states. Nor could they afford to lose Ohio as they had lost New York. The Republican party sought to recapture New York, and consolidate and expand existing power, both within the states and on a national level. So it was that the battle over control of the governing apparatus in these states—a battle already fraught with meaning—became a struggle for the health of the country's two major political parties as well.[29]

THE RADICAL REPUBLICANS AND A PRINCIPLED
PARTY PATRIOTISM

The tendency to conflate Republicanism with loyalty and Democracy with treason assumed two forms during the war years. First, Radical Republicans like George Julian argued that with Lincoln's election, the principles of the Republican Party had become the principles of the nation. The Radicals—a group of Republican politicians whose refusal to compromise on the slavery question distinguished them from other Republicans—were usually from or had roots in New England. They represented rural areas or small towns in New York, Pennsylvania, New England, and those parts of the Midwest characterized by New England migration. Radical senators included Charles Sumner from Massachusetts, Zachariah Chandler from Michigan, and Benjamin F. Wade from Ohio. Radical congressmen included Owen Lovejoy from Illinois, Joshua Giddings from Ohio, and Julian.[30]

For the Radicals, the formation of the Republican Party, the Republican victory in 1860, and, in fact, the Civil War itself were the fruition of years of labor for antislavery—a cause many believed to be a religious as well as a national imperative. Never party men in the traditional sense, they embraced the Republican Party only because it represented antislavery principles. Any attempt to dilute those principles met with disdain or even outrage. Julian, for example, had little patience with the Union Party, which he believed moved the Republican Party away from its antislavery tenets and towards the principles of the Democracy. "Republicanism is not like a garment, to be put on or laid aside for our own convenience," he argued in February 1863, "but an enduring principle, which can never be abandoned without faithlessness to the country." The Union Party movement was "utterly preposterous" to Julian; "simply a shallow expedient for dividing the spoils of office, at the cost of the practical surrender of the principles for which Republicans had so zealously contended."[31]

Barring that surrender, loyalty to the nation could only be expressed through loyalty to the Republican Party. This point the Radicals made clear time and again. No true statesman, argued Benjamin Wade in a speech titled "Patriots and Traitors," would fetter the power of the national state while it struggled for its very life. Yet Democrats and only Democrats could be found assailing the administration for the assumption of "tyrannical" powers; and those guilty of such attacks were rarely heard condemning the Confederates. Wade would brook no interference from traitors disguised as civil libertarians: "Do you think that we will stand by," he queried, "yielding to your argument, while you fetter our legs, and bind our arms with the Constitution of the United States so that you may stab it to death?" Such Democratic dissembling stood in sharp contrast to the purity of the Republicans, who, as Zachariah Chandler explained to a crowd in Michigan, compared favorably with the apostles themselves—the apostles, after all, had at least one traitor.[32]

Republicanism was also synonymous with loyalty because only Republicans could be found promoting a vigorous war for antislavery principles. This argument was powerfully articulated by the Committee on the Conduct of the War, a joint congressional committee established in December 1861 to investigate the failures of the war effort. The committee published a series of reports detailing the results of its investigations into government corruption, rebel atrocities, and the failings of Democratic generals, reports that were published in newspapers and pamphlets.[33]

The most politically potent of these reports concerned General George B. McClellan, a self-impressed, condescending man who let his abhorrence of abolition be known early in the war. His subsequent reluctance to lead troops into battle and defiance of orders led many radicals to suspect him of deliberate sabotage. On April 6, 1863, the committee released its report on McClellan. At best, the Democratic general appeared a bumbling fool; at worst, he was a traitor. The committee's conclusions had implications for the loyalty not just of McClellan, but of the entire Democracy. The report, according to Chandler, was "splendid. . . . It kills copperheads *dead*. . . . The testimony is perfectly damning." For if a Democratic Union general could not be trusted to fight for the new nation, could any Democrat?[34]

The Republican Party's embrace of antislavery principles underlay the Radicals' understanding of party loyalty. But the second form that the conflation of Republicanism and patriotism assumed, illustrated by the Union Party, the rhetoric of numerous partisan papers and leaders, and the partisan Union Leagues, found its meaning not in principles, but in wartime necessity and the need for unity. Indeed, particularly as war gave way to revolution, moderate Republican leaders argued that it did not serve the Republican Party to address the issues at all. "The essential thing," wrote Murat Halstead of the *Cincinnati Commercial* to Secretary of the Treasury Salmon Chase, "is to keep the administration out of sight as much as possible, and talk of the cause of nationality and nothing else." Though at times the partisan presses conducted focused debates concerning the issues, equally often such discussions quickly degenerated into attacks on the opposing party's loyalty.[35]

To the extent that the goal of such rhetoric was to pry supporters away from the Democratic Party, Republicans faced a daunting task. The Democracy boasted legions of loyal, even devout supporters. It had a long history, sacred heroes, and hallowed traditions. To the project of undermining this well-entrenched opposition party, Republicans brought the resources of mid-nineteenth-century partisan culture.

THE UNION PARTY AND NO-PARTY PATRIOTISM

With battles raging throughout the South and elections staged like clockwork across the North, newspapers kept readers informed of the ever-changing military and political balance of power. Partisan papers almost without exception, few missed an opportunity to frame the news in terms of their party's particular concerns or ideals. In Illinois, Indiana, and Ohio, Democratic newspapers bemoaned the loss of the Mississippi River trade; in all four states, they complained about the war debt, taxes, unemployment, the threat of black migrants, violations of civil liberties, and infringements on states' rights.

Republican responses to these complaints varied, but a common underlying theme, increasing in frequency as the conflict wore on, was the need to remain united against the greatest threat the Union had ever faced. And, in this country marked so profoundly by partisan discord, unity meant, more than anything else, bipartisanship.

It was in this spirit—rhetorically at least—that the fusion "Union" Party was founded. Town by town, state by state, Republican Party organizations abandoned the name that had ushered them into office, and, with it, the promulgation of the party's more radical principles. No longer would anti-slavery speak for this rechristened party. Instead, the Union Party's sole doctrine was to save the Union. All leaders were committed, all measures enacted, toward that end and that end alone.

There is no modern reliable history of the Union Party. Thus it is difficult to know precisely how many state organizations existed in the early years of the war. Illinois, Indiana, Ohio, and New York all had Union parties, as did California, Massachusetts, and Wisconsin, and presumably many other states as well. In 1864, the national Republican convention assumed the label, and Lincoln himself ran on the Union ticket.[36]

The Republican Party in Ohio underwent its official metamorphosis in the summer of 1861. In preparation for the approaching gubernatorial elections, Republicans—echoing the call that preceded the creation of the Republican Party itself—announced a bipartisan convention of "all loyal citizens of Ohio who are in favor of the maintenance of the Government, and of the vigorous and continued prosecution of the war." Across the state, local party organizations followed suit, urging Democrats to join them in a party to save the Union. Some Republicans even suggested that a joint convention be held, with offices distributed equally between the two parties. Most Democrats, fond of their own party and suspicious of the no-party claims of the Union Party, demurred. But a small number of Democrats joined the Ohio Union movement.[37]

Union tickets appeared in counties throughout Illinois, Indiana, and New York in the fall 1861 municipal elections. By 1862, Republican organizations in Illinois, Indiana, and New York sponsored statewide Union Party conventions, and the Union Party strategy prevailed in all four states for the remainder of the war. At times this strategy appeared to benefit Republicans: in Ohio, for example, the fusionist movement was credited with placing Union Party members in the executive mansion and both houses of the 1861 legislature. In Illinois, the Union Party claimed responsibility for enticing more "Egyptians," or southern Illinois Democrats, into the party. At times this strategy did not succeed: all four states lost their Republican majorities in the autumn 1862 elections.[38]

But win or lose, the Union Party strategy invariably kept Democrats on the defensive with respect to loyalty to nation. It allowed Republicans to claim, as did Indiana governor Oliver P. Morton, that with the war *they* had chosen "to lay down the partisan on the altar of [their] country." Republicans gleefully declared that "in this hour of our nation's trial, our Country is our Party." Indeed, some declared their party defunct: "No one claims that there is in existence a Republican party," argued the *Cincinnati Daily Gazette,* "except in the sense of believers in republicanism."[39]

Democrats repeatedly challenged these claims. And in fact, though it did attract some Democrats, there was little about the Union Party to suggest that it existed outside the aegis of the Republican Party. Despite Republican assurances that the Union movement was not "a trick to coax Democrats into our Republican parlor," the Union Party was, in effect, a political strategy, a tactic employed when useful and abandoned when less so: in some places Republicans ran under the Union name one election, as Republicans the next.[40]

Nonetheless, Republicans continued to insist that loyalty to country demanded the surrender of all party concerns and identities. To effect this surrender on the part of Democrats was no simple task, and though the creation of an allegedly bipartisan party was one approach, Republicans employed a number of other strategies as well.

Alert to the obstacles that Democratic traditions placed in the path of such sacrifice, they attempted to subsume the Democratic heritage under the Union Party umbrella. They plastered Stephen Douglas's plea to sacrifice party at the head of their newspapers, claiming him, along with Thomas Jefferson and Andrew Jackson, as their own. Democrats who did not follow in the spiritual footsteps of their heroes were labeled "spurious" or "sham" Democrats. While this charge was originally leveled by Jacksonian Democrat-turned-Republican Francis P. Blair in response to the Kansas-Nebraska Act—"as a Democrat of the Jefferson, Jackson, and Van Buren school," he took grave issue with "this spurious Democracy"—with the war almost any Democratic complaint could elicit the accusation. Confronted with complaints about the suspension of habeas corpus, Republican congressman John A. Bingham from Ohio exploded: "These men who strike at the last great experiment of republican government among men. Who are they? . . . There is not a Jacksonian Democrat in this conspiracy. . . . They are not the Douglas Democrats. . . . They are pretenders, hypocritical pretenders of Democracy. . . . They call themselves Democrats; they are simply Northern traitors. . . . They are no more Democrats than the Devil himself." Although they claimed to support the war, these "so-called Democrats" were lying. Real Democrats worthy of the Democratic tradition had joined the Union Party.[41]

Why, then, did so many Democrats cling to this spurious Democracy? One Republican answer was that Democrats who refused to abandon their organization were slaves to party. "[The] war finds us in party harness," argued James Hughes, an Indianapolis War Democrat, "with our minds chained down to party ideas and organizations." For a generation Democrats had dominated the presidency, and Democratic national loyalty had become dependent on the benefits to party such dominance procured. Thus, as Ohio Republicans explained, the Democracy was without "loyalty to country unless the Democratic party controls it and enjoys the official spoil." In this analysis, all expressed concerns were construed as partyism, including Democratic complaints about the loss of the Mississippi River trade, the Morrill tariff, the draft, taxes, and the suspension of habeas corpus. Democratic patriotic proclamations must also be met with skepticism, for, in the words of the *Albany Evening Journal,* "That men will bear false witness for party's sake is a melancholy truth."[42]

Republicans brought another tactic to the task of discouraging Democratic voters: they attempted to revive a nearly moribund tradition, fear of party. Though their own party had been only recently founded on an awareness and acceptance of the idea of parties, like their Whig progenitors, Republicans hoped that antipartyism might divest the Democracy of a bit of its stature. Parties, they warned, were the "sunken rock on which governments had been wrecked." Too often they served as a cover for evil intent: since the war had begun, party spirit had "made many apologies for treason." Republicans condemned the "haughty gods of party pride," and even quoted George Washington's farewell address, replete with warnings about the dangers that party presented to republican government.[43]

It was but a short step from fear of party to the Republicans' next suggestion: that parties be eliminated not just for the duration of the war, but beyond. Though most Republicans assured the Democracy that it could resume its prewar role once the Union had been saved, a few prominent Republicans expressed their hopes that the Union Party would usher in another "one-party era." In a speech to the Indiana state legislature, which was later published in pamphlet form, Governor Morton urged that "the voice of party . . . be hushed . . . let us rise above these paltry considerations, and inaugurate the era when there shall be but one party, and that for our country." James Hughes agreed: "Let us do this first," he argued as he urged the men and women of Indianapolis to surrender their wartime party affiliations, "then we can restore old party organizations if necessary. I will do the Republicans the justice to say they do not now wish to restore their old party."[44]

Partyism offered one explanation for Democratic intractability. But Republicans also proposed another, more disturbing possibility: the Democracy had become a front for the Confederacy. While old school Democrats labored for the Union cause under the guise of the Union Party, those who refused to join them had merely stolen the Democratic party label: as the *New York Tribune* explained, "In the livery of Democracy they hope more effectively to serve the cause of treason." Republicans called on Union lovers everywhere to "spurn" these Democrats much as they would the Rebels themselves.[45]

THE REPUBLICAN CONSTRUCTION OF TREASON

"The Democratic organization is everywhere showing its affiliation with the rebellion," the *Cincinnati Daily Gazette* noted in July of 1863, "and is fastening eternal infamy to its name." From secession to Appomattox, Republicans invoked an almost uninterrupted litany of charges against the Democratic Party, charges that suggested its defilement by association with the Southern rebels. Former Democratic Party leaders led the Confederate government and held commissions in its army. Democrats were "joyfully claimed by rebels as the friends of rebellion," with, Republicans pointed out, just cause: Democrats lent assistance to the Confederacy by criticizing and embarrassing the government, giving speeches and publishing tracts critical of the war, and discouraging volunteers. When not engaged in frontal attacks on the war and the administration, they appealed to the "prejudices and passions of the ignorant . . . by making up side issues" designed "merely to aid the rebels in putting down the constitution, law, and all liberty." Under the guise of the democratic process, their party machinations worked to "hold the people of the North still" while the South overturned the government.[46]

As it happened, Republican charges rested on a modicum of truth. Ambivalence about the war, particularly after the Emancipation Proclamation formalized its revolutionary nature, was widespread, especially within the Democracy. When there was resistance to the draft, it generally came from Democrats. The southern portions of Illinois, Indiana, and Ohio did harbor Democrats who actively opposed the war; a few even actively advocated an alliance with the rebels. In New York, resistance to the war assumed revolutionary tones in the summer of 1863, when draft riots rocked the city for three days. Confederates no doubt took comfort from that movement.

But it is important to note that most Republicans were not targeting a few Democratic secessionists or draft resisters. The net they cast was far broader: there could be no loyal wartime Democrats outside the purview of the Union Party. As a single-issue party, the Union Party sought to unite loyal men from both parties behind the vigorous prosecution of the war. As long as that party offered candidates driven "purely by a lofty patriotism," Democrats who could not "find it in their scrupulous consciences to vote for a man who agree[d] with them about the war," but differed with them on slavery— or on any other issue, ranging from taxes to conscription, from currency to civil liberties—could not be truly loyal. Indeed, those Democrats who did abandon their party for the Union or Republican Party were considered to have "converted from Democracy to loyalty."[47]

Thus Republicans tarred practicing Democrats of *all* stripes with the opprobrium of treason. Mere association with the party could raise questions about one's loyalty: for some Republicans, the wearing of Democratic emblems such as a hickory branch, a butternut, or even the head of Liberty was considered traitorous. Though only a minority of Democrats were actually opposed to the war, Democratic electoral tickets were routinely labeled "Copperhead" tickets, and dismissed as treasonous.[48]

Such generalities appeared particularly contrived when applied to local elections. For years, city and county elections had been cast dramatically in national terms. Now, with the entire opposition party not just corrupt but traitorous, this practice lent these small contests, with their language of apocalypse and doom, an unprecedented significance. "The duty of voting the Union ticket on Monday is a sacred one," proclaimed the *Cincinnati Daily Gazette* concerning an election for city solicitor and city engineer in the spring of 1863. "This is no ordinary contest. It is not whether this party or that party, in a partisan sense, shall succeed, but whether the cause of our country, or that of VALLANDIGHAM submissionists shall triumph." Though only two years earlier the same paper had urged its readers to dismiss Democratic charges that Republican candidates were abolitionists, "keeping Municipal affairs separate from . . . National politics," and examine the candidates' "individual qualifications" instead, the *Gazette* now admitted that it had not examined qualifications, "preferring to put the question on the necessity for supporting our soldiers in the field by fidelity in political offices at home. All party considerations were subordinated to the national cause. . . . There is a principle at stake—a question of unconditional loyalty. . . . Choose, then, under which flag you will serve."[49]

The movement to taint the entire Democratic Party by virtue of its association with the Confederacy was periodically energized by rumors of vast Democratic conspiracies to aid and abet the rebellion. Endemic more to the Midwest than to New York, beginning with the fall 1861 elections, reports of secret societies dedicated to the destruction of the Northern government and the Union—societies staffed without exception by Democrats—appeared regularly in Illinois, Indiana, and Ohio newspapers.[50]

The societies these reports claim to have discovered did in fact exist. But, as historian Frank Klement has shown, they were chiefly a product of fantasy, both on the part of their inept founders *and* their Republican detractors. The "Knights of the Golden Circle" (KGC), a Republican favorite in Illinois and Indiana, is a case in point. Founded in the 1850s by lawyer, teacher, doctor, and feckless schemer George Washington Lamb Bickley, the KGC was originally dedicated to establishing an empire for Americans in Mexico. Bickley traveled throughout the South, in disguise and tracked by creditors, searching for men willing to pay a ten-dollar fee to join his largely nonexistent organization.[51]

Were it not for the intervention of Washington politics and partisan scheming, it is unlikely that Northerners would ever have heard about Bickley and his Knights of the Golden Circle. But when rumors of a secret society pledged to prevent Lincoln's inauguration located conspirators inside Buchanan's cabinet, the KGC was among the names bandied about. Though a congressional investigation turned up no such conspiracy, the idea of a secret society dedicated to the overthrow of the Union had entered Northern political parlance, and the Knights of the Golden Circle soon became its most colorful emblem.[52]

Two other secret organizations rumored to be sponsored by Democrats and intent on treason received attention from the Republican press during the war. But investigations into both the Sons of Liberty and the Order of the American Knights revealed that neither society had large membership rosters or functioned in any consistent, concerted manner. In fact, there is no evidence to suggest that a single significant treasonous society existed at any point during the war. Though Northerners, lacking the benefit of the research of later generations of historians, had no way of knowing this, political leaders did. Not one of the numerous investigations of political bodies or reputed societies produced compelling or even credible evidence. The evidence that was produced was piecemeal and invariably suspect, consisting of conflicting accounts, forged letters, and testimonies of criminals or prisoners.[53]

But it was the genius of the Republican Party to assign to these bumbling organizations a vast and expanding membership, rigorous operations, and evil intent. Embattled party leaders blended fact with fiction to produce harrowing accounts of intrigue, sabotage, and treason. The *Chicago Tribune* reported that the Knights of the Golden Circle boasted one hundred thousand "oath-bound, armed men," "determined to get up a fire in the rear of the armies of the Union." One account placed the nationwide membership of the Order of the American Knights at nearly one million. Another claimed that the KGC was "thoroughly organized in every Northern state" and "among our neighbors in Canada, and . . . the nobility, aristocracy, and moneyed classes in England."[54]

With membership of these treasonous societies allegedly growing daily, political gatherings that might, on the surface, seem merely adversarial assumed a more ominous tone. "It has been rumored around for some days," observed the *Chicago Tribune* in February 1862, "that there were many Knights of the Golden Circle and members of the Mutual Protection Societies in the [Illinois Constitutional Convention]. . . . The number of K.G.C.s has been placed so high as to come within a few votes of the majority." Thus the convention, a state-based attempt to wrest control of the state's governing apparatus from Republicans, was portrayed instead as but one project of the internationally based KGC, an organization that had planned the assassination of President Lincoln, armed the South for years before the insurrection, and was continuing in its quest to "seek the overthrow of the great American Union."[55]

Just as rumors of treasonous Democratic conspiracies strengthened the association between Democrats and rebels, so too did the actions and treatment of Clement Vallandigham, Ohio's ex-congressman and gubernatorial hopeful. Vallandigham, who called for peace from the floor of the House of Representatives in January 1863 and was arrested for "expressed or implied treason" in May of that year, was the Democrat Republicans loved to hate. He was an "arch-traitor" of the caliber of Burr and Arnold; he was a "pimp" of Jefferson Davis, a "renegade miscreant." And, unfortunately for the future of the Union, he was not necessarily an exception to the Democratic rule. On the contrary, in Republican speeches and papers, Vallandigham became representative of the evil that lurked in Democratic shadows. As the *Cincinnati Daily Gazette* noted in its discussion of the Democratic ticket in a local spring 1863 election, "Every vote cast for the candidates on the so-called Democratic ticket will count as a vote for submission to rebels under the head of such men as VALLANDIGHAM."[56]

In May 1863, Vallandigham delivered a speech calling on Northerners to express their opposition to the war at the polls. Four days later, he was arrested for violation of General Ambrose Burnside's General Order No. 38, which declared that anyone committing "expressed or implied treason" would be tried as a spy or a traitor, and, if convicted, would suffer death or banishment. Vallandigham was tried in a military court, convicted, and exiled to the Confederacy. He made his way north to Canada; from Canada he pursued his candidacy for the governorship of Ohio. The gubernatorial contest between the exiled Vallandigham and his opponent, War Democrat and Union Party candidate John Brough, captured the attention of Americans North and South. For Northern Republicans, a Vallandigham victory would be devastating; for Southerners, a sign that the Union could not sustain its commitment. But Vallandigham's candidacy was a double-edged sword. Republicans surely

In May 1863, following an incendiary speech, Clement Vallandigham was arrested for violating General Burnside's General Order No. 38, which declared that anyone committing "expressed or implied treason" would be tried as a spy or a traitor. Vallandigham was tried in a military court, convicted, and exiled to the Confederacy. Throughout much of the war, Vallandigham served as a foil for Republicans who sought to portray the Democracy as a seedbed of treason. (The arrest of Clement Vallandigham, leader of the Peace Democrats, May 1863. *Frank Leslie's Illustrated Newspaper.* Collection of the New York Historical Society, negative no. 75042.)

relished the prospect of a campaign against a convicted traitor, a traitor now officially representing the Democratic Party. Vallandigham's candidacy alone might encourage Democrats to think twice about their chosen party. The campaign summer of 1863, marked by name-calling, heated debates, brawls, and even murder, then culminated in victory for Brough.[57]

With Brough's triumph, Vallandigham no longer seemed to represent much of a threat to Republicans or the Union. But in June 1864, Vallandigham returned to Ohio from exile. Hearing rumors of his return, alarmed Republicans demanded his immediate arrest and deportation. Cooler heads prevailed: as Murat Halstead wrote, "It would be a great mistake now to arrest

Vallandigham. . . . Sensible Republicans without exception say the best thing to do is let him alone." Horace Greeley agreed: "He will do good here." Greeley wrote in the *Tribune,* "His running for Governor last year was worth fifty thousand votes to the Unionists of Ohio. Can't we get him on the Copperhead ticket as Vice-President?" Though Vallandigham's name did not appear on the Democratic national ticket in 1864, it was frequently seen in the Republican campaign literature of that year.[58]

But even as Republicans painted this picture of a Democracy rife with partyism, conspiracy, and treason, their own party-building efforts proceeded apace. Party newspapers and politicians were adept at portraying Republicans as patriots and Democrats as infidels. Beginning in the fall of 1862, they received help from a national network remembered by William O. Stoddard, a personal secretary to President Lincoln, as "the most perfect party skeleton ever put together for utter efficiency of political machine work": the popular, partisan Union Leagues. These leagues were distinct from, and will be considered independently of, the three elite metropolitan Union Leagues that form the focus of the following chapter. For while the elite leagues proclaimed a nationalist vision and a nationalist patriotism, the popular leagues were profoundly partisan. Offering association-minded Americans membership in a secret society, the popular Union Leagues defined both the nation and patriotism in terms of the Republican Party.[59]

THE UNION LEAGUES

Throughout the spring and summer of 1863, a strange, clandestine ritual repeated itself in meeting rooms, lodges, storefronts, and halls across the North. Prospective initiates to a new patriotic society entered the outer chamber of the local Union League headquarters. There a high-ranking official rehearsed the league's objectives: "to preserve Liberty and the Union of these United States; to maintain the Constitution . . . to sustain the existing administration in putting down the enemies of the Government, and thwarting the designs of traitors and disloyalists." The candidates pledged themselves to secrecy, then were asked a number of questions: Were they opposed to secession or disunion? Did they acknowledge that their "first and highest allegiance" was to the United States national government?[60]

Candidates who passed this first trial were escorted into the meeting itself. The room was dark, its only light the "fire of liberty" which burned on an altar. The altar also held a United States flag, a ballot box, a gavel, and a

Bible. Incense wafted through the air. The candidates sang "Rally 'Round the Flag, Boys" as they gravely paraded to the altar. An official spoke: it was the league's solemn charge that "neither domestic nor foreign traitors" be allowed "to destroy this nation." Applicants pledged to carry out the league's objectives and were introduced to the symbols and secret meanings of the league. Members then headed off into the night, pledged to recruit more "true Union men" for induction into this covert patriotic society.[61]

The Union-wide repetition of this ritual, or of rituals closely resembling it, reflected the stunning growth of a movement that began in the fall of 1862 and claimed almost one million members by the autumn of 1864. The first wartime Union League was founded in Pekin, Illinois, in the early autumn of 1862, by George F. Harlow, commission merchant and Republican Party founder. As depression and war weariness engulfed the region, Harlow and his local Republican associates watched the state Democratic Party gain influence in Illinois politics. Concerned about the fate of the Union war effort and of the Republican Party, they formed a secret society "whereby true Union men could be known and depended upon in an emergency."[62]

Within a few months, the idea had spread to surrounding towns and counties. Traveling agents administered the league's oath to local political leaders and provided the new councils with league charters. The effort received support from Illinois governor Richard Yates. Soon the movement spread beyond the state, and by the summer of 1863, Union Leagues had been organized throughout the North. In May 1863 a national convention was held in Cleveland, Ohio. One hundred and seventy-one delegates from eighteen states were in attendance.[63]

In retrospect, the rapid growth of secret societies dedicated to the Union is not surprising. Mid-nineteenth-century Americans loved secrecy and ritual—by the 1840s, a proliferation of quasi-Masonic clubs, temperance clubs, and nativist clubs operated in secrecy. Historian Mark Carnes has proposed that such societies were rooted in the gender anxieties of the mid–nineteenth century, as secret fraternal rituals offered men an alternative to the increasingly feminized religious practices and culture of the day.[64]

But for Republicans, the secret rituals of the Union Leagues served an additional purpose—like the Sanitary Fairs, they offered a sense of excitement, belonging, and importance in a local forum of the distant nation-state. Members saw themselves acting out valuable roles as American citizens: if, as party leaders claimed, the Democracy threatened to subvert the Union, secret league activities could be critical to their nation's survival.

Pledged to the promotion of loyalty to the nation, league members held meetings, sponsored rallies, and distributed literature. But their efforts to encourage loyalty did not stop there. Though rhetorically a nonpartisan organization, like the Union Party, the leagues were in fact markedly partisan. Local and state league officials were usually local and state Republican Party officials. James M. Edmunds, president of the national league from 1863 to 1869, had previously been chairman of the Michigan State Republican Central Committee and was reputed to be "one of the best informed and most capable politicians in the country."[65]

Not surprisingly, the league's definition of patriotism was usually synonymous with Republicanism. In fact, over time, any pretense of bipartisanship collapsed under the weight of party exigencies. League houses served as distribution centers for partisan literature, including that produced by the metropolitan publication societies. Local councils packaged Republican newspapers and sent them to Union soldiers. Members policed polls and rallies, guarded conscription tables, and in other ways discouraged any criticism of Lincoln, Republicans, or the war. Not content to wait for treasonous behavior to surface, Union Leagues also formed vigilante committees to ferret out persons of suspect patriotism and report them to the United States War Department. Democratic secret societies were also a favorite target.[66]

If there was irony to be found in the fact that Republicans labored under cover of darkness even as they condemned Democratic societies for the clandestine nature of *their* operations, Union Leaguers did not acknowledge it. In fact, the very secret nature of the leagues reinforced the dialectic wherein Republicanism equaled loyalty and Democracy equaled treason. The covert nature of the league's work was both justified by and seemed to confirm the Democracy's own undercover attempts at subversion. Moreover, the leagues' ceremony provided a means of ritual affirmation of loyalty. Theatrical initiation rites, combined with bizarre systems of identification, allowed members to make ritual statements of their own position *not* among the ranks of the Democratic disloyal, but in the armies of the Republican faithful.[67]

THE DEMOCRATIC RESPONSE TO REPUBLICAN NOTIONS OF PATRIOTISM

Not surprisingly, Democrats did not accept Republican constructions of patriotism. Point by point, they challenged the Republican Party's interpretation of the Civil War partisan dynamic. Contrary to Republican claims,

Republicans had not sacrificed their party; such pretensions were "a sharp Republican trick to demoralize the Democratic Party." Where Republicans felt confident as a party, they held Republican conventions; where they doubted their power, they hid behind the Union Party, from which "their pimps prate of no-party." Indiana governor Oliver P. Morton, for example, claimed that his enrollment of seventy thousand Democratic soldiers was one indication of his willingness to lay down the partisan. Democrats were out-raged: "To receive Democrats into the Army is the Governor's comprehen-sive idea of laying down the partisan upon the altar of his country," they remonstrated. Morton refused to appoint Democrats to civil positions, even those vacated by Democrats enlisting in the army. Growing tired of Repub-lican claims to be above party, Democrats asserted, "It is high time that these hypocritical professions of no-partyism should cease, for they are too glar-ingly false to deceive the most simple."[68]

To combat Republican claims that parties as institutions should be sus-pended in wartime, Democrats invoked Jefferson to challenge the Republi-cans' Washington: the *New York World* quoted a letter Jefferson had written to John Taylor, arguing that "in every free and deliberating society, there must, from the nature of man, be opposite parties. Perhaps this party divi-sion is necessary to induce each to watch and debate to the people the pro-ceedings of the other." Wartime was no time to abandon the watch. With public patronage "overgrown and enormous," the people's "rigorous scru-tiny and wakeful vigilance" was needed now more than ever.[69]

Democrats also rejected Republican claims that the Union Party was the wartime representative of Democratic traditions, history, and values. "To ask Democrats to say that their political life is a lie," argued an Indianapolis paper, "and their professions have been a hypocrisy, is rather much. . . . Democrats are joint heirs with Republicans of this Government, joint guardians of the public liberties, joint architects of its fortunes and equally interested in its future destiny."[70]

As Democrats argued the validity of their wartime party, they insisted that their behavior within that party was unassailable. Mere opposition to the ever-changing policies of the administration did not, they argued, constitute infi-delity to country, "unless the great body of solid citizens are expected to shift like a weather cock at every shifting of the breeze." As the *New York World* pointed out after Lincoln issued the preliminary Emancipation Proclama-tion, the president himself had argued against emancipation as a policy. They protested, then, "against the introduction of a test of loyalty by which the president would have been convicted of treason at any time since his inauguration up to within the last few weeks."[71]

When Republicans persisted in labeling Democratic candidates traitors, even those who voted men and money for the war, Democrats complained bitterly: "If all democrats are traitors, we have the singular phenomena of a Union army comprised mainly of democratic traitors . . . of a war carried on by monies contributed mostly by democratic and traitorous bankers . . . and [by] traitorous democratic generals. . . . If democrats are traitors, they have a very singular way of showing their treason."[72]

Viewed through the lens of the Democracy, then, Republican definitions of loyalty were patently partisan. They demanded that a citizen "bow the knee to the Republican calf" and lay down "his principles and manliness upon the altar of Republicanism." "Let us hear then no more of this whimpering about loyalty," declared the *Albany Atlas and Argus* in 1863. "Because men happen to differ in political opinions or about the best means of restoring the Union, it does not follow that they are disloyal."[73]

Rejecting Republican arguments that expressions of discontent equaled partyism or, worse yet, treason, Democrats invoked republican tenets concerning the rights of citizens of a republic. They pointed to the difference between "supporting the government and supporting the administration": "These men are not the government; they are not the country. They are, for a brief period, the instruments of conducting the affairs of the government and the country." The administration was staffed with mere men, "the people's servants"; Americans were well qualified to judge the conduct of those servants. It was, in fact, a patriot's duty to keep the leaders in check, and he who failed to do so, "is as false to his duty, as much a traitor to his country, as the man who deserts to the enemy."[74]

As Democrats framed their own ideas of loyalty to the nation—ideas rooted in republican traditions of liberty, vigilance, and civic virtue—their rhetoric was at times reminiscent of the revolutionary idealism of Thomas Paine. But Democratic ideas of national identity differed markedly from those suggested by Paine, who had written antislavery tracts as early as 1775, and who called on Americans to "forget not the hapless African" in their plans for a new government. Democrats envisioned a nation which might, in fact should, forget the "hapless African," for to them America was a nation for white men only.[75]

The Democratic belief that the nation was intended for whites alone—a belief Stephen Douglas had articulated frequently in the 1850s—was expressed often during the war. "Ours is a government of white men," asserted the *Indianapolis Daily State Sentinel* in July 1861. Though Republicans might argue that the founders intended to include blacks in the declaration, "all men are created equal," as John McShea, Jr., an Albany, New York, Democrat, pointed out, the proof of their error lay with the declaration's author, a slave owner who had not emancipated his own slaves. "It is plain, Sir," McShea asserted, "that Thomas Jefferson and the founders of this government meant to establish it for white men."[76]

Democrats thus regularly decried Republican war measures not just because they threatened American civil liberties and federalist traditions, but also because they jeopardized the very nature of the American polity. The enlistment of African-American troops, for example, was met by many Democrats with outrage: abolitionists, they claimed, were "attempting to degrade the country by placing a poor, miserable and subjective race in the position which white men alone should occupy. Is it possible that the people of the North, the descendants of a proud and imperious race, will permit the Negro to be armed and placed by his side in maintaining a white man's government?" A parade in Dayton, Ohio, featured a wagon bearing thirty-four women in white dresses (together representing the thirty-four states) and a sign proclaiming "Fathers and Brothers, protect us from Despotism and Negro Equality." As a New York paper proclaimed, Northerners had "more to fear today from the prejudices of an American congress as to negro emancipation than from the bayonets of a rebellious foe."[77]

Democratic constructions of white American identity invoked images of historic intent and racial integrity; but they also regularly enlisted Northerners' fears of competition. They painted a picture of a zero-sum game, in which each and every gain for black Americans would result in a loss for whites. The *Indianapolis Daily State Sentinel* accused the Republican administration of policies that supported "vagabond Negroes in idleness" while adding to the "burdens of the farmer and laborer." The *New York World* predicted "a swarthy inundation of negro laborers . . . cheapening white labor by black competition." The specter of "hordes" of freedmen migrating north and competing with whites for scarce land and scarcer employment was common.[78]

Because a Democratic America was a white America, patriotism to that nation, though on one level defined by republican tenets of civic duty and assertion, had another meaning as well. Democrats linked the notion of patriotism to the defense of a white man's government. Thus, much as patriotism for the radicals was yoked to the pursuit of antislavery, loyalty for

many Democrats meant antiabolitionism. "The Lincoln Catechism," a sa-
tirical antiadministration pamphlet published in 1864, declared that the
Republican Party proposed to change the name of the nation to "New Af-
rica," and that the Republican-taught meaning of "patriot" was "a man who
loves his country less, and the negro more." Clement Vallandigham was more
overt: "Whoever feels it is his duty to fight armed rebels at the South, let
him enlist at once," he proclaimed. "Whoever remains at home, it is his duty
to join with me against Abolition rebels in our midst. This is loyalty; this is
fidelity to the Union."[79]

In July 1863, Democratic concerns about civil liberties, the growth of the
national state, and abolitionism came together with long-standing class, racial, and political tensions in the New York City draft riots. Though the riots
took the nation by surprise, New York was a volatile environment. There the
nation's richest lived side by side with its poorest. If many of the city's wealthy
profited from wartime investments, for the poor, the burdens of war—including rising prices, declining real wages, and job insecurity—were immense.
The prospect of black migrants fueled working-class discontent. Fernando
Wood, a leading city official and head of one of the city's two Democratic
machines, was a dedicated peace advocate. And Horatio Seymour's outspoken
opposition to the draft led many to believe that he would not allow its enforcement in New York. On July 4, 1863, Seymour went even further, appearing
to sanction violence if the draft should be effected despite his best efforts:
"Remember this," he entreated his Democratic audience, "—that the bloody
and treasonable doctrine of public necessity can be proclaimed by a mob as
well as by a government."[80]

The draft against which the New Yorkers rioted was the result of the
Enrollment Act of 1863. While many Democrats objected to the draft law on
the grounds of states' rights and civil liberties, its most controversial provision was a clause offering draftees a commutation fee of $300, a provision
which fueled a growing working-class conviction that the war was a rich man's
war and a poor man's fight. In New York, opposition was further informed
by what many perceived to be inequities in the quotas established for Democratic districts in New York State.[81]

In June 1863, Governor Seymour received a telegram from Washington
requesting twenty thousand militia to drive Lee out of Pennsylvania. Seymour
complied, and the city was left without military protection. On Saturday,
July 11, provost marshals arrived in New York City and drafting began. The
governor did not intervene. On Monday morning, July 13, the riots began.[82]

The riots, according to Iver Bernstein, had two distinct stages. The initial rioting was in effect a demonstration, directed against the Republican administration and its class-biased Enrollment Act. But by late Monday, the crowd had begun to shift its focus. No longer did it confine its attacks to symbols of the Republican Party and the wartime administration; in the second phase of the riots, participants turned their animosity increasingly toward the black community and Protestant upper-middle-class reform institutions. Swarms of angry rioters attacked blacks in the streets and dragged them out of their homes. They tortured, killed, and mutilated their victims, as tolerant and even approving crowds looked on. They set fire to an orphanage for black children, a home for aging prostitutes, and two Protestant missions, among other targets. Seymour declared the city in a state of insurrection, and troops were brought in from Pennsylvania to subdue the rioters. On July 17, five days after they had begun, the riots ended. One hundred five men, women, and children had been killed.[83]

The Colored Orphan Asylum on Fifth Avenue became the target of racial hatred and violence during the New York City draft riots. Rioters razed then burned the building. One hundred five men, women, and children were killed in the riots. (Burning of the Colored Orphan Asylum, New York City draft riots, July 1863. *Harper's Weekly*. Collection of the New York Historical Society, negative no. 30033.)

The riots were, in a sense, the Republicans' worst fears realized. They represented both the potential for the disintegration of the war effort throughout the North and a rejection of the Republican vision. Yet almost immediately, it became clear that the riots, like Democratic secret societies and Vallandigham, could work to Republican advantage. Republicans blamed Democrats and the Democratic press for the riots. Seymour's salutation to the rioters—in an attempt to restore calm, he addressed a gathering as "my friends"—drew extensive censure. Because only Democrats had opposed the draft, the riots served to validate the Republican conflation of Democracy with treason, Republicanism with loyalty.[84]

Moreover, the riots worked to discredit Democratic notions of white national identity, an effect catalyzed by the heroic performance of black troops one day after the rioting in New York ended. On July 18, the African-American Fifty-fourth Massachusetts Colored Infantry led an assault on the nearly impenetrable Fort Wagner. Though the attack was not successful, the courage and valor of the black regiment captured the North's attention. As James McPherson notes, "Few Republican newspapers failed to point the moral: black men who fought for the Union deserved more respect than white men who fought against it."[85]

Indeed, just as the riots worked to challenge the Democracy's racist notions of national identity, they also marked a turning point for Republican constructs of nationality. If civil liberties and white supremacy informed Democratic notions of patriotism and national identity, as the war progressed, many Republicans promulgated a definition of American identity that, while restrictive and partisan, accommodated African-Americans.

But could this new definition triumph at the polls? As the North headed into the summer of 1864, it suffered heavy losses in fierce engagements at the Battle of the Wilderness, Spotsylvania, Cold Harbor, and Petersburg. Peace activists stepped up their campaign to end the war and began to acquire more influence in the Democratic Party. Though Democrats chose George McClellan, a War Democrat, as their presidential candidate, they selected George H. Pendleton, a prominent Copperhead associated with Vallandigham, as his running mate and voted a peace plank into the Democratic platform.[86]

To stave off the Democratic threat, Republicans drew from the panoply of methods they had developed over the course of the war. They ran on the Union Party ticket, not just on the state level, but on the national level as well: in June 1864, the National Union Convention—effectively the Republican Party convention—opened in Baltimore and nominated Lincoln for a second term. As the campaign swung into gear, charges of secret societies and conspiracies proliferated, culminating in the "Holt Report," a fourteen-thousand-word government publication detailing the activities of a new Democratic secret society. Prepared by Judge Advocate General Joseph Holt, the report argued that half a million Northerners belonged to the Order of the American Knights, an offshoot of the defunct Knights of the Golden Circle. Led by Clement Vallandigham, the order's intentions included aiding the rebels with arms and intelligence and establishing a northwestern confederacy. The report was published in October and met with skepticism, even among Republican officials; it was nonetheless printed as a pamphlet and widely circulated throughout the North. The Union Leagues played their part as the "perfect party skeleton . . . for utter efficiency of political machine work," distributing literature, sponsoring rallies, and policing polls.[87]

But in the end, it was the efforts of David Farragut, William Tecumseh Sherman, and the Union's sailors and soldiers that tipped the scales in the Republicans' favor. In August Farragut led the Union Navy in a victory at Mobile Bay; in early September, Sherman captured Atlanta. Granted new hope that the war might soon be over, Northerners rallied behind the incumbent. Lincoln swept the election, garnering 55 percent of the popular vote—the first president to win by such a sizeable margin since Jackson in 1828. For the moment, the Republican definition of national identity was ascendant.[88]

"A Profound National Devotion"

The Metropolitan Union Leagues

Edward Everett Hale was a member of Boston's Brahmin caste and a patriot by birth. His uncle, Edward Everett, was a renowned statesman who would deliver the two-hour oration that preceded Lincoln's Gettysburg Address; his great Uncle, Nathan Hale, had died a martyr to the Revolutionary cause, his devotion to country still on his lips. Though at times his family's class pride superseded its national pride—as a child he was forbidden to mention the name of his esteemed great-uncle, as death by hanging was a class embarrassment—Edward Everett Hale grew up with the understanding that his was a distinguished, patriotic lineage, destined for national leadership.[1]

During the Civil War, Hale, a Unitarian minister and avid writer, did not volunteer for service. Instead, he devoted his energies to sermons and articles designed to sustain and encourage the embattled North. He became a member of two elite nationalist organizations, the Union League and the Loyal Publication Society. "The Man Without a Country," the short story that opens this book, was the most dramatic product of Hale's patriotic efforts.[2]

But the message in Hale's story was not his alone. Throughout the latter half of the war, the elite Union Leagues in Philadelphia, New York, and Boston devoted themselves to transforming Americans' contractual notions of patriotism and nation into unquestioning, even organic, ideas of loyalty and national identity. The Union League movement was, as we have seen, a nationwide phenomenon: hundreds of clubs were formed in cities and towns across the North during the course of the war. All the leagues shared a founding premise, that of cultivating loyalty to the nation. But outside Philadelphia, New York, and Boston, the Union Leagues had a more popular, distinctly partisan nature.

The Union League to which Hale belonged stood in marked contrast to such societies. These were gentlemen's clubs, with limited membership, lavish quarters, abundant treasuries, and a focus on a nationalist, rather than partisan, patriotism. Although the Philadelphia League made a weak and somewhat abortive effort to organize leagues in its immediate environs, for the most part the elite clubs did not participate in the spread of the league throughout the North and, in fact, were often at odds with or embarrassed by the popular leagues. The Boston organization chose the name "Union Club" to distinguish itself from the Union Leagues, and for several years officials in the New York City Union League Club considered changing their name so that they would not be confused with the popular leagues of the same name in New York City and New York State.[3]

Begun as gentlemen's clubs in the midst of the social chaos generated by sectional conflict and civil war, these leagues quickly acquired a more complex character. The leagues brought an embattled intellectual and professional elite together with powerful business interests in a coalition designed to rally support for the Union and strengthen the national state. They pursued the task of constructing a transcendent patriotism on two distinct levels. First, through the creative appropriation of an upper-class institution, league founders hoped to cultivate a nationalist patriotism among the metropolitan elite, forging a cohesive upper class in the process. They created exclusive gentlemen's clubs whose chief criteria were loyalty to the nation and support of the national administration.

For Northerners who did not qualify as elites, league members had a different approach: they sponsored and wrote literature for publication societies. The pamphlets and broadsides produced by these societies were designed to rally Northerners behind the war, assert control over an increasingly unruly working class, and inculcate a preeminent national loyalty. They employed a multitude of arguments, battling partisanship, defending specific government policies, painting the North as a free labor Mecca, and, like Hale's "The Man Without a Country," portraying the nation-state as an organic entity central to the fulfillment of self and freedom.

THE ANTEBELLUM METROPOLITAN ELITE

Several scholars, among them Amy Bridges, Robert Dahl, and Sam Bass Warner, have described the process whereby political, economic, and social power, coexisting in the urban merchant elite throughout the eighteenth and the early nineteenth centuries, were separated in the mid–nineteenth century. In the earlier period, elites and masses alike believed that there was an identifiable public interest, a common good that transcended particular concerns. The gentry "ruled," bringing notions of noblesse oblige, governmental activism, and economic regulation to the pursuit of that common interest.[4]

By the mid–nineteenth century, however, dramatic economic, social, and political changes had reconfigured power relations in urban America. The cotton trade fueled an economic boom in New York City; in Philadelphia manufacturing and finance flourished; and Boston was transformed by the textile industry. Industrialization and immigration reshaped class relations, populations exploded, and universal white manhood suffrage empowered the masses. As the merchant elite faced the demands of a transfigured political economy, many withdrew from political office to attend to newly specialized vocations, or were displaced by a new breed of politician wielding the weapons of political democracy and party machines.[5]

But if the merchant elite withdrew from officeholding, they did not withdraw from politics. Their survival as a class depended on political power, which implied power to enact duties, issue permits, expand infrastructure, secure land grants, impose taxes, and grant franchises, charters, or monopolies. Merchants and politicians initially worked hand in glove: the politicians organized the electorate and sought office, while the merchants financed their efforts and served on councils. By the 1850s, however, further changes in the cities' class and political structure had undermined this "amicable division of labor." Increasingly, politicians looked directly to the masses for support, and in exchange, protected the voters'—not the merchants'—interests. As Amy Bridges writes, "By forsaking the offices of governments and distancing themselves from the populace, the wealthy had lost control of city government."[6]

If urban elites felt their control over the new professional politicians slipping away, they also felt their influence over the masses waning. During the forties and fifties, all three cities witnessed antiabolitionist, antiblack, nativist, and/or labor riots. In Philadelphia, nativist rioting in the mid-forties resulted in the consolidation in 1854 of twenty-seven municipalities into one city; the goal was to bring the inhabitants of the fifteen hundred farms included in those municipalities under the authority of the city's police. But one effect was to bring huge numbers of Democrats into the voting population; the Whig, Free-Soil, and Know-Nothing elite, who later joined forces in the Republican Party, were forced to seek new support among the working classes. In New York, class tensions erupted in the 1849 Astor Place riots, leading to unprecedented intervention by city and state authorities. The state militia fired on the crowd, and twenty-two people were killed. In Boston, Irish immigration upset the preexisting political and social order and fueled nativist rioting. With no "moral consensus" on which to stake their claim to authority, a beleaguered patriciate faced an increasingly restive, disorderly working class.[7]

Threatened by professional politicians, fearing anarchy in an age of class politics, the embattled elite soon found itself rocked from within as well, as slavery and secession divided the cities' upper and middle classes. In Philadelphia, secession and the war for Union drove a wedge between men with familial or business ties to the South and the conservative Whig-Republicans who otherwise dominated the city's elite. In New York, cultural and economic concerns united many of the city's professionals, merchants, industrialists, and bankers behind the war but fueled a simmering feud between an older patrician class troubled by the "experience of commerce" and one segment of the rising merchant class. In Boston, the battle over slavery jeopardized a long-standing Brahmin-Whig hegemony, pitting Cotton and Conscience Whigs against one another.[8]

The toll the war took on urban upper- and middle-class solidarity was clearly illustrated by the fate of urban gentlemen's clubs, which, in mid-nineteenth-century America, all but constituted "society." In Philadelphia the Wistar Party, a sixty-three-year-old association evolved from the tradition of weekly entertainments at the home of Dr. Caspar Wistar, disbanded shortly after the war began. The Philadelphia Club continued its meetings, but they became increasingly tense and unpleasant, as did meetings of the Somerset and Forest Clubs in Boston and those of the old Union Club of New York City.[9]

Although the rush to patriotic unity muted many of these conflicts early in the war, by the autumn of 1862 battlefield defeats, the burgeoning role of the federal government, and the change in war aims heralded by the Preliminary Emancipation Proclamation had loosened wartime restraints on expressions of discontent. As defeatism escalated, the elite in each of these cities confronted its particular divisions in distinct yet similar ways.

THE UNION LEAGUE OF PHILADELPHIA

In Philadelphia, the discontented were by no means in the minority. Given Pennsylvania's geographical proximity to the South, many of Philadelphia's most prominent families were of Southern origin. They maintained close ties to their Southern kin and sent their sons to Southern schools. Philadelphians were linked to the South economically as well: their banks negotiated the cotton that left Charleston for Liverpool; they discounted the bills of exchange for Virginia tobacco. Moreover, the South provided a market both for the foreign goods that passed through Philadelphia's ports and for the city's own manufactured products. Whatever their political affiliations prior to the sectional struggle, once the war began, the men and women with close Southern ties allied with the Democrats, and some even overtly with the South.[10]

For wealthy Philadelphians without Southern ties, politics prior to 1854 meant membership in the Whig Party, for that party best represented the interests and ideals of a manufacturing city's elite. With secession, Philadelphia's Unionists believed that the very foundation of their prosperity as a class had been placed in jeopardy. The perpetuation of the nation on Northern terms was necessary to the continued existence of the commercial and manufacturing interests. Though for years those interests had taken the Union, with its lawful environment, internal improvements, and tariffs for granted, with the war, Philadelphia's business elite could no longer afford that luxury. Morton McMichael, editor of the *Philadelphia North American,* spoke for many when he argued that the South's secession was "a question of simple law and order against anarchy. It is a question which vitally concerns every man's safety in business." Two days later he reiterated this theme:

> We . . . live under the national law. If that is broken down, our interests, our property, and our lives may be lost in the disorder which will ensue. . . . Do our merchants expect to preserve their business when the authority of the Union is gone in the Mississippi Valley. . . . Can their trade to any state be of value if there are no courts or laws to aid the recovery of debts? Nothing but ruin awaits all business interests of ours . . . if the doctrines of the Secession leaders are to prevail.

McMichael warned those "who have obtained to such prosperity in the United States" that if they were to "remain in peace and prosperity at all, . . . there must be a powerful and united effort made now to sustain the government." Thus the *North American* supported a war to strengthen the national state and combat Southern political power.[11]

As the war escalated, the tensions between the two factions of the Philadelphia elite intensified as well. The publication in 1862 of Charles Ingersoll's pro-Southern pamphlet, "Letter to a Friend in a Slave State," marked the end of the elite dissenters' restraint. As defeatism spread from meetings and rallies into the social clubs of the wealthy and renowned, the Unionist patriciate expressed dismay. Judge J. I. Clark Hare, a prominent Whig jurist, bemoaned the rising status accorded the disloyal in Philadelphia. "The thought that seemed to move Judge Hare the most," reported George Boker, secretary of the Philadelphia Union League, "was that while we, the inhabitants of a loyal city, were thus cast down before the ill fortunes of our country, men who were almost leagued with the Southern traitors were walking with high heads among our people, openly exalting in our discomfiture, and eagerly waiting for the day of our utter overthrow." As a director of that league later explained, "The thoroughly aroused loyalists of Philadelphia had to establish and maintain their social position," and, in the process, protect the prosperity that that position both reflected and enabled.[12]

And so the Unionist elite laid plans for a new kind of social club. With fidelity to the Union as its cornerstone, this fashionable club would wage a battle for the loyalty of the upper class through the manipulation of powerful symbols of status and prestige. If successful, it would weld that class into a cohesive force, strengthening the Unionist faction at home in their battles for political power and social control in the service of their class, as well as throughout the nation, where the irresoluteness of the people seemed to threaten an end to the Union as the elite knew it.

In November 1862, Morton McMichael, Judge J. I. Clark Hare, George Henry Boker, poet, playwright, and son of a Philadelphia financier, and Benjamin Gerhard, a wealthy businessman, met to discuss plans for an association which would honor the nation and exclude the disloyal. The new club called for "unqualified loyalty to the Government of the United States and unwavering support of the suppression of the rebellion." Membership was by invitation only; those eligible must meet the founders' requirements for social standing as well as for patriotism. Philadelphians who could not meet these requirements would be refused social and business relations with club members, for the time had arrived when "sympathy with [armed rebellion] should in social and commercial life meet the frown of the patriotic and the true. Disloyalty must be made unprofitable." The original draft called for associates to refrain from "all social intercourse and dealings with disloyal persons." Thus the "primary object" of the organization would be "to discountenance and rebuke by moral and social influences, all disloyalty to the Federal Government."[13]

The opulence of the Philadelphia Union League House was designed to enhance the appeal of this elite gentlemen's club, whose chief criterion was loyalty to the Union. (Philadelphia Union League House. *Frank Leslie's Illustrated Newspaper.* Collection of the New York Historical Society, negative no. 75043.)

To enhance the social appeal of the Philadelphia club, large sums of money were invested in elegant quarters. "No effort nor reasonable expense has been spared in the Reading Room, the Telegraphic News and the Restaurant, to make our house an inviting centre of instruction and convenience," noted Boker of the Chestnut Street clubhouse. Those expenses included the purchase (at a reduced price) of Thomas Sully's equestrian portrait of George Washington, originally commissioned for Congress in 1842. Further adding to the club's attraction for the elite was the fact that it was modeled closely on the style of the dissolved Wistar Party. The "cards of invitation" issued by the new club were almost replicas of the Wistar's. Appearing only eighteen months after the demise of that prestigious association, the Union Club appeared to be assuming the role of successor. But it was ostracizing—even blacklisting—those members of society who entertained Southern sympathies. The reaction among local Democrats was one of outrage: a local Copperhead paper printed the names and addresses of club members, suggesting that those gentlemen's houses would soon be destroyed.[14]

THE NEW YORK UNION LEAGUE

As the Union Club took shape in Philadelphia, plans for a similar club were being made in New York City, where a small but vocal segment of the city's commercial and manufacturing class opposed the evolving war aims and measures of the Lincoln administration. This largely Democratic contingent did support the war for the Union. But they argued against emancipation and a transformation of the South's political economy, fearing both the impact of the disruption of Southern labor relations on the production and export of agricultural products and the implications of black suffrage for the Democratic Party. Often recent arrivals to New York, these men worked closely with the city's politicians, catered to the immigrant masses, advocated free trade, and supported the kind of "international republicanism" typified by the "Young America" movement. August Belmont, a prominent financier and Democratic Party leader, was a spokesperson for this vision.[15]

The men who founded the New York Union League took strong objection to Belmont and his cohort. Like their counterparts in Philadelphia, they understood the centrality of the state to the continued prosperity of the nation as they knew it. But the New York Union League was also rooted in a cultural critique of Belmont and his national vision. Its chief founders were professionals and intellectuals, including Henry Bellows, prominent Unitarian minister; Frederick Law Olmsted, Sanitary Commission secretary and Central Park superintendent; George Templeton Strong, lawyer; and Wolcott Gibbs, prominent physician. These men faced challenges both to their political influence and to their vision of a moral, cohesive society. In their view, laissez-faire and mass democracy represented perhaps the greatest threats to that vision. They hoped that a new spate of institutions might help bind together a society in decay. In the war they saw an opportunity to restore their power and enact their vision, in part through the strengthening of the national state and national identity. All four men were already members of the United States Sanitary Commission, an association designed to coordinate the volunteer and medical war efforts, but whose "animating idea," according to Bellows, was "the nation as super-eminent above the states."[16]

Thus league founders hoped that the New York club would assert the authority of the older mercantile class against that of Belmont and the "arrivistes." Writing to Wolcott Gibbs in November 1862, Frederick Law Olmsted outlined his hopes and explained his rationale for a nationalist gentlemen's club in New York. The members of this new club, the "hereditary natural aristocracy," would be distinguished from the "parvenus; we are rich, they are vulgar." Olmsted pointed specifically to August Belmont and Henry G. Stebbins (a member of the Belmont clique) as examples of the latter. Olmsted's new gentlemen's club, an association of the "legitimate descendants and arms bearers of the old dukes of our land," would define loyalty in such a manner as to exclude Belmont and Stebbins, even if they professed support for the war.[17]

Olmsted's vision of the club as a cultural weapon in a war for class survival had yet another dimension. In his view, the new generation of young wealthy men did not understand the obligations and duties of an elite upper class. In an elaborate membership plan, Olmsted expressed his hopes that the club might attract "promising young men" and indoctrinate them to the ways of the nationalist elite. "Gentlemen in the European sense," these young men were "men of leisure" who "don't understand what their place can be in American society." As a result, they were "greatly tempted to go over to the devil (boss devil)."[18]

The Union League had to teach young rich Americans where their allegiances must lie, constructing a self-consciously nationalist elite to govern in the process. Olmsted hoped that in the leagues the youthful rich might be "sought for and drawn in and nursed and nourished with care." "Established men" could "fraternize with them, to welcome and hold every true man of them in fraternity." Such fraternization would not only help to shape a nationalist mind-set; it would help socialize a new generation of wealth to the ways of the nationalist upper class, thus helping to perpetuate that class while cultivating a political governing elite from the youthful rich: "so soon they may govern us if they will." To accomplish this task, "good rooms with something to do is alone essential. . . . Billiards and reading and smoking at least." The Union Club, then, would both shore up the patriotism of the wavering elite by virtue of its status and serve as a forum within which the upper class could know and form one another.[19]

To be effective in uniting the city's elite behind the war and against the views of Belmont's circle, the New York League's founders understood that they needed a coalition of professionals like themselves with the city's commercial, financial, and manufacturing classes. "Leading merchants are essential to our success," Strong wrote in his diary. With "a very respectable catalogue of moneyed men . . . we may make the thing work." Such a coalition was not at all unrealistic. If before the war the city's merchants, bankers, and industrialists had differed in their approach to the sectional crisis—many merchants and bankers feared losing the benefits that Southern markets and the cotton trade provided, and favored compromise at any cost, while industrialists viewed slavery as a threat to Northern workers' right to rise, and thus opposed compromise—with the war, the majority of these men rallied behind the Union and the Republican administration. They understood that the national state represented court-enforced contracts, tariffs, and an expanding infrastructure. Moreover, as the war progressed, New York City's elite assumed a disproportionately heavy portion of the government's debt. As they poured individual or corporate savings into war bonds, their stake in the war and the nation it was being fought to preserve escalated. As New York's Chamber of Commerce noted in its annual report of 1863–64, the war had engendered a "vast pecuniary obligation" to suppress the rebellion.[20]

Thus the New York Union League was founded to unite the city's business elite with its professionals and intellectuals behind a strong national state and a vigorous prosecution of the war. The club took shape in the early spring of 1863, as Bellows, Strong, Olmsted, and Gibbs refined their project and began screening potential members. On March 20 the organization held its first official meeting and elected officers. In its choice of officers the New York club revealed its reliance upon the commercial class: Robert B. Minturn, head of the second largest shipping and shipbuilding firm in the nation, was elected president; and William H. Aspinwall, banker and shipping and commission merchant; Moses Taylor, shipping and sugar merchant; and Alexander T. Stewart, dry goods merchant, were among the vice presidents. In his diary, Strong expressed his delight in finding "strong representatives of capital and commerce . . . interested and active."[21]

The New York League vowed to "make the Union League Club House in its appointments, as complete as any in the world." They rented an unoccupied family home—"one of the most splendid mansions of the metropolis"—on the corner of Seventeenth and Broadway, facing Union Square, for six thousand dollars a year; twenty thousand more was set aside to furnish and carpet it. The house would provide a meeting room, committee rooms, two billiard rooms, and a bar. Temporarily, meals would be catered, but plans were made to build a restaurant "upon a scale commensurate with the dignity of what ought speedily to become the largest and most influential club in America."[22]

Like its counterpart in Philadelphia, the New York club caused some consternation among those excluded by its criteria. Strong gleefully observed the opposition's discomfiture: "It is delightful to perceive that 'respectable' Copperheads begin to be aware of this club, and to squirm as if it irritated them somehow." Describing an encounter at the opera with a gentleman who claimed he disapproved of a club founded on a political basis and had therefore chosen to decline an offer of membership, Strong wrote, "Very funny; for in all our talk about organization and tests of admission, the name of William Butler Duncan has been familiarly used as a convenient . . . specimen of the class we would not admit on any terms."[23]

THE BOSTON UNION CLUB

If in New York and Philadelphia the impetus for the Union Clubs came in part from an attempt to secure the moral and social advantage for a faction of the cities' elite, in Boston the club served to bring the city's two upper-class factions closer together, if only temporarily. For much of the antebellum period, Boston Brahmin society was noted for its cohesiveness and its ability to withstand challenge. In *The Unitarian Conscience,* Daniel Walker Howe describes the alliance between Harvard moralists and Boston businessmen: the moralists provided a rationale for capitalism, and the merchants granted them positions of cultural and moral leadership. In the 1830s, when textile manufacturing engendered a new economic elite, the old merchant elite adapted by financing the new industry, forging business alliances, and intermarrying. But the sectional conflict called commitments and interest into the open, and as Cotton Whigs fretted over the potential loss of Southern markets and business connections, Conscience Whigs insisted that slavery would expand no more. After the attack on Fort Sumter, Boston's formerly Whig and now Republican elite had closed ranks once again, but the Emancipation Proclamation and plans for black troops presented yet another challenge.[24]

In the Somerset Club, "the state of feeling was more conspicuously critical than patriotic" wrote Martin Brimmer, graduate of Harvard Law School and son of a wealthy former mayor of Boston. "Some privately denounced the war in all its aspects; some attacked indiscriminately all the acts of the government . . . ; some were indifferent; some were wavering; some, with the best intentions, were made doubtful or timid by the tone of people about them. For those, and there were happily many of them, who were unhesitating in their support of the war, there was no common centre, no rallying place."[25]

In February 1863, a committee of fourteen of Boston's elite, including Harvard scholar Charles E. Norton and John Murray Forbes, one of the nation's leading railroad magnates and a United States Sanitary Commission founder, issued invitations to membership in a society of "clubbable men." In its desire to serve as a point of conflux for diverse members of the upper class, the club officially eschewed political action and elected Edward Everett, John Bell's running mate on the 1860 Constitutional Union ticket, as league president. The membership rolls of the Boston Union Club bear testimony to its success in this endeavor: members of the city's mercantile and manufacturing elite—the Lowells, the Lawrences, the Appletons, and the Brookses—joined, as did many of New England's most prominent intellectual and literary men, including Ralph Waldo Emerson, Edward Everett Hale, Oliver Wendell Holmes, and James Russell Lowell.[26]

Much as it had in Philadelphia and New York City, the Union League in Boston set the tone for the elite of the city, establishing national patriotism and fidelity to the administration as the standard of behavior in high society. As Oliver Wendell Holmes observed, the club would both serve as a locus for ardent supporters of the administration and attract those whose chief concerns were social, for "once a rallying point is given for all who mean hearty loyalty, the weak brethren who do not know what they believe will walk in with their white cravats and vacuous features, and leave the malignants in the only position they are ashamed of—that of being in the minority."[27]

As a result of the metropolitan Union Leagues, for many of the urban upper and middle classes, patriotism became a requisite part of life in society. As one contemporary later noted, "[The League's] effect was to make patriotism fashionable. Its political power consisted . . . in informing the rich and fashionable that they would lose caste if they became Copperheads." By the end of the leagues' first year, league membership in Philadelphia had grown to 985. The membership list of the New York club read like a Who's Who in New York City, with a total of 528 members, and the Boston club boasted over 400 members. Democrats and Republicans alike were members. Those who were not members pretended to be: According to Strong, Charles Gould told William C. Russell

that the Union League Club was a most praiseworthy institution which every loyal citizen of New York ought to join at once. He [Charles Gould] had done a great deal to set it going and worked for it until he saw it fairly established and likely to succeed, and then he had resigned because he had so many engagements that he really couldn't—and so forth. Whereas Charles Gould and Prosper M. Wetmore have from the first been recognized as embodiments of corrupt, mercenary, self-seeking sham-patriotism, and as representing a dirty set of false-hearted hack stump orators and wire-pullers, vigilantly to be excluded.[28]

THE NATIONALISM OF THE METROPOLITAN ELITE

It was the promise of status and profit that coaxed the wavering elite into the metropolitan Union Leagues; but once there, it was clear that though these clubs offered luxurious meeting rooms, elegant restaurants, and elite company, they were not ordinary gentlemen's clubs. The leagues organized Committees on Enlistments, which raised tens of thousands of troops for the Union, sponsored speakers who addressed national topics, celebrated national anniversaries "which could be turned to account in affecting public sentiment," and appointed committees to carry out various other war-supporting measures. They also participated in electoral races: setting aside its claim to nonpartisanship, the Philadelphia League campaigned in the 1863 gubernatorial race; both the Philadelphia and New York Leagues staunchly supported Lincoln in 1864. Through their publication societies, examined later, the Union Leagues advocated on behalf of the national loan, income taxes, the draft, emancipation, and black troops. Charting the course for the metropolitan elite to follow, they suggested that loyalty to country entailed championing a vigorous war effort, sustaining the war administration, and supporting the unprecedented growth of the national state.[29]

But perhaps the most striking statement that the leagues made concerning the meaning of national patriotism for the upper class lay in their support for emancipation and their active role in the mustering of African-American troops. This was, after all, a class of men many of whom, as Sven Beckert points out in a study of the New York City bourgeoisie, had agitated for compromise with the South at any cost prior to the war. Their support of such measures as the Fugitive Slave and Kansas-Nebraska Acts was rooted in a strong desire to see the South, with its markets and cotton production, remain as a part of the Union. Similarly, their vehement opposition to secession and support of the Northern war effort were in large part responses to the threat to the authority of a national state which protected and fostered their business concerns.[30]

The leagues were not, then, abolitionist organizations, though individuals ethically committed to the abolition of slavery did join. But they were deeply concerned about the fate of the national state. Hence many members supported both emancipation and the deployment of black troops chiefly as war measures. Moreover, with the Emancipation Proclamation, antiblack sentiment itself stood to undercut support for the national cause. In Philadelphia and New York, the campaigns that the Union Leagues undertook to raise and then showcase black troops were designed to aid the nation in its battles against both Southern secession and Northern resistance to increasingly radical war measures.

In June 1863, the Union League of Philadelphia organized a Supervisory Committee for the Enlistment of Colored Troops and began raising money and recruiting men. On July 24, the first regiment joined the national forces as the Third United States Regiment, Colored Troops. On October 3, the troops paraded through downtown Philadelphia and then marched for review in front of General George Cadwalader, who observed the parade from the steps of the Union League house. With no police escorts, the white officers carried loaded arms; the Sixth Regiment carried unloaded muskets, while the Eighth Regiment marched unarmed. A loud, "secretly hostile or openly jubilant" crowd thronged the streets; the parade was reportedly without incident.[31]

The New York League also recruited black troops and staged a similar parade only eight months after the draft riots had exposed the deep frustrations and antiblack sentiment of the Irish working class. One account, perhaps apocryphal, suggests that it was during those riots, as they sat armed behind locked doors and barricaded windows, that league members devised their plans. "If they got out of this thing alive, they would make the club defy public sentiment by raising and equipping a regiment of Negro troops and sending them to the front. More than that, they would march these freed men through the city streets." Particularly after the draft riots, it was important that Americans learn that such sentiments were not patriotic—that loyalty was more important than color. Over the winter the regiment was assembled, and the soldiers trained on Riker's Island.[32]

On March 5, 1864, the regiment marched from the dock at the East Twenty-sixth Street wharf to the league building at Union Square, where an estimated one hundred thousand people had gathered to view the presentation of colors to the new regiment. In a dramatic and symbolic gesture, the "Mothers, Wives, and Sisters of the Members of the Union League Club" stood on a grandstand erected in front of the clubhouse and presented the troops with their flags and an address signed by 189 prominent society women. This list included Mrs. John Jacob Astor and Mrs. John Jay. The address first recognized the Union League for its "liberality and intelligent patriotism," then turned to a truly remarkable tribute to the troops: "When you look at this flag and rush to battle . . . remember that it is also an emblem of love and honor from the daughters of this great metropolis to her brave champions in the field, and that they will anxiously watch your career, glorying in your heroism, ministering to you when wounded and ill, and honoring your martyrdom with benedictions and with tears." Following an elaborate reception, the troops paraded through New York City as planned, accompanied by flag bearers, one hundred policemen, and a military band.[33]

What was remarkable about this tribute was its dramatic transgression of mid-nineteenth-century white cultural norms. The intermingling of white women and black men spoke to Northerners' deepest racial fears. Yet here were the city's elite white women, vowing to love and honor the black soldiers, to nurse those who were wounded back to health, and to weep over those who died. It was a striking statement of the role that emancipation and the arming of blacks had assumed in the league's version of patriotism.

Although Union League support for black troops was rooted in a desire to see the nation strengthened and preserved—in contrast to the abolitionists, who, as we shall see, used a burgeoning national sentiment to promote egalitarian ideals—the result was still to broaden the definition of patriotism in America. Loyalty, not race, defined a patriot. Although this message was intended in part for the participants of the city's recent draft riots, it held meaning for elites as well: if the upper-class men who flocked to the leagues were to enjoy its perquisites of social prestige, they would have to embrace its evolving policies toward African-Americans as well.[34]

Thus, through the appropriation of gentlemen's clubs, league leaders rallied their class behind the war. As the cities' most prominent professionals, businessmen, and intellectuals followed the lure of status and profit into the Union Clubs, patriotism, which began with the swearing of unwavering loyalty, soon meant support for the vigorous prosecution of the war, an expanding national state, emancipation, and black troops. Moreover, by bringing the upper class's wealth, power, and prestige to the problem of wartime support, Union League leaders modeled their superior brand of loyalty and displayed their credentials to govern. Claiming the exclusive mantle of patriotism, they reclaimed some of the cultural and social authority that had escaped them prior to the war.

But support from the cities' elite alone would not win the war. If defeatism within the upper classes could be mitigated through the manipulation of status concerns, a different approach was required for the great majority of Americans.

THE UNION LEAGUES AND THE MASSES

For the founders of the Union League, the masses had always presented a special problem. As a group, league founders had little respect for the common man and disdained democracy. Representatives of their cities' intelligentsia as well as their professional and capitalist classes, some feared unfettered democracy for its impact on culture, or the "training and refinement of . . . tastes, ideas, and manners"; others recognized it as a threat to property. But most agreed that popular assertiveness threatened social stability. Charles Eliot Norton, the editor for the Boston Loyal Publication Society, argued that the masses were without "counsel, restraint or education." "It is not, then," he advised, "to the people that we look for wisdom and intelligence . . . they could not, if they would, rescue themselves from evil"; hence the upper class must accept its role as guardian. George T. Strong likened the people to a contagious disease: "Neither the blind masses, the swinish multitude, that rule us under our accursed system of universal suffrage, nor the case of typhoid, can be expected to exercise self-control."[35]

Elite fears of democratic passions were temporarily assuaged when the populace rallied following the attack on Fort Sumter. Labor union branches closed, labor meetings were canceled, and strikes were called off as workers rushed to enlist in the Union cause. But as the war progressed, Union defeats, a burgeoning national state, and increasingly revolutionary war aims fed growing disillusionment with the war and its Republican advocates. Economic tensions and class conflict further antagonized the people: mounting taxes and wartime inflation denied workers the prosperity the nation as a whole seemed to be enjoying. Eggs increased from fifteen to twenty-five cents in a two-year period; potatoes and bread nearly doubled. In Pennsylvania, prices jumped 110 to 200 percent between March 1861 and November 1862; wages lagged behind.[36]

In the early months of the war, workers did little in the way of organizing to combat high prices and stagnant wages. But by late 1862, as business and industry flourished, organization appeared necessary. Skilled and semiskilled tradesmen began to demand higher wages. By early 1863, labor was experiencing what Philip Foner has called "a revival of trade unionism." New unions were established; old unions grew; strikes abounded. In

1862 New York City witnessed thirteen tradewide strikes; in 1863 that number rose to twenty-nine, and in 1864, there were forty-two tradewide strikes. In June 1863, *Fincher's Trade Review* ran a series on "The Upheaving Masses in Motion!"[37]

Such upheaval was anathema to the founders of the Union League, who feared that, in addition to jeopardizing the social order, labor's assertions stood to undermine the war effort. "The subject of labor is getting to be the great question of the country," wrote Philadelphia League member E. B. Ward to fellow member Henry C. Carey. Even Forbes, who, almost alone among the leagues' elite, claimed that "true democracy" was "a particular hobby," feared the impact of "wak[ing] up the laboring classes" on the war. (Forbes's fears were not confined to labor's impact on the war: as a railroad manager he fought labor organization and believed that agitators ought to be dismissed, regardless of their length of service.)[38]

In fact, most workers remained surprisingly loyal: some were Democrats and some Republicans, but the vast majority continued to support the government. But league members, who feared for the loyalty not only of eastern labor but of the midwestern masses as well, were convinced that Northern anarchy and Southern victory were certain if free reign were given to popular discontent. Democratic victories in the 1862 fall elections served as a tocsin to the Unionist elite across the country; thus, long before the July 1863 draft riots appeared to give shape to their fears, the Unionist upper classes of Philadelphia, New York, and Boston embarked on a campaign to remind the masses for whom the war was being waged, and to instruct them in a more deferential patriotism.[39]

In February 1863, at a meeting of the Philadelphia Union League, Benjamin Gerhard moved that a Board of Publications be established to "disseminate patriotic principles amongst a larger and more distant audience, whose minds could only be reached through the agency of printed documents." The resultant Board of Publication of the Union League in Philadelphia boasted three committees and twenty-seven members.[40]

Lyndley Smith, a prominent sugar refiner, chaired the finance committee, which collected $250 each from ninety-six league members. Smith's business and social connections helped him secure an additional $10,000, and by the end of 1863, a total of $35,000 had been raised by subscription.[41] A publications committee, headed by ironmaster and economist Stephen Colwell, solicited articles and pamphlets from members and associates, and sent them on to a distribution committee.[42] On average ten thousand copies of each pamphlet were printed, but actual publications per pamphlet ranged from four thousand to one hundred thousand.[43]

Recipients were varied and numerous. Pamphlets were sent to Union Leagues in other cities, where they were kept in reading rooms for on-site perusal and circulated to surrounding districts. In remote areas, particularly in the Midwest and far West, pamphlets were sent to postmasters who arranged their delivery to shops and homes. Union League literature was also sent to individuals, including league members in New York and Boston, who considered it for their own publication societies, and to clergy. Soldiers were an important target: pamphlets were sent to various aid societies, chaplains, a Union Volunteer refreshment saloon, army hospitals, and military installations. Pamphlets were also printed in German and distributed in southeastern Pennsylvania. By the end of 1864 the Board of Publication of the Union League in Philadelphia had produced and distributed over two million pamphlets. As George H. Boker, secretary of the Philadelphia League, boasted, "There is scarcely a post-town, from Maine to California, which has not received a package of our publications."[44]

At the same time that the Philadelphia League was making provisions for its Board of Publications, members of New York's intellectual and social elite organized a similar association: on February 14, 1863, the Loyal Publication Society was formed. Its stated object was "to publish and distribute tracts, papers, and journals of unquestionable loyalty, throughout the United States, in the cities and in the country, in the Army and Navy, and in hospitals, and thus to diffuse knowledge and stimulate a broad national patriotism." Charles King, president of Columbia College, served as the society's first president, but within a few months he had resigned, and was replaced by Francis Lieber, a political scientist who also taught at Columbia.[45] While aimed for the most part at soldiers, the New York Society, like its Philadelphia counterpart, sent pamphlets to a myriad of associations and individuals. The Loyal Publication Society published ninety separate pamphlets, distributing nine hundred thousand copies of them. An unhappy New York Democrat testified to the effectiveness of the society's distribution committee: "You can hardly go into a public office or store, but you will see such documents on tables, counters, and even *posted* as handbills."[46]

In Boston, a different sort of publication society held its first meeting on March 10, 1863. While the last of the societies to take official form, in fact, the Boston association traced its roots back to the summer of 1862, when railroad magnate John Murray Forbes conceived the idea of circulating pro-Union editorials from leading journals to smaller papers. For a short time Forbes undertook the project himself: he wrote to editors to request that they reprint a number of copies of worthy articles and send them to him for distribution.[47]

In July and again in August 1862, Forbes wrote to William Curtis Noyes to discuss the possibility of an organization devoted to such activity. In March 1863, Forbes sent out a flyer inviting "50 or so" men to subscribe to the project. Illustrating the extent to which the society represented Boston's leading intellectuals as well as its capitalists and professionals, Charles Russell Lowell, Charles Eliot Norton, Henry Wadsworth Longfellow, and George Livermore joined him in signing the invitation. Edward Everett Hale served on the executive committee, and Harvard scholar Charles E. Norton became the society's editor.[48]

As the head of the society's executive committee, Forbes brought with him the experience and know-how of one of the nation's most successful railroad capitalists. Forbes was the prime mover behind the Michigan Central Railroad; the Chicago, Burlington, and Quincy System; and the Hannibal and St. Joseph Railroad. For years he had written letters and articles pleading the case for the railroads; he understood the importance of building goodwill and was well accustomed to constructing arguments that proclaimed the shared interests of the railroad managers, their potential investors, and the communities through which the roads would pass. With the war he shifted his talent and his time to the production and reproduction of patriotic literature. Though shortly after Norton had been installed as editor Forbes announced his withdrawal from an active role, in fact Forbes was a driving force throughout the life of the society. He wrote Norton as often as several times a week, shaping policy and content, insisting that one theme or another be pressed.[49]

At first the New England Loyal Publication Society limited its efforts to culling, copying, and sending out articles, but soon it expanded its purview and began producing its own "broadsides." These broadsides included three or four articles as well as an original editorial written by a society member. At one point the society estimated that it sent its broadsides to nine hundred papers, that two hundred papers copied them regularly, and that each of them had an average of one thousand subscribers. If each copy reached only three readers, then a single broadside could reach six hundred thousand people.[50]

ARGUMENTS FOR THE UNION

From the beginning, the publication societies directed their efforts at the masses. The New York Society was founded initially for the purpose of educating the rank-and-file Union troops; in Boston, Forbes wrote to William Curtis Noyes, "It is pretty clear that your leaders are 'marching on' in New York, and it is now mainly important to enlighten the working classes." Years later, a member of Philadelphia's Board of Publication reflected, "Those devoted loyalists realized to the full the imperative necessity for stimulating a healthy national sentiment among the class from which recruits were chiefly to come . . . and then there was the 'average man' to be looked after; toned up in his conception of duty."[51]

Stimulating a "healthy national sentiment" among a discouraged people in the midst of a long war was a challenge. The pamphlets and broadsides brought a variety of approaches to this task. To bolster the spirits of a war-weary public, many placed the war in historical perspective. They warned against the expectation of a speedy success and pointed to precedents of long wars ending in national honor. Some placed not only the war but the North's shortcomings in historical context: "We do not monopolize executive imbecility, nor are our military blunders without parallel or precedent."[52]

Many pamphlets invoked the voice of the soldiers to instill resolve in readers. After all, if the soldiers, who bore the brunt of the suffering, could resist defeatism, what right did the people have to succumb? As one soldier, quoted in a New York pamphlet, said, "It makes the blood boil within my veins, to think we came out here to fight for the Government, while they at home are fighting against the Government . . . when we are enduring the hardships of a soldier, and exposing ourselves to sickness and death, they are at home making political capital out of it." Soldiers pleading for support of the government were joined by their dead brethren: "Our soldiers bid us to stand by the government," read one, "our slain soldiers bid us . . . loud above all, comes down the voice of heaven: 'Stand by the Government!'"[53]

One of the most common complaints alleged among the soldiers and echoed by authors of numerous pamphlets was the persistent elevation of party above country. A Philadelphia pamphlet called party politics "one of the great sins of the day." Francis Lieber's "No Party Now But All for Country" explained the threats that the war presented the North, and urged its readers to respond as they would in any emergency: "When we are ailing, we do not take medicine by party prescription. . . . When a house is on fire and a child cries for help at the window above, shall the firemen at the engine be allowed to trifle away the precious time in party bickerings?" Though such reproaches were frequent, and though each publication society made claims to nonpartisanship—Forbes, for example insisted his goal was to "sink and obliterate the old party names"—in their practice, the societies were consistently Republican. In January of 1863, while laying the groundwork for his enterprise, Forbes asked Samuel G. Ward to help him locate "*vigorous* Republicans to help us with brains as much as money and not *bore* us too much." Like the Union or Republican Party papers, the publication societies linked the Democrats with the Confederacy, and suggested that true Democrats—Democrats in the Jacksonian or Douglas tradition—voted Republican. The Democratic Party was "openly and shamelessly the servant of the slave power"; and though the rank and file of the party might still have the public welfare at heart, the party "occupies a position which means its success threatens grave evils." Partisan appeals intensified before elections: in September 1863, as the autumn elections approached, Forbes wrote to Norton to encourage him to press this theme: "I think now is the time to push hard the wolves in sheep's clothing who pretend to be democrats."[54]

Though often dismissed as partisan concerns, Northerners' complaints about the growing nation-state and its increasingly radical policies also received serious attention. Constitutional issues were addressed in pamphlets such as "Our National Constitution: Its Adaptation to a State of War or Insurrection" and "The War Powers of the President and the Legislative Powers of Congress, in Relation to the Rebellion, Treason, and Slavery." Many pamphlets defended the expansion of the national government through extensive discussions of individual policies, including the suspension of the writ of habeas corpus, conscription, legal tender, the national loan, the Emancipation Proclamation, and the support of black troops.[55]

While the latter two policies were occasionally defended on constitutional grounds, they were primarily heralded for the benefits they would bring to Northern whites. One of the more striking examples of this approach engaged its readers in a grotesque exercise wherein the respective wartime worth of a white Northern man and a black Southern woman were tediously calculated. Applying a complex formula, the author concluded, "Although negros are not men, yet for all purposes of war one black slave woman is equal to four northern white men." Other broadsides argued that, beyond crippling the South's economy, abolition provided a larger market for Northern manufactures, freed up capital, and created a workforce anxious to labor for money.

The raising of black troops was similarly regarded. It robbed the South of valuable resources while conserving equally valuable Northern resources: "A nigger killed in battle, a white man saved." Black troops would be acclimated to the hostile Southern climate, could help "hold the nation" after the war, and would help train the freedmen in productive occupations.[56]

But as the war progressed, increasing numbers of pamphlets and broadsides argued that slavery was morally wrong and that blacks had a right to "equal treatment." Forbes, who believed that the question of black troops was "the most important practical point of the day," included articles from abolition papers in his broadsides, including Frederick Douglass's "Men of Color, To Arms!" and excerpts from several of Wendell Phillips's speeches. Even these appeals, however, remained within the framework of the society leaders' elitism. As Forbes himself explained in October 1864, "I am essentially a conservative, . . . have rather a prejudice against philanthropists, and have been anti-slavery more because slavery is anti-republican, anti-peace, anti-material progress, anti-civilization than upon the higher and purer ground that it is wicked and unjust to the slave. I have no special love for the African, anymore than for the low-class Irish." His goal for the society—that it be "not anti-slavery, except incidentally, but . . . [for] the vigorous prosecution of the war"—reflected this view, as did the New England Society's support of colonization.[57]

Moving beyond the defense of specific policies, many pamphlets undertook a discussion of what the nation itself represented. Some tailored their vision to specific groups. German-born Francis Lieber wrote a pamphlet that compared the South with the Germany emigrants had left behind: "If a German wants to have a stew of states, he never need come for it to America." The ideas that animated Germans were unity of country and civil freedom. They arrived on American shores expecting the rights of free citizenry, the rewards of skill and industry, "no privilege debarring merit." In the North those rights and rewards awaited the immigrant, but in the South, a Confederate leader had warned his colleagues that "no state can endure in which the laboring class has political rights." Pamphlets or broadsides directed at the Irish invoked Ireland's liberation tradition, portraying the American nation as fitting comfortably within that tradition. "The Irish Patriot: Daniel O'Connell's Legacy to Irish Americans" invoked an Irish hero's comparison of black slavery to the oppression of the Irish.[58]

Other pamphlets painted the nation as the foundation of Americans' wealth and prosperity. They described the vast resources of the nation: one writer, explaining why war bonds were selling well, enthused, "They buy on the past history of the country, on its rapid growth, on its unsurpassed prospects for the future. . . . They believe in the value of one million square miles of lands . . . in the thousands of millions of mineral wealth folded in its vast embrace." Such nation-building pamphlets spent up to fifty pages detailing the territorial area, population, immigration, material wealth, and natural resources of the land and illustrating how favorably the United States compared to other countries. This argument was aimed in particular at midwesterners, who tended to identify more with the South than they did with the North. Alarmed at this tendency, Forbes urged Norton to emphasize the "community of interest" between the Midwest and the North. Norton responded with a number of articles that explained that it was the Union, not the South, which was the "cornerstone of prosperity." The Mississippi had almost ceased to be an outlet for midwestern goods; the Midwest was now no more dependent on the Southern market than it was on the Mexican or Central American markets. Another broadside assured its readers that cotton growing in Texas would be a profitable enterprise for white men once the South was subdued and slavery abolished.[59]

The idea that the nation represented prosperity was, in a sense, reminiscent of the arguments that Jay Cooke made in his bond campaign literature. But these arguments also fit within another tradition. For years now, Northerners had been expressing the view that the nation's prosperity was the natural result of their unique democratic, free labor society. The publication societies' literature set out to convince Northerners that the Civil War was being waged to preserve that order, an order which operated in the people's—and most notably, workers'—behalf.

A WAR FOR FREE LABOR

In March 1863, in a letter to Charles Norton, Forbes wrote of his desire to persuade the people of the "true issue" of the war: "Democracy versus Aristocracy." "I think we can do most good," he explained, "by showing how completely this is the war of a class, and a small one, against the people everywhere." In December he pressed Norton again: "The North will never be firmly united until the truth is more widely spread that this is a war of slave aristocracy versus the people North and South."[60]

The notion of the war as a battle between two societies—between aristocracy and democracy—was not, of course, unique to the publication societies. Republicans already believed antislavery to be only one part of a broader movement "from absolutism to democracy, aristocracy to equality, backwardness to modernity." At the heart of that movement lay a belief in "free labor"—"labor not subject to the coercions of slavery—and enjoying the opportunity for physical mobility and social advancement." With this promise ever in view, Republicans proclaimed the dignity of labor and glorified Northern society. To the extent that poverty and popular discontent persisted in this ideal society, Republicans believed that the masses must be brought to understand the community of interest they shared with capital, and somehow be afforded the opportunities that escaped them in the eastern cities: westward migration, supported by a homestead act, was a Republican panacea. Since, as New York's Loyal Publication Society's president Lieber argued, "the mob disregards property," the solution was to encourage them to acquire property and reach "a state of substantial independence," or middle-class status. Even in Philadelphia, New York, and Boston, where industrial concentration was greatest and for most workers mobility was a fantasy, workers were moved by stories of individual successes. Thus Republicans celebrated the North's comparatively democratic, free labor society, defined as it was in opposition to Southern slave society.[61]

If not all Americans understood the war in its free labor context, it was the task of the publication societies to change that. Forbes worried that both midwesterners and Northern labor did not comprehend the nature and implications of the war. "Just imagine," Forbes wrote Norton, "what would be the changed condition of things if our Northern people saw [the war] in its light and stood shoulder to shoulder! Let it be our task to get light."[62]

So Norton faithfully carried out his charge: the society's publications consistently presented the free labor nature of the war. "The deadliest struggle," one broadside declared, "is between civilization and barbarism—freedom and slavery—republicanism and aristocracy—loyalty and treason." "We *are* a nation of mechanics," a second broadside exclaimed, "and by this sign, we will conquer." The war was a battle for the right of white men north and south to labor without restraint: "The true glory of the war is not that it liberates the black but the white men of the South."[63]

Pamphlets from the Philadelphia and New York societies joined the New England association in this campaign. The North was described in all its glory: the virtues of its schools, its churches, its voting booths, and its free labor system extolled. One pamphlet pronounced, "The United States . . . truly the land—the very paradise of labor . . . labor here makes all men equal. . . . In no country is labor more prized or honored, or better paid than here! Even capital, which in Europe controls labor, here becomes subordinate to and serves labor." But if America was, as the title of another pamphlet proclaimed, "For Free Working Men," it would not remain that way for long if the South was not stopped. "Mechanics, Farmers, and Laborers, Read! How Slavery Injures the Free Working Man": Southern victory, the pamphlets warned, would be followed by the establishment of privileged orders, a franchise enjoyed by nobility and gentry alone, the abolishment of free schools, and amalgamation of blacks with poor whites, with "both . . . reduced to slavery."[64]

THE ORGANIC SOCIETY, UNCONDITIONAL LOYALTY, AND THE REALIZATION OF SELF

Once the masses understood that the war had been undertaken on their behalf, it remained only for them to be "toned up in [their] conception of duty." Duty varied, as Henry Bellows was reported to have told a camp of Union soldiers, according to "one's position and surroundings." Though George T. Strong had acknowledged the difficulties of unconditional loyalty during deliberations on qualifications for league membership—"No one can be expected to pledge himself to uphold whatever any set of men at Washington or elsewhere may hereafter think proper to do"—no such understanding was granted the masses. The marches of black soldiers down the streets of Philadelphia and New York may have broadened the definition of patriotism by removing race as a factor, but they offered another prescription in its place. Iver Bernstein argues that "through their open association with the black poor, merchants sought to counteract working class disloyalty publicly by exhibiting an ideal relationship between classes." The Union League could "uphold the city's blacks as a model deferential working class because of their indisputable status as victims."[65]

The true patriot, then, was deferential and unquestioning: "A man must be either for his country or against his country," averred General Benjamin Butler in a widely circulated pamphlet. "He cannot be throwing impediments all the time in the way of the progress of his Government under pretense that he is helping some other portion of his country." Even if dissension was considered acceptable in times of peace—a claim that many league members disputed—war demanded silence and support: "We are in the midst of a civil war," a pamphlet on financial war measures reminded Americans. "Men and money are necessary for [the nation's] protection, . . . the national life must be preserved. . . . Sir, with all my objections to the financial system of the country, I feel it to be my duty to support that system *until the war is over*."[66]

Many pamphlets spoke to the discontent that Americans might feel but must not express: "The present Government was not the Government of my choice," acknowledged General Butler as he addressed soldiers in the field. "—I did not vote for it, or any part of it, but it is the Government of my country . . . and as long as I believe that Government to be honestly administered, I will throw a mantle over any mistakes that I think it has made, and support it heartily. . . . I am a traitor and a false man if I alter in my support. . . . No man who opposed his country in time of war ever profited." A New England broadside argued that even a democratic government could not survive if its members were not willing to cease discussion when called upon to do so by the crisis of the nation and the authority of the government. Americans were not, it pointed out, "living together as a debating club."[67]

That wartime patriotism implied unquestioning support of the government's policies was a common theme in the pamphlet literature; but for some Union Leaguers, unqualified loyalty was not simply a wartime concomitant. Like Philip Nolan in "The Man Without a Country," these men argued, Americans were singularly unappreciative of the nation and the role it played in their lives. During the war, a handful of Northern intellectuals set out to cultivate a new form of patriotism—an Old World "loyalty"— among Americans, whose ideas of consensual government informed contractual views of their duties as citizens. According to these men, the contractual premise was flawed: the nation was not the product of a contract; it was an organism, whose growth was natural and good. Loyalty to such a nation must be unconditional, much like the love a mother gives her child. As historian George Fredrickson explains, "Americans needed to think of themselves as subjects, having the blind duty to uphold a traditional way of life, rather than as free individuals claiming their rights under the constitution."[68]

The idea of an organic society was not unique to the Union League. This tenet had roots both in German political theory—Francis Lieber, who had studied Hegel, held that the Constitution was "an organism of national life . . . not a mere league of independent states or nations"—and in Unitarianism. According to historian Daniel Walker Howe, Unitarians in the early nineteenth century believed that "the ideal commonwealth was an organic unit, composed, like a living body, of interrelated parts, each contributing its essential function." It existed as an "aid to the expression of human purposes." Unitarians rejected the notion of a social compact, arguing that affections were more important to the stability of society than self-interest.

But if "social cohesion depended on emotional appeals, it was obviously necessary to envelop institutions in some kind of mystical aura."[69]

It is not surprising, then, to find New England Loyal Publication Society's editor Charles Norton, son of the prominent Unitarian Andrews Norton, arguing that "our nation was never, in truth, founded. . . . It was not made by man; it is no discovery or invention, but a natural growth." Boston League member Alexander H. Bullock was an elegant spokesman for such organicism: for him a nation was not an "aggregate of individuals, but . . . a power and a life, . . . the agency and instrumentality among the providence of God and the designs of His glory. We are indeed a part of it, but only for a moment. . . . The organism of a nation! It enfolds and blesses races; it perpetuates traditions, ideas, examples, principles . . . it is government!"[70]

A citizen's obligations to such a nation were profound, transcending any of the notions of patriotism that had heretofore characterized the American polity. Americans' attitudes toward their leaders in particular required revision. In a sermon titled "Unconditional Loyalty," the Unitarian minister Henry Bellows argued that

> the Head of a Nation is a sacred person. . . . There is something in the chief magistrate infinitely more important than his personal qualities, his judgment, his intelligence, his rectitude. It is his office, his representative character as the National Head. He can truly say with Louis XIV, 'The State—it is I. Dishonor me, and you disgrace the nation.' . . . To rally 'round the President—without question or dispute—is the first and most sacred duty of loyal citizens.[71]

Bellows's sermon, delivered early in 1863, was published as a pamphlet by the New York society later that year; it also appeared in numerous Northern newspapers and was republished by the Board of Publication in Philadelphia in September. That same month, the Philadelphia board published another sermon with a similar tone: "I hold that the President of the United States, according to the scriptures, is the minister of God," the Reverend William B. Stewart proclaimed. "The powers that be are ordained of God. . . . The President, with the constitution in his hand, can say to those who denounce him . . . as Louis XIV of France said to his opponents, 'The Government, it is I.' "[72]

Harsh as it may have seemed, such silent obedience was not without its rewards. In fact, for those who considered this tenet in its entirety, the maxim of unquestioning loyalty to a nation and the state which embodied that nation represented the sole path to freedom—to the realization of self. "Liberty . . . true liberty requires a *country*," Lieber insisted. It was only through identification with and obedience to the nation that the mystical spirit of a people could be fulfilled. Embracing the implications—if not the philosophical foundations—of both Hegelian romanticism and Unitarian organicism, league members called for Americans to recognize the nation as the sole route to freedom. They enveloped the nation-state with the Unitarian "mystical aura" in prose: "We live not our lives merely," averred Bullock, "but we live a *state* consciousness that runs back and prefigures among the eternities, blending with the ages past and bidding the next ones hail." Without that state, "in obeyed and felt majesty, there is no development for man, no mission for woman, no sleep for children. How sublime the life of a nation!"[73]

Though popular in elite intellectual and literary circles, it is doubtful that this notion of freedom through patriotic obedience gained much acceptance among a people whose Revolutionary heritage defied Old World precepts of hierarchy and authority. But the same ideas, when set forward without political science preachments or philosophical anachronisms, could evoke Americans' deepest fears of atomization, of the individual, in Tocqueville's words, "confine[d] . . . entirely within the solitude of his own heart." In Edward Everett Hale's "The Man Without a Country," the organic vision was made palatable to Americans.[74]

Hale's emotional, firsthand—albeit fictional—account of the spiritual cost of disloyalty provided a concrete counterpoint to the theoretical patriotism of league sermons and tracts. Compelling in its detail, fantastic yet believable, the narrative aimed to tap its readers' emotions: as Hale himself confessed, "my own tears blotted the paper of the original manuscript."[75]

"The Man Without a Country" was inspired by exiled Copperhead Clement Vallandigham's bid for the Ohio governorship in the fall of 1863, and, more specifically, by Vallandigham's assertion that he "did not want to belong to a nation which would compel by arms the loyalty of any of its citizens; he did not want to belong to the United States." Although Hale campaigned to get the story published before the Ohio gubernatorial election so that he might influence the outcome, the story actually appeared in *Atlantic Monthly* in December 1863, two months after Vallandigham's defeat.[76]

The story is narrated by Frederic Ingham, an old shipmate of Philip Nolan's, and begins as Ingham discovers Nolan's death notice in the paper. Nolan, a privileged wealthy westerner, a "gay, dashing, bright young fellow," had been one of Aaron Burr's accomplices. Though his role was small, though his fellow conspirators escaped with minor sentences, Nolan's crime is his irreverence, and for this he is exiled not to another country, but to an endless journey on the seas. It is during that journey that Nolan learns what it means to be without a country. Through Ingham, Hale relates a series of incidents that reveal Nolan's evolving, and eventually obsessive, patriotism. Taking turns reading aloud to pass the time on the ship, the sailors unwittingly hand a book of poems to Nolan just at the point in Sir Walter Scott's "The Lay of the Minstrel" where he is to read a tragically ironic passage:

> Breathes there a man with soul so dead
> who never to himself has said
> This is my own, my native land
> Whose heart has ne'er within him burned
> As home his footsteps he hath turned
> From wandering on a foreign strand?
> For him no minstrel raptures swell;
> High though his titles, proud his name,
> Boundless his wealth as wish may claim,
> Despite these titles, power and pelf,
> The wretch, concentrated all in self.

Nolan turns white while reading the passage, "gags" and "chokes," then flings the book into the ocean and retires to his cabin, from which he does not emerge for two months.

When a great ball is held on board the ship, Nolan hopes it may be his chance to hear the news from home. There is a celebrated Southern beauty on board; perhaps she has not heard of his sentence. Bowing to the woman, he secures a dance with her. As the dance is a contra dance, there is little time for talk, but there is, as Hale avers, "chances for tongues and sounds, as well as for eyes and blushes." Nolan woos the Southern beauty with flattery and casual conversation, then, "a little pale," he asks what she has heard from home. He is instantly rebuffed. The object of his failed seduction is not romantic love but word from the states: country is a more primal need than love or sex.

In the South Atlantic in the first days after the slave-trade treaty, Nolan's ship overhauls a small schooner with slaves aboard. Acting as a Portuguese interpreter, Nolan tells the slaves that they are free and will be taken to Cape Palmas. The slaves protest, and Nolan must translate their emotional protestations: they wish to go not to Cape Palmas, but home to their own beloved countries. Returning to the ship in a dinghy, Nolan turns to the young Ingham: "Remember, boy, that behind all these men you have to do with, behind officers and Government and people even, there is the 'Country Herself,' your country, and that you belong to her as you belong to your own mother."

Philip Nolan's deathbed visitor violates the terms of Nolan's sentence and fills in the dated U.S. map that decorates his room. Hale wrote that the suffering of the "Man Without a Country" was designed to teach Americans "that the country is in itself an entity. It is a Being," and to show how meaningless life outside of that entity must be. (Philip Nolan on his deathbed, from Edward Everett Hale, *The Man Without a Country,* 1893 edition.)

Nolan's dying wish is to hear what has become of his beloved country. His deathbed visitor violates the terms of Nolan's sentence and at last shares with Nolan the events of the previous fifty years. He fills Nolan's dated map in, and describes the glory that has become the United States. He tells him of "old Scott and Jackson," of steamboats and railroads and inventions, of

West Point and the Smithsonian and the Capitol and Lincoln, of "the gran-
deur of his country and its prosperity." He has not the heart to tell him of
the war. Nolan dies within the hour and is buried at sea.

"The Man Without a Country" was an instant success. It remained in print
throughout the war, and was reprinted intermittently for years afterward.
In spite of this success, Hale expressed regret that his hopes for anonymity
were not realized: he had hoped that the public would believe his story was
true. Told in a first-person narrative, the story is peppered with statements
that lead the reader to that assumption: "this I know" or "this I have been
told" precede many of the narrator's revelations. A myriad of historic details
adds to the story's verisimilitude: the ship on which Nolan dies is named after
a real vessel which had been lost at sea just two years before the story's publication; the sailors and captains had names similar to real historic figures.
Even the ship's alleged longitude and latitude at the time of Nolan's death,
which, claimed Hale, initially placed the *Levant* at the top of the Andes as a
hint to clever readers of the story's fictional nature, was changed before
publication—perhaps, Hale admitted, by himself—to place the ship not far
from where she had in fact disappeared.[77]

In spite of the fact that Hale's name appeared in the index, most readers
apparently assumed the story was factual. Many wrote to say they had known
Nolan or Ingham; some expressed horror that the government would effect
such a cruel punishment. Retired sailors wrote Hale to say they remembered
Ingham, and a rumor that Nolan had actually been pardoned circulated.[78]

Years later, Hale reflected that he had set out to teach Americans "that
the country is in itself an entity. It is a Being," and to show how meaningless
life outside of that entity must be. Nolan does not miss friends or family or
art or women. He is not even called by name: because his buttons bore no
insignias, the sailors called him "Plain buttons." He has been completely
stripped of all identity, because without country, there is no identity.[79]

Like Philip Nolan, Civil War Northerners stood to lose their country and
little comprehended the enormous cost. If intellectual tracts did not resonate, Nolan's suffering was palpable. The pathos of his tale was an admoni-
tion: infidelity to country could mean loss of country, an awful fate not even
poor Nolan deserved. Hale's story dramatized this maxim, and brought it into
living rooms, reading rooms, and libraries across the North. It was a provoca-
tive notion for a people who appeared at times to have more invested in their
state, local, or even partisan identities than they did in their role as members of a nation.

"Until the Ideas of Massachusetts Kiss the Gulf of Mexico"

The Abolitionist Vision of Nation and Patriotism

For the conservative intellectuals who formed the core of the elite metropolitan Union Leagues, the realization and exaltation of the nation was an end in itself; emancipation and the employment of black troops the means to that end. But to another set of activists, it was not the nation that represented the fulfillment of reason and therefore of humankind, but the ideals embodied in this particular nation's credo. For the abolitionists, the United States was not a nation worth saving—or even a nation at all—until it lived up to the ideals it had set forth in the Declaration of Independence. Abolitionists across the North welcomed the war and the burgeoning national sentiment it engendered as the means to the ends toward which they had labored for decades: freedom, equality, and justice for all, regardless of race.[1]

For the first year and a half of the war, the abolitionists' hopes rose and fell with the fate of Union troops and the administration's ever-changing war policy. With the September 1862 Preliminary Emancipation Proclamation, it appeared to many abolitionists that their hopes might at last be realized. But Republican losses in the autumn elections, rising defeatism, and Lincoln's Annual Message to Congress—in which he proposed an amendment offering compensation to any state that emancipated its slaves before 1900—soon intervened. Many began to doubt that the president would carry out his plans for the Proclamation.[2]

On January 1, 1863, abolitionists gathered in Boston's Music Hall and Tremont Temple to await word of Lincoln's pronouncement. Among the over six thousand women and men assembled in the two halls were Wendell Phillips, Frederick Douglass, and Anna Dickinson. As Douglass later recounted, it was an occasion "of both hope and fear . . . whether we should survive or perish, depended in large measure upon the coming of this proclamation." The vigil began early in the day, as, amid speeches and songs, the abolitionists waited to celebrate "the new departure." At seven-thirty in the evening anxious organizers established a line of messengers between Boston's telegraph office and Tremont Temple. "Eight, nine and ten o'clock came and went," wrote Douglass, "but still no word." The audience listened politely to the speeches, but all eyes were on the door. The crowd grew despondent. "Every moment chilled our hopes and strengthened our fears."[3]

At last a man burst into the hall, "with a face fairly illuminated," and exclaimed, "It is coming! It is on the wires!" The effect on the crowd, reported Douglass, was "startling beyond description." As the Proclamation was read, the crowd erupted. "I never saw Joy before," wrote Douglass. "Men, women, young and old, were up; hats and bonnets were in the air." "It was one of the most affecting and thrilling occasions I ever witnessed, and a worthy celebration of the first step on the part of the nation in its departure from the thralldom of ages."[4]

As the abolitionists soon came to understand, it was, in fact, *only* a first step. But if the Emancipation Proclamation was a turning point in the war for all Americans, it was a particularly meaningful one for the abolitionists. With emancipation, war became revolution. The Proclamation was a signal that the product of that revolution might be a nation built upon a foundation of freedom and justice; and that loyalty to that nation might be consistent with the devoted pursuit of those ideals.

Historians have long acknowledged that abolitionist agitation helped lay the groundwork for the politicization of the slavery question and, ultimately, for civil war. Influenced variously by the Enlightenment, rationalism, republican notions of liberty, evangelism, and a Jacksonian reverence for the individual, abolitionists from the colonial period onward fought to pierce the silence that enveloped the slavery question in American society and politics. Beginning in the 1830s, this battle took the form of an organized movement dedicated to abolition through "moral suasion"—the conversion of millions of Americans to the recognition that slavery was a sin and must be eradicated. By 1840 these men and women had succeeded in introducing slavery into politics, and a group of antislavery politicians emerged to take up the battle.[5]

With the attack on Fort Sumter, nearly all abolitionists recognized that their movement faced a turning point. Where moral suasion had failed, the war might succeed: the national state would emerge as an instrument of national liberation, destroying both slavery and the aristocratic society it had produced. With few exceptions, abolitionists embraced the war, declaring that it signaled the death of slavery and the birth of a new America. It was their most fervent hope that this new America would be dedicated to the proposition that all men—of all colors—were created equal.[6]

But the shift from individual conscience as the agent of change to a focus on the state was not without peril. Abolitionists supported the empowerment of the national state because they believed that those powers would position the nation as a guarantor of an enlarged liberty. As the war progressed, however, it was not at all clear that these hopes were well founded. In August 1861, General John C. Frémont took a bold initiative, declaring martial law in Missouri and issuing an order to free the slaves of the state's Rebels. Abolitionists across the North celebrated. Days later, Lincoln revoked the edict. In May 1862, General David Hunter declared martial law in Florida, Georgia, and South Carolina, and, like Frémont, freed the slaves in all three states. Again, Lincoln countermanded the order. As late as August 1862, Lincoln seemed to suggest that he did not share the abolitionists' vision: in a letter to Horace Greeley, editor of the *New York Tribune,* he wrote that his "paramount object" was to save the Union, and that he would do it "without freeing *any* slave" if he could."[7]

Abolitionists labored to keep their perspective on the war in plain view of the North. In the beginning their ideas were considered not just controversial, but inflammatory. As the war progressed, however, their belief that slavery was at the center of the conflict and that abolition was the only solution began to gain acceptance. Increasingly, abolitionists attracted large, even friendly crowds. Three in particular—Wendell Phillips, Frederick Douglass, and Anna Dickinson—emerged as the movement's leading orators. Over the course of the war these three abolitionists spoke to hundreds of thousands of Northerners. As the abolitionists' most popular speakers, they played the lead role in constructing the abolitionist version of a transcendent nationalism.[8]

The power of Phillips, Douglass, and Dickinson to move Northerners cannot be understood outside the context of nineteenth-century oratorical culture. A legacy of the Revolution, this culture placed oratory and rhetorical discourse at the center of the education of the citizens of a republic; or, as the century progressed, the conversion of voters in a democracy. In a preradio, pretelevision age, platform speeches were often two to three hours in duration. Oratory was a respected art form; gifted orators were respected artists.[9]

This oratorical culture received an institutional grounding in 1826, with the lyceum movement. Josiah Holbrook, the movement's founder, envisioned a nationwide network of local associations where citizens of all ages would gather to hear lectures and debates. With few opportunities for the exchange of information and ideas available to them, Americans embraced the lyceum, and the movement flourished. On the eve of the Civil War, lyceums could be found in nearly every Northern state. Aided by advances in railroad and telegraph technology, the local, informal nature of the meetings had given way to what was in effect a vast national lecture circuit, wherein professional lecturers traveled from town to town and spoke in large halls to capacity crowds. In this "golden age of American oratory," these men and women were often speakers of national renown, including such figures as Henry Ward Beecher, Oliver Wendell Holmes, and Ralph Waldo Emerson. In spite of such eminence, most lecturers could be heard for an admission price of about twenty-five cents.[10]

With the attack on Fort Sumter, American lyceum lectures focused almost exclusively on the war. Through this medium, as well as through their writings, Phillips, Douglass, and Dickinson became national figures. Together they reached millions of Northerners, spreading their ideas about the meaning of the nation they hoped the war would create, and of loyalty to that nation.[11]

WENDELL PHILLIPS

Wendell Phillips was without question the abolitionists' most prominent wartime orator. "As a popular speaker, we doubt that there is his superior in the country," claimed a journalist after hearing Phillips lecture in 1850. During the war his popularity soared: his speeches were heard by an estimated fifty thousand men and women and read by over five million in the winter of 1861–62 alone. By 1863, a political adviser to General Benjamin F. Butler could write, "Phillips . . . manufactures a vast amount of popular opinion. No man will speak oftener or to wider audiences in America."[12]

The weight of this responsibility could not have fallen on more qualified, dedicated shoulders. Born in Boston in 1811, Phillips grew up in Beacon Hill's Brahmin society. His parents were Calvinists and Federalists; his father was Boston's first mayor. As a child Phillips absorbed a sense of Calvinist duty and discipline, as well as a deep appreciation for American history and its

A member of Boston's Brahmin society, Phillips became one of the country's most popular speakers during the war. (Wendell Phillips, premier Civil War abolitionist spokesperson.)

heroes. Indeed, Phillips could easily have seen himself as a part of that history: when his father died in 1823, he was buried between Samuel Adams and James Otis.[13]

Phillips's aristocratic and Revolutionary heritage lent him confidence and authority; but it was not just his background that informed his manufacture of public opinion. Phillips was a theorist and singularly self-conscious molder of public opinion. He believed that history was moving toward an age of true democracy. In the United States, leaders were but "servants of the people"; and it was through those people that further democratic progress would take place. There was, he declared, "no law that can abide one moment when popular opinion demands its abrogation."[14]

It was Phillips's role to stimulate and direct that public opinion. To do so, he would "use the very tools by which it was formed." If Americans lived in a market, he argued, "we would seek to prove only that slavery is an unprofitable investment." If the nation were "one great, pure, church," he would speak only of God and morality. But Phillips and his fellow Northerners lived in the world. No one approach would suffice to reach all; Phillips would employ all tools "such as an honest man may touch."[15]

Eschewing politics, Phillips worked to keep images of the desirable—not the practical, the popular, or even the possible—before his audience. If slavery was a sin, then immediate emancipation—not compromise with the South—was called for. If the Union countenanced slavery, then disunion was in order. "My curse be on the Constitution of these United States!" he proclaimed. Such bold statements were not designed to enhance the abolitionists' popularity or enlarge their following, but to shock a complacent, unmindful public into thinking deeply about the issue of slavery. His priority, as he made clear from the beginning, was not the nation, for even a "true nationality" was "nothing . . . when weighed against justice." Phillips "put no value on the Union," which was, by 1860, "a name—and nothing more."[16]

But on April 13, 1861, the North made a giant leap in Phillips's direction. The popular reaction to the attack on Fort Sumter took Phillips and his colleagues by surprise. They began to consider the possibility that the war might do what thirty years of abolitionist labor had not. Phillips eschewed politics; and he had little faith in the United States government. But he understood that most Americans "still linger[ed] in [their] father's prejudice for the Union." That prejudice might now be put to good use: public opinion moved faster now than in normal times. Phillips recognized that these were what he would later call "formative hours," a time when "the national purpose and thought grows and ripens in thirty days as much as ordinary years bring it forward." Keeping images of the good society before the public, he strove to recreate the nation on truer grounds.[17]

On April 21, 1861, four thousand people crowded into Boston's spacious Music Hall, anxious to hear what Wendell Phillips had to say about the newly proclaimed war for the Union. The platform on which Phillips was to speak had been "profusely" decorated with the Stars and Stripes, and the hall about him was decked with laurel and evergreen. As Phillips entered the hall, the crowd greeted him with "hearty, irrepressible rounds of applause."[18]

Within minutes of speaking, Phillips made it clear that he now embraced the Union's cause. "[For] the first time in my anti-slavery life," he proclaimed, "I speak under the stars and stripes. . . . No matter what the past has been or said; today the slave asks God for a sight of this banner, and counts it the pledge of his redemption." The declaration of war and the outpouring of support in the North had convinced Phillips that, though "hitherto [the Union] may have meant what you thought, or what I did; today, it represents sovereignty and justice." Abandoning disunion, Phillips yoked his dreams of the good society to the war, the national state, and a new national identity. For the next four years, his speeches focused on what the nation could and should mean, and on what patriotism to that nation entailed.[19]

The nation on which Phillips pinned his hopes had as its sheet anchor the tenets proclaimed in the Declaration of Independence. "The cornerstone of our government," he told his listeners three months after the war had begun, "the spirit of '76, was the full liberty of each and every human being." But the Declaration's promise of liberty and equality had been betrayed, both by the limited vision of the masses and by the perfidy of their leaders. Though the people had endeavored to live up to the nation's lofty motto as they understood it, its full implications had escaped them. The same, however, could not be said for the founders themselves. It was the "faithless compromise" of 1787 that had doomed America. The founders had enshrined slavery into the Constitution, and "60 years of infamy" had followed. The war was the inevitable result of that infamy.[20]

With the war, Northerners had a chance to recapture the squandered glory of the Revolutionary years. The Constitution of 1787 was "a blurred and tattered parchment. . . . It is gone," Phillips told his audience at a Fourth of July speech in Framingham, Massachusetts, in 1861. The people might now rebuild their government—"you and I are to have a voice in the moulding. The part which Henry and Madison, which Hancock and Adams, played in '87, we are to play today. . . . Today we plant fresh seed. Mr. Lincoln and the Administration are pausing, waiting. The furrow is opened."[21]

Phillips painted a picture of the Union he envisioned in his first speech as a unionist, on April 21 in Boston's Music Hall. "Years hence," he predicted, "when the smoke of this conflict clears away, the world will see under our banner all tongues, all creeds, all races—one brotherhood—and on the banks of the Potomac, the Genius of Liberty, robed in light, four and thirty stars for her diadem, broken chains under feet, and an olive branch in her right hand." He repeated this theme of a multiracial, egalitarian America throughout the war. The United States would be an empire that knew "neither black nor white, neither Saxon nor Indian, but [held] an equal scepter over all. . . . An empire, the home of every race, every creed, every tongue."[22]

Clearly, the realization of Phillips's vision required first that the nation's four million slaves be emancipated. Phillips recognized that this was not the intention of many of the Union's leaders. Lincoln was conducting the war, he argued in August 1862, with an eye toward the preservation of slavery. But in this democratic age, where public opinion governed more powerfully than leaders, Lincoln was but a servant of the people, "and he is honestly waiting, like any other servant, for the people to come and send him on any errand they wish." If Lincoln truly believed the American public wished him to free the slaves, he would free them.[23]

For the first year and a half of the war, then, Phillips urged the Northern public to insist that the war be a war for freedom. The Revolution had been a holy war, he proclaimed, but this was "a holier and the last,—that for LIBERTY." Phillips called on Northerners to help him "take back that name which I endeavored to write on the forehead of Abraham Lincoln, of Springfield—'the slave-hound of Illinois'; and instead of it, . . . to write on that same honored brow, 'Liberator of four million bond men; first President of the *free* United States of America.'"[24]

At times this appeal for a war for emancipation and an egalitarian nation took the form of a defense of black equality. In 1861, Phillips delivered a speech on Toussaint L'Ouverture, the leader of the Saint Dominique rebellion. In an age where theories of race superiority abounded, Phillips pointed to the nation of Haiti and to L'Ouverture as evidence of the fact that "Negro blood, instead of standing at the bottom of the list, is entitled, if judged either by its great men or its masses, either by its courage, its purpose, or its endurance, to a place as near ours as any other blood known in history."[25]

In this speech, Phillips stated the principle toward which he believed public opinion must be led: abolition was essential because all races were equal. But Phillips had decided years prior to the war that he would not confine himself to any one approach to abolition; that he would use any tools "such as an honest man may touch." Phillips set many of his arguments in the framework of less controversial tenets. Perhaps the most pervasive of these was his argument that the destruction of slavery was essential to the perpetuation of the Union as a free labor society.

"This nation is made up of different ages," he told his audience in 1861. "Not homogeneous, but a mixed mass of different centuries. The North *thinks*—can appreciate argument—is the nineteenth century. . . . The South *dreams,* it is the thirteenth and fourteenth century—baron and serf, noble and slave." The North took "every child in the cradle" and placed beside it "virtue and knowledge," intelligence and industry. The white South eschewed labor; it was marked by ignorance and indolence. The war, argued Phillips, was a struggle between "slaveholders and free labor," between barbarism and civilization. Like many of his fellow abolitionists, Phillips promoted a war for the destruction of not just slavery, but of "the intellectual, social, aristocratic South." Sewing machines, reaping machines, voting booths, "ideas and types," would form the basis of the new nation.[26]

With the Emancipation Proclamation, Phillips shifted his focus. Emancipation alone was not enough: if the war ended without a guarantee of black freedom *and* black rights, all that had been achieved might be lost. Phillips moved ahead of the public yet again. He began to urge Americans to insist upon a lasting and meaningful freedom for the nation's slaves as well as for its white citizens.

"Now to my mind, an American Abolitionist, when he asks freedom for the Negro, means effectually freedom," he argued in a speech before the Massachusetts Anti-Slavery Society, "real freedom, something that can maintain and vindicate itself." Again, Phillips located his notion of freedom in the tradition of the Declaration of Independence. "Our philosophy of government, since the 4th day of July, 1776," he noted, "is that no class is safe, no freedom real, no emancipation is effectual, which does not place into the hands of the man himself, the power to protect his own rights." For Phillips, this power initially meant the suffrage; by 1864, it meant land as well.[27]

Phillips's advocacy of black suffrage and land for the freedmen marked another step forward in the evolution of his relationship with the national state. As an agitator, he worked to convince Americans who feared or distrusted centralized government that the new egalitarian nation that was to emerge from the war required a newly empowered state to protect it. "Build the State at once!" he proclaimed in August 1864. And as his conception of the national state grew, so too did his efforts to cultivate a preeminent national identity. In fact, like the conservative intellectuals who labored through the Union Leagues to effect a national mind-set, Phillips began to urge Northerners to abandon their prewar conception of themselves as a confederacy of sovereign states and embrace a new transcendent nationalism. He proposed to "lead the minds of the people into the new channel of national rights." "We are all Americans, with but one object," he told his listeners, "to save and glorify our nationality."[28]

Indeed, at times Phillips waxed so eloquently about the nation that his rhetoric sounded remarkably like that of the Union Leagues. In this age of nation-building, in the context of an insecure American national identity, Phillips drew from his agitator's toolbox yet another instrument with which to construct the good society. The war, he told his audience in May 1862, was "the momentous struggle of a great nation for existence and perpetuity. We have been planted as one; the normal idea of the nation is that it is to be one and indivisible."[29]

Of course, Phillips's nation differed from that of the romantic nationalists in one crucial respect—as he explained, the "gradual unfolding of the great elements of our national life" was inspired not by the advent of a newly disciplined and obedient citizenry, but by the prospect of emancipation and equal rights for all. Thus this tendency to glorify the nation found its fullest expression after the Emancipation Proclamation. The battle between North and South was "but the prelude to an immortal marriage," he told a crowd at Boston's Music Hall on January 4, 1863. "The Union of the future is to be as indestructible as the granite that underlies the continent; and the cement is . . . to be . . . the blood of the brave hearts that have made Virginia more than equal to Belgium." Almost two years later, he was still appealing to Northerners' nationalist proclivities, this time interweaving his themes of a just, multiracial, free labor society:

> Now we are struggling with the antagonism of two ideas—the idea of Massachusetts that every man is equal before the law, and the idea of the South that labor is disgraceful. My goal is a homogeneous nationality which shall weld Boston and New Orleans, New York and Charleston into one thunderbolt, and make us able to control the continent. Then the nations of Europe will respect us. . . . In my nationality there is but one idea—the harmonizing and equal mingling of all races. . . . I would leave no stone unturned until the ideas of Massachusetts kiss the gulf of Mexico . . . when that is accomplished, we shall be the strongest, noblest nation on earth, and every one of us will be proud to say, I am an American citizen.[30]

Like his understanding of the nation, Phillips's definition of patriotism fluctuated with his belief that the growing national state would be used to promote justice. Early in the war, Phillips called on Northerners to express their loyalty not through acquiescence, but in active, even vigorous terms.[31] "If I am to love my country," he told a crowd in December of 1861, "it must be loveable; if I am to honor it, it must be worthy of respect." It was the duty of citizens truly committed to a republican system of self-government to critically examine government policy, to formulate and then to express their opinions, no matter how unpopular. "Such criticism is always every thinking man's duty," he argued. "War excuses no man from this duty." He urged his listeners to show tolerance toward those who disagreed with them: "No mobs . . . to silence those whom events have not converted. . . . We are strong enough to tolerate dissent."[32]

But Phillips recognized that a powerful historical tradition circumscribed Americans' ability to think clearly about hard moral truths. Americans "defiled their consciences" not so much in fear or favor to their superiors, but rather in unthinking deference to them. They looked to the founders in awe and felt their inferiority. Obsessed with discovering the founders' thoughts or intentions on any given subject, they were unable to examine issues objectively. Phillips had long lectured Americans on the need to look beyond the writings and deeds of the fathers, to the principles for which they stood and the implications that those principles had for the present. As he told an audience in a speech on the Pilgrims delivered in December 1855, "The Pilgrims of 1620 would be, in 1855, not in Plymouth, but in Kansas."[33]

Who, then, were the true patriots of the war? Not the women and men who stood staunchly behind the government and leapt to perform its every bidding, though they might wear the outward garb of loyalty. There was, explained Phillips, "nothing so hard to see as your own time. Emerson once said of Webster, 'He knew the patriots of '76 well, but would not have known the patriots of his own day if he had met them in the street.'" America's heroes were those who struggled to forge the nation-state as a tool of liberty and equality. "Waste no time in showing that you are right," Phillips told his fellow believers at Boston's Music Hall. "Take it for granted. We are the Constitution and the patriots, everything else is treason."[34]

Phillips moved seamlessly from a patriotism rooted in the assertion of conscience to the idea that the only true patriots were working for abolition. But the exercise of individual conscience did not inevitably lead to abolitionism. Though Phillips initially cautioned against suppressing discontent, as the war progressed, he refined this notion. If the nation truly meant justice, and if the assertions of the war protesters threatened the fulfillment of that meaning, the prerogatives of the nation might be said to override those of a democratic citizenry.

Thus, when the administration's detractors challenged the constitutionality of the expanding national state, Phillips gambled. He explicitly urged

Americans to jettison their contractual views of nationality, replacing them
with the idea that the nation had a life and destiny of its own, one that could
not be restrained by the exercise of individual rights. "Man does not make
Unions," he argued in January 1863, two weeks after the Emancipation Proclamation, "and it is hardly possible for man to break them . . . one would think,
by the way men talk, that a Union was made by parchment." In a striking
departure from his earlier rhetoric, Phillips invoked an old world model of
nationality. "We are either a nation, or we are not. If we are a nation . . . if,
like England and France, we are one people, indivisible,—then . . . no parchment could bar us from the use of any power within our reach to save the
nationality. . . . Do you suppose any agreement could bar the Queen of England or the Emperor of France from saving [their] country in the hour of
peril? How absurd! The nation knows no limits."[35]

Phillips asked Northerners to show their patriotism by respecting the
power and autonomy of the emerging nation-state. When, in August 1862,
Lincoln suspended the writ of habeas corpus, an act that would allow the
arrest and detention of war protestors, Phillips endorsed his actions. "It is
necessary to do anything to save the ship," he asserted. "It is a mere question of whether you prefer the despotism of Washington or that of Richmond.
I prefer Washington."[36]

But the changes Phillips hoped for were slow to come. Though the Emancipation Proclamation had taken the sting out of Lincoln's revocation of both
Frémont's and Hunter's emancipation edicts, for the abolitionists, the good
society remained elusive. In December 1863, Lincoln proposed a plan offering
amnesty to any citizen of the Confederacy (some military and elected officers
excluded) who swore future loyalty to the Constitution and agreed to obey all
laws pertaining to the abolition of slavery. Once a mere 10 percent of any state's
voting population took this oath, that state could organize a new state government. The plan made no provisions for enfranchising blacks, nor did it suggest that the government would do anything to ensure what Phillips had called
an "effectual" freedom—one that could "maintain and vindicate itself." For
Phillips the plan made freedom for blacks a "sham"; it "perpetuate[d] slavery
under a softer name." An alternative plan more amenable to the abolitionists was set forth in the summer of 1864. The Wade-Davis bill required that
50 percent of a Southern state's population swear fidelity to the Constitution
before a state constitutional convention could be held. Only those willing to
take an "Ironclad Oath," pledging obedience to the Constitution in the future
and denying involvement in the present rebellion—could vote for delegates.

The bill included a provision for equality before the law regardless of race, though it did not enact black suffrage. Lincoln's pocket veto of the Wade-Davis bill enraged abolitionists, including Phillips, who seemed to be watching the nation he had hoped to build crumble before his eyes.[37]

Confronting these setbacks to his hopes for an egalitarian nation, Phillips revived his conception of an assertive, conscience-based patriotism. He became increasingly critical of Lincoln, and campaigned against him in 1864. When his critics accused him of disloyalty, he defended himself in terms that established how far removed his understanding of loyalty was from that which his nation of "no limits"—the nation which no parchment could restrain— might have suggested:

> Remember Mr. President, we are American, not European. We live under the Constitution of the United States, not English or French rule; Any man . . . who raises today the war cry, "Stand by the Administration" and does not take into account that limitation . . . forfeits his franchise under the free institutions of the fathers, and binds his lips, like a vassal of the Czar, to a lifelong allegiance. . . . I am only a Constitutional American citizen. . . . I have a right to say whether my interests shall be committed to this principle.[38]

Phillips unequivocally asserted his right to oppose the administration. In light of his loyalty to the principles of liberty, he argued, anything but opposition was in fact disloyalty. He contrasted his own actions to the Democratic war protesters on the grounds that he supported the war that was to create a nation of liberty and justice, while they opposed it.[39]

This, then, was the governing principle behind Phillips's definition of the nation and patriotism. Much as the power he would grant to the state was contingent upon its exercise in the interest of equality and justice, so his understanding of loyalty was, in the end, defined by the exercise of not just any conscience, but one rooted in the fundamental principles of the Declaration of Independence. The vision that guided him always was one of social justice and equality. In the Civil War years Phillips oscillated between hope and frustration as he and his abolitionist colleagues sought to lead the American people in the creation of a nation-state true to that vision.

FREDERICK DOUGLASS

Wendell Phillips could speak with authority about the meaning of the nation and patriotism in part because he himself claimed status as a scion of the founding fathers. Few abolitionist speakers rivaled his power or his popularity. The one man who did also staked a unique claim to his authority, though it could not have been more different from Phillips's. Frederick Douglass spent his early years not on Beacon Hill, but on a plantation in Maryland, the child of a white man and a slave.

Douglass was twenty when he engineered his escape from slavery, settling down with his wife in New Bedford, Massachusetts, in 1838. Through speeches given first at a church, then at antislavery meetings under the tutelage of William Lloyd Garrison, this strikingly talented and articulate man rose to prominence. As an orator he was a compelling figure: tall, muscular, with a voice one contemporary described as rivaling "Webster's in its richness, and in the depth and sonorousness of its cadence." His oratorical power was compounded by his status as an ex-slave: he was, as historian David Blight asserted, "the greatest living challenge to the American paradox of slavery and freedom." In his speeches Douglass wove tales from his personal experience as a slave with reports of Northern prejudice; scattered throughout these speeches were Garrisonian expressions of moral suasion.[40]

But like many black abolitionists, Douglass soon became impatient with Garrison and his cohort. Champions of the ideas of equality and justice, these white men and women were nonetheless guilty of racial condescension. Moreover, Douglass found the abstractions of Garrison's nonresistance a luxury the black man could ill afford. If politics could in any sense advance the prospects for emancipation, then he could not support its eschewal. In 1847, Douglass founded his own newspaper, the *North Star;* less than a year later, his paper endorsed the Free Soil Party. By 1851, Douglass had rejected the Garrisonian notion of a proslavery Constitution, arguing instead that the Constitution contained within it the promise of equality, regardless of race.[41]

Douglass, like Phillips, struggled over his decision to tie his hopes for emancipation and racial equality to the American government. But unlike Phillips, in opting for America Douglass gambled twice: once on an alliance with the state, and again on the ultimate good faith of whites. Not all black leaders took this course. Martin Delaney and H. Ford Douglas, prominent black abolitionists, urged African-Americans to abandon the notion that they would ever realize their freedom in white America. Emigration and even rebellion—H. Ford Douglas announced his willingness to "join a foreign enemy and fight against [this government]"—represented alternative courses.[42]

But Douglas and Delaney were in the minority among black abolitionists. In choosing to place his faith in America, Douglass was operating within what

Douglass's nationalism asserted the centrality of African-Americans to American national identity. (Frederick Douglass, leading
African-American abolitionist. From frontispiece to his 1855 au-
tobiography, *My Bondage and My Freedom.*)

Vincent Harding has called "the Great Tradition of Black Protest," a primary
component of which was, by the 1840s, an assertion of the American identity
of blacks and of their role within the nation. In the face of white efforts to
colonize blacks and black efforts to emigrate, the majority of African-American editors and abolitionists insisted that the best hope for the black race lay
in the United States. As Charles Ray, editor of the *Colored American,* wrote in
1840, "It is our duty and privilege to claim an equal place among the American people, to identify ourselves with American interests, and to exert all the
power and influence we have, to break down the disabilities under which we
labor, and look to become a happy people in this extended country."[43]

Douglass's faith in the future of blacks in the United States was part of a
larger faith which informed his thinking during the war years. Like Phillips,

he believed that the world was moving inexorably toward an era of liberty and justice. But unlike Phillips, Douglass regularly couched his notions of progress in terms of Providence and the millennium.

Providentialism and millennialism pervaded American popular culture in the mid–nineteenth century. But Douglass's millennialism had a distinctly abolitionist quality. The path to righteousness, he told his audiences, was marked by an ongoing conflict "between . . . good and evil, liberty and slavery, . . . the glorious light of love, and the appalling darkness of human selfishness and sin." The outcome of this struggle would be the final perfection of the race: all humans living together, free and equal, each bringing the best of his or her race to bear on high civilization. The "sacredness" of humanity would be recognized, and race would become insignificant.[44]

In Douglass's view, the United States was to play an important part in this process. But events in the 1850s undermined many black leaders' faith in the prospect of a free and just America. The Fugitive Slave Law of 1850 mandated federal assistance in the return of any Northern black accused of being a runaway slave. In the 1857 Dred Scott case, the Supreme Court announced that any black person descended from slaves could not be an American citizen. Even Douglass, whose faith in America far exceeded that of many of his black contemporaries, finally endorsed a movement to emigrate to Haiti, and planned a trip to investigate the island in early April 1861.[45]

With the war, Douglass's faith revived. His view of America as the best hope for blacks merged with his belief in the nation's providential mission, and he began to argue a position that black leaders across the North were coming to believe: the war was an act of God, the newly empowered state a tool to free the slaves and uplift the nation. For Douglass, blacks would play a central role in that process.[46]

In his wartime speeches and editorials, Douglass set forth his understanding of the United States as a chosen nation. From the beginning, he argued, its doctrines, enshrined in the Declaration of Independence, had shone as a beacon light. Not only the nation's principles, but the unique makeup of its population fitted it as the site of the perfection of the human race. The nation's "mighty heart" beat "with the best blood of all nations." Here the European joined the African, the Asian, the Mexican, and the Native American. God had selected America, he argued, as a testing ground for "the faithful application of the principle of perfect civil equality to the people of all races."[47]

The promise of America resided in its principles and its people; but slavery had betrayed the promise and corrupted the very soul of the nation. As a result, America had a dual national identity. With freedom in the North and slavery in the South, the nation "had degenerated into a compromise, so that an American wherever met with is simply a bundle of contradictions, incongruities, and absurdities." The "National Head" was "bowed down, and our face is mantled with shame and confusion."[48]

This crisis in national identity would by necessity resolve itself in one direction or the other. If Americans recognized that the cause of the war, and of their own fall from grace, was slavery; if they acted on that recognition with wisdom, strength and courage, then "righteousness" would exalt the nation; and that nation would assume its rightful place as "a queen among the nations of the earth." But the alternative to national glory was national shame; to national elevation, national debasement. If Americans shrank from the duty that this war imposed, the great American experiment in democratic government and human perfection would fail, and the nation would perish. Its name would be added to that long list of nations vanished from the map; and American Republicanism would become but a "hissing and a byword to a mocking earth."[49]

Thus, in the context of a racist culture and a white ethnocentric national identity, Douglass insisted that the incorporation of African-Americans into the American polity was essential to that polity's existence and integrity. Though the vicissitudes of black advances and disappointments would at times shake this vision, throughout the war, he persisted in predicating his image of American identity on black inclusion. He argued that African-Americans had made incomparable, inestimable contributions to their country. They had worked the land and made it fertile; they had "watered the soil with their tears and enriched it with their blood." Southern slaves had worked nearly single-handedly to produce the riches of the South, while black laborers had contributed to the prosperity of the North. Moreover, the black population was unwavering in its patriotism: black troops had fought in the Revolution and the War of 1812. Notwithstanding the current administration's reluctance to enlist African-Americans, black men stood ready to fight for their country again.[50]

While Douglass called on whites to officially welcome blacks as members of the American family, in fact, he argued, blacks were already an integral part of the nation. "Go to California and dig gold; the black man is there," he told his audience at Tremont Temple in February 1862. "Go to war with Mexico, . . . and the black man is there. Go down into . . . South Carolina, and the black man is there . . . as your friend, to give you . . . more trustworthy information than you can find among all the poor white loyal trash you can scare up in that region. . . . We shall never leave you."[51]

Blacks were central to the fate of America not only because of their contributions, but also for the role they alone could play in the achievement of the nation's mission. If America were to become the Christian, egalitarian, and multiracial nation that God intended, it would be necessary for her people to overcome prejudice. Thus, whites could learn the lessons necessary for their redemption through blacks. "The allotments of Providence," Douglass proclaimed in February 1862, "seem to make the black man of America the open book out of which the American people are to learn lessons of wisdom, power, and goodness." Those lessons would prepare the nation for its role as a beacon light for all the nations of the world, both in terms of political liberty and equality before the law, and in terms of the recognition and appreciation of the fundamental humanity of mankind, regardless of race. "Over the bleeding back of the American bondman," Douglass proclaimed, "we shall learn mercy. In the very extreme difference of color and features of the Negro and the Anglo Saxon, shall be learned the highest ideals of the sacredness of man and the fullness and perfection of human brotherhood." The treatment of the nation's blacks would be the measure of her progress: "The destiny of the colored American," Douglass told his audience in 1862, "however this mighty war shall terminate, is the destiny of America."[52]

Thus, loyal Americans would push their leaders for an abolition war, empower a national state to effect an abolition peace, and guarantee equal rights to all regardless of race. These themes Douglass repeated throughout the war. But African-Americans themselves would also play a central role in the active forging of a new, revitalized America. As blacks joined the Northern army, as they donned military uniforms, fought and died for the Union, and waged a battle for equal pay, they were, Douglass argued, making the nation their own. And in doing so, they helped move that nation closer to the millennium. Thus one of the principal models of patriotism in Douglass's rhetoric became that of the black soldier.[53]

From the outset of the war, Douglass was one of the country's foremost proponents of black enlistment. The admission of African-Americans into the United States Army would serve several purposes. First, as Douglass made clear, if black troops were allowed to fight, the war would become a war for abolition. Black soldiers could be *formed into a liberating army, to march into the South and raise the banner of Emancipation among the slaves."* Second, Douglass recognized that by fighting for the Union, African-American men would establish a claim to citizenship. This notion was rooted in the classical republican assumption that service in a militia was an honor, and implied a right to citizenship. "Once let a black man get upon his person the brass letters, U.S., let him get an Eagle on his button, and a musket on his shoulder and bullets in his pocket, and there is no power on earth which can deny that he has earned his right to citizenship." Blacks fought for the true meaning of America not only by helping to create an abolition war, but also by creating a biracial citizenry. The black man's service could be viewed as exemplary action—as prefiguring equal participation in the new, trans-formed republic.[54]

Black soldiers' demands for equal pay fortified this image. Though recruiters had promised African-Americans the same compensation as that which their white counterparts received, black soldiers were in fact paid not as soldiers, but as laborers. They received $10.00 per month minus $3.00 for clothing, while whites performing the same duties received $13.00 per month plus a $3.50 allowance for clothing. Black protest was immediate and vociferous. A movement to demand equal pay was mobilized, aided by sympathetic officers. Soldiers and their families wrote letters to put pressure on President Lincoln and Secretary of War Edwin M. Stanton to reverse the policy; some black soldiers refused to accept any pay if not equal pay. Though Douglass contin-ued to urge African-Americans to enlist in the face of this discrimination, he saw the danger of such inequality. "Our work will not be done," he argued in December 1863, "until the colored man is admitted a full member in good and regular standing into the American body politic." This was the first ver-sion of the new republic; there could be no second-class citizenship.[55]

As the unequal treatment of black soldiers suggested, the war was testing Douglass's vision. Like all abolitionists, he grew increasingly frustrated with the administration's vacillations. He had staked his hopes, as well as the lives of two sons who enlisted in the Union Army, on the belief that as the war progressed, blacks would be incorporated into the nation—first as soldiers, then as citizens. Black troops had not even been welcome in the Union Army until early 1863; upon acceptance, they faced not only unequal pay, but unequal status: black officers did not receive commissions. Douglass defended the administration's decision to withhold commissions from blacks, and con-tinued to recruit African-American soldiers in spite of unequal pay. But even he felt compelled to suspend his recruitment efforts in the summer of 1863, three months after the Confederate Congress announced its plans to treat captured black soldiers as slaves in rebellion—effectively, to execute them.

Abolitionists waited for a retaliatory statement from Lincoln. But throughout May, June, and most of July, none was forthcoming. Lincoln finally responded on July 30, proclaiming that "for every soldier of the United States killed in violation of the laws of war a rebel soldier shall be executed . . . for every one enslaved . . . a rebel soldier shall be placed at hard labor." Douglass resumed recruitment.[56]

His unhappiness with Lincoln notwithstanding, Douglass supported the president for reelection in 1864. His role in the campaign was minor compared to that of other abolitionists. Douglass's own explanation for the difference spoke volumes about how little the nation had progressed toward his ideals of equality: "I am not doing much in this presidential canvass," he wrote to Theodore Tilton in October 1864, "for the reason that the Republican committees do not wish to expose themselves to the charge of being the 'N—r' party. The Negro is the deformed child, which is put out of the room when company comes." If black soldiers could not be paid as much as white ones, neither could a black leader hope to obtain equal status with a white leader. American national identity continued to be contaminated by pervasive racism.[57]

Douglass's faith would be tested again and again. Nonetheless, he continued to hold forth the hope that the war would produce a new nation, one that would embrace blacks. Though the millennium he predicted failed to materialize, his appraisal of the role of black troops in the war and in the nation's renewal was in part vindicated. As black troops heroically fought and died for the Union; as they waged battles for equal pay, they did in fact change the meaning of the war, and thereby, the meaning of the nation. Through their service to the republic, they sought and acquired citizenship; through their battles for equal pay, they demanded equality before the law—a notion later enshrined into the Constitution in the Fourteenth Amendment. As the emblems of Douglass's true patriots, they moved the nation closer to what Douglass believed God intended it to be.[58]

ANNA DICKINSON

Historians have long recognized Phillips and Douglass for their contributions to Civil War popular political discourse. But it was Anna Dickinson who, perhaps more than any other abolitionist orator, captured the imagination and affection of the wartime Northern public. "There never was such enthusiasm over an orator in this country," wrote Elizabeth Cady Stanton, Susan B. Anthony, and Matilda Jocelyn Gage with feminist pride in their *History of*

Woman Suffrage. Only eighteen when the war began, by war's end Dickinson had become a national figure, renowned for her ability to electrify audiences with her impassioned rhetoric. Wendell Phillips confessed that she brought tears to his eyes; Lincoln himself heard her speak and was reported to have "enjoyed the lecture . . . exceedingly." In light of her youth and her sex, her talent was a source of awe: Dickinson was a phenomenon. Northerners embraced her as the nation's savior: they regaled her with music, flowers, and jewelry. She was heralded as a "Joan D'Arc," an oratorical prodigy sent from God "to bear the banners of Liberty and the Republic to victory."[59]

Dickinson inherited both her abolitionist commitments and her oratorical genius. She was born in 1842, the child of Quaker abolitionists whose home served as a stop on the underground railroad. At the age of two she lost her father to a heart attack, suffered at the conclusion of a fervent anti-slavery speech. Dickinson herself gave her first public speech—a spontaneous retort to a man who asserted his contempt for women's rights—at a Quaker meeting in January 1860. Over the next year her reputation grew, and by the close of 1860 she had established herself as a new but accomplished abolitionist speaker.[60]

The outbreak of war evoked in Dickinson the same enthusiastic, hopeful response experienced by abolitionists throughout the North. She spoke frequently in favor of the North in her home state of Pennsylvania. In October 1861, she came to the attention of William Lloyd Garrison. Like Phillips and Douglass, she was shepherded in the early part of her career by this zealous founder of the American Anti-Slavery Society.[61]

In February 1863, Dickinson received an invitation which would catapult her to a position of fame and adulation. Benjamin Prescott, the secretary of the Republican State Committee in New Hampshire, asked her to campaign for the Republican Party in the March 1863 gubernatorial contest. The first Northern state to hold elections following the Democratic upset in the fall of 1862, New Hampshire was considered crucial for the Republicans: the election would serve as a harbinger of continuing dissatisfaction with the war administration or of Republican victories in the offing.[62]

From early February to the eve of the March 10 election, Dickinson campaigned throughout the state. At each stop, she was "serenaded, feasted, and feted . . . eulogized by the press and the people." When the New Hampshire Republicans claimed victory, newspapers, politicians, and the governor-elect himself credited Dickinson. The campaign in New Hampshire was followed almost immediately by one in Connecticut. When similar results obtained,

Dickinson's youth, gender, and dramatic oratory led to her description as the "Joan of Arc" for the Union cause. (Anna Dickinson,
Civil War abolitionist)

Dickinson's fame was secured. "If ever such events were accomplished by
human agency," proclaimed a Massachusetts judge, "that girl saved Connecticut and New Hampshire to the Union." A correspondent of a Connecticut
paper wrote "God makes only one such woman in an age—and no one who
has witnessed the wonderful power of this modern Joan of Arc, can doubt
that she has been raised up for some great purpose."[63]

As word of Dickinson spread, she received invitations to speak in cities across the North, including Boston, New York, and Philadelphia. Soon even Wendell Phillips found himself beseeching Dickinson to make room in her schedule to speak at an abolitionist meeting. In 1864, she delivered a speech in Washington, D.C., to an audience which included the president. As Dickinson spoke to capacity crowds in Cooper Union, Music Hall, and eventually, in the Hall of the House of Representatives, she set forth a number of by-then familiar arguments. Slavery, she asserted, was at the heart of the war. The South, not the North, was responsible for the conflict. An examination of American history revealed a series of aggressions enacted by the Slave Power against the Union, culminating in this battle between democracy and aristocracy, free labor and slavery. As allies of the South, Northern Democrats were to be held culpable as well. In contrast, Dickinson extolled the virtues of the North, the sacrifice of Union soldiers, and the heroism of the North's African-American troops.[64]

Contemporary critics were quick to point out this lack of originality. Her themes, reported one paper, were culled from the speeches of Wendell Phillips and "stale Tribune editorials." The few historians who have studied her concur: Dickinson's fame was based on her oratorical talent—not on brilliance of insight or analysis.[65]

But if Dickinson's themes were the stock themes of abolitionism, her presentation of them contained its own originality. Indeed, while Phillips and Douglass developed powerful ideas about the nation-state and patriotism, Dickinson's contributions cannot be fully understood without an examination of her unique presentation. Much as the Sanitary Fairs offered a tangible version of ideas of culture and sacrifice; just as "The Man Without a Country" concretized the abstract tenets of the romantic nationalists; so Dickinson's speeches rendered palpable the evil of the South, the virtues of the North, and the duties incumbent upon the nation's patriots.

Dickinson's speeches frequently opened with a poetic, historical, or classical allusion; a familiar reference bound to resonate with her audience. She then moved to a war-related but nonetheless sweeping point—for example, the South's responsibility for the failure of the Union—and proceeded to take her listeners through a rapid-fire series of facts and figures to substantiate it. Reviews of her speeches often mentioned this "profusion of thought and illustration": the "energetic sentences, crammed full of undeniable facts."[66]

Dickinson's oratorical style compounded the persuasive effect of this approach. "Her sentences are mostly long, rolling, and tempestuous," wrote a reporter from the *Chicago Tribune,* "gathering strength as they progress in duration, until at last they sweep all before them in their irresistible might." The audience—no matter how skeptical upon entering the hall—was generally caught up in the torrent. One doubter, "prejudiced against her at the start," described his conversion: "She had not spoken ten minutes before all prejudices were dispelled; thirty minutes, and not a man in the house could be found who would admit that he ever had any prejudices; sixty minutes, and she held fifteen hundred people breathless with admiration and astonishment; two hours, and she had raised her entire audience to a pitch of enthusiasm which was perfectly irresistible."[67]

As Dickinson commanded her audiences' attention, her focus often narrowed: if the South was responsible for the war, so too were the Democrats, looking "tamely on while rebellion was festering in the land." Again, she presented her audience with a multitude of examples, naming Democrat after Democrat who had contributed to the onset or perpetuation of the war: Hadn't James Buchanan been in office at the outset of the war? Hadn't General Robert Patterson—a Democrat—permitted the rout at Bull Run? And finally, in many of her speeches, Dickinson focused her lens even more narrowly, bringing her scrutiny to bear upon the bête noire of abolitionists and Radicals alike, General George B. McClellan.[68]

McClellan's resistance to antislavery—and indeed, to battle—led many abolitionists to suspect his commitment to the Union. Some, including Wendell Phillips, alluded to the possibility that his behavior was treasonous. In the fall of 1861, Dickinson stated in no uncertain terms what had been on the minds of radicals for months: "Future history will show," she announced in a speech delivered at the annual meeting of the Pennsylvania Anti-Slavery Society only a few days after the Union defeat at Balls Bluff, "that this battle was lost not through ignorance and incompetence, but through the treason of the commanding general, George B. McClellan." The subsequent furor caused by her accusation led her to abandon this charge of outright treason. But Dickinson had discovered a powerful tool: by scourging McClellan, she gave human form to the enemy. Much as Vallandigham served as the countersymbol of a patriot for the Republicans, for Dickinson, McClellan personified the forces which prevented the triumph of an abolition war, and therefore of the nation. Though McClellan had been relieved of command in the fall of 1862, by the spring of 1863 he was a leading candidate for the Democratic presidential nomination. In May of that year, in a speech titled "The Day—The Cause," Dickinson detailed his blunders, one by one. He had "waited month after month" to strike, "while his army was dying at the rate of four thousand a month from disease alone, and at last, when the feelings of the country drove him down to Manassas, . . . he found it defended by empty entrenchments with wooden guns." He had taken eighty thousand men to Yorktown and "sat down, week after week, to do what? To attack? Not at all. To settle down, rooted in the mud." Six weeks later he had marched into Yorktown and discovered it "garrisoned by just one single black man." Now, she proclaimed, "he has left the scenes of battle for the company of New York traitors, and spends his time dining and feasting." Dickinson thus defined patriotism first by offering a counterexample: McClellan's assertion of limited war aims, his seeming sabotage of Northern military initiative, and his association with defeatist Democrats rendered him a near-traitor.[69]

But Dickinson also offered her audiences positive models of patriotism. If Democratic generals had sabotaged the war effort, Northerners need only look to the Army's Republican generals for examples of patriotic heroes. Again, Dickinson offered specific names—Greble, Winthrop, Ellsworth, Baker, Saxton, Hunter—and offered what one reporter called "thrilling examples" of their heroics. Frémont in particular—"the man that dared to . . . take liberty as his watchword, and Freedom and Truth as his battle shout; who dared to come out for truth, regardless of the world's expediency, and hurl a thunderbolt against the foe" presented a stark and compelling contrast to the ineffective, defeatist McClellan. True patriots, she suggested, had the courage and commitment to conduct a war for abolition.[70]

Dickinson also lauded the Union soldiers. She had spent a summer visiting and caring for soldiers in a Union hospital in Philadelphia and incorporated the stories she had heard into her speeches. Anecdotes of individual daring and determination punctuated her oratory: in November 1863, she regaled a capacity Chicago crowd with the tale of a black soldier who, on the death of the standard bearer of colors, wrapped the flag around his person and became "a living standard, crying aloud, 'Come on, boys! I'm good for a single moment!'" His unfathomable courage rallied the regiment; and the North swept to victory.[71]

Indeed, the willingness of Union soldiers to sacrifice for their country became a regular theme in Dickinson's speeches. War, she argued, had developed the nation's "noble, self-sacrificing courage and honor, confirming it as it was confirmed never before. This element of self-sacrifice is a great thing in us as a people." Again, Dickinson dramatized her point by use of specific, personal examples: "I never see a common soldier without the profoundest respect," she proclaimed in a speech given first in Washington D.C.'s Hall of Representatives and then across the North:

> There he comes in his faded blue! Maybe he limps a little. Perhaps he goes over the ground painfully on crutches or with a cane. If you smile and nod to him he cannot return the salute for want of a right hand; or perhaps a stray ball has made his face beautiful by a ghastly scar. He endured the hardships of the Southwest campaign, and endured them without a murmur; until he was attacked at Port Hudson. Or perhaps he remembers Antietam, where for hours he stood while the fiery rain of shot and shell fell around him. . . . He carries with him Wagner, and as we turn to look at him we know that he did not flinch or shrink on that slippery slope. . . . The nation honors him living, and mourns him, the private soldier, dead. Where he sleeps is sacred ground, and the people will pile his monuments on the blood-stained turf where he fell, dying that a great cause might live.[72]

If Dickinson's celebration of the nation's education in sacrifice was reminiscent of the rhetoric of the Sanitary Commission, her use of Union soldiers to personalize the North's cause evoked images of the Sanitary Fairs. But Dickinson's use of the soldiers differed from both the commission's and the fairs' in an important way. The commission leadership was most concerned that the nation become as one; suffering and sacrifice were vehicles to that process. In the Sanitary Fairs, the soldiers represented a model of a patriotism defined by sacrifice, but that sacrifice was devoid of ideological content.

As an abolitionist, Dickinson had a different perspective. She acknowledged that the North had been slow to recognize the greater meaning of the contest; but after piling "mountains of slain," it had at last "reached the point where we learned God's lesson." The ground had been "crimsoned with the best blood of the land," not to preserve the Union as it was, but that that land "might bring forth its harvest of liberty!" The sacrifice of the nation's young men had at last taught the North that the war was a "death struggle between freedom and slavery."[73]

And only by pursuing that battle to its "bitter end" could the North do justice to its slain. There was, Dickinson told a Philadelphia audience in May 1863, "no arm of compromise in all the North long enough to stretch across the sea of blood that has been spilled, and the mountain of 200,000 human beings packed between the North and the South." She reiterated this theme in Washington before an audience that included the president: "We stand pledged by the remains of those heroic dead to fight for 'Justice, Truth, and

Freedom.'" For Dickinson, the sacrifice of the soldiers could not be under-stood outside of the struggle for the abolitionist nation.[74]

The Northern public embraced Anna Dickinson—at times, no doubt, in spite of her abolitionist message. Her popularity was due in part to the nov-elty of her situation: her talent belied her youth; her sex belied her very pres-ence on the platform. It was this latter point that challenged Republicans, who strove to exploit her novelty while avoiding any fallout from her violation of gender norms. They struggled to fit her into nineteenth-century gender categories; to find labels for her more in keeping with the genteel, benevolent Sanitary Fair workers than the firebrand female abolitionist that she was. "How logical, picturesque, thrilling is her speech," wrote the *Springfield Republican* in May 1863, "how her eyes flash, beam, and tremble into tears—how Cassandra-like, with strong voice, she utters her message of woe; and anon, as Juliet, sinks into tenderness, pathos, music." She had a "fine femi-nine eloquence," wrote a New York paper, while another paper noted her "earnest, soul-glowing face." When Pennsylvania congressman William D. Kelley introduced Dickinson to a Connecticut audience, he assured his lis-teners that she was "as good a daughter and sister as she was gifted as a woman."[75]

Despite Republican efforts to place her in accepted female spheres, Demo-crats had a field day with Dickinson's transgression of gender categories. "This is a very ridiculous matter," proclaimed the *New York Journal of Commerce*. "The province of woman is too well understood to need explanation now. She is the home angel, not the politician." Though Republicans might find her manner pleasing, the *New York World* found her "an ordinary-looking person, with a harsh voice, unfeminine manner, and a parrot-like flow of words." Her "indecencies of speech would have disgraced a pot-house brawler of the other sex." This "feminine effrontery" was but "the falsehoods of the war committee set off with the sneers of a virago."[76]

The real Dickinson evaded the categories of either party. If she was not a virago, neither was she Juliet. Try though the Republicans might to downplay the radical aspects of the role she assumed, Dickinson was in fact violating gender norms; moreover, she was an outspoken feminist. Her first public speech had been on women's rights, and she continued to speak to that issue during the war. Her lectures included such titles as "Woman's Vot-ing," "A Plea for Women," and "Woman's Work and Wages." In them she challenged the political, social, and even physical superiority of men, at one point challenging the "puny, bewhiskered, beringed, beperfumed popinjays of Chestnut Street" to "stand up before her and talk about women's physical inferiority to men." More important, she called on Northerners to incorporate women into the body politic. In November 1862, she told a Boston audience that if women had represented the Union during the sectional crisis, there would have been no war. Drawing an analogy between the management of a home and that of the country, she further suggested that a woman would never have tolerated McClellan: "It would not have taken a woman or housekeeper two years to discover that a person was incompetent, and to discharge him."[77]

But Dickinson's feminist vision played only a minor role in her wartime oratory. Like her fellow feminist abolitionists Elizabeth Cady Stanton and Susan B. Anthony, she subordinated the claims of her sex to those of the slave in the hope that women would also reap the benefits of a nation dedicated to "universal freedom, universal suffrage, and universal justice." While never denying her beliefs, she rarely volunteered them in the course of her speeches on the war. Her response to a Democratic editor who condemned her as a "spiritualist, a strong-minded woman, [and] an expounder of woman's rights" was revealing: She denied the first charge, ignored the second, and deflected the third with humor. "I wish that for once the women of Hartford had a chance to vote," she said. "The editor of the *Hartford Times* would be nowhere."[78]

As a young female, a feminist, an abolitionist, and an orator with broad appeal, Dickinson defied contemporary gender categories. Perhaps this is why Northerners could best understand her as a Joan of Arc: a young woman, both maiden and warrior, "sent as from on high to save the state." Like the epic heroine in France's nationalist saga, Dickinson's startling emergence and fiery patriotism marked her for a leading role in America's transcendent national drama. It was to the delight and clear benefit of abolitionists across the North that it was *their* nation-state—one committed to the notions of equality and justice—that this heaven-sent messenger had come to save.[79]

THE ABOLITIONISTS' LEGACY

With the passage of the Thirteenth Amendment in January 1865, many abolitionists believed that their work was done. William Lloyd Garrison led a movement to disband the American Anti-Slavery Society (AASS), the movement's chief institutional vehicle. But others, Phillips, Douglass, and Dickinson among them, disagreed. As Phillips argued, abolitionists were fighting for "absolute equality before the law; absolute civil equality . . . and I shall never leave the Negro until, so far as God gives me the power, I achieve it." In May 1865, the AASS voted to continue its existence, with Phillips replacing Garrison as president.[80]

For the next four years, Phillips, Douglass, and Dickinson campaigned for the fulfillment of their vision of the nation. In a testament to their concern that it be an egalitarian nation—for lacking that, it was not, to them, a nation at all—all three opposed the Fourteenth Amendment. Though that amendment defined national citizenship in terms that included blacks and established the supremacy of the nation over the states in its guarantee of "equal protection of the laws," it also recognized the right of states to exclude blacks from the franchise. As Douglass explained, "To tell me that I am an equal American citizen, and, in the same breath, tell me that my right to vote may be constitutionally taken away from me by some other equal citizen . . . is to tell me that my citizenship is but an empty name."[81]

Abolitionist hopes rested not with the Fourteenth but with the Fifteenth Amendment, which guaranteed suffrage to male citizens regardless of race. Indeed, Phillips, Douglass, and Dickinson each played important roles in that amendment's formulation and passage. In September 1866, at a Southern Loyalists' Convention in Philadelphia, the issue of black suffrage threatened to break up the assembly of prominent Republicans. Border state delegates bolted, and the convention appeared at an end. Douglass and Dickinson assumed charge; and Dickinson took the floor. Her speech entranced the Southern men who made up the audience, many of whom had never heard a woman speak publicly. "When she sat down," Douglass would later write, "I felt that the battle was half won." Douglass himself also spoke, and the convention approved resolutions that later became the Fifteenth Amendment.[82]

Phillips's contribution to the amendment's passage was more ironic. In 1869, the House approved a version of the amendment that forbade the abridgement of voting rights for reasons of "race, color, or previous condition of servitude." Concerned that failure to forbid restriction of the franchise on the additional grounds of education or property ownership would lay the basis for the eventual disenfranchisement of blacks, the Senate passed another formulation of the amendment that added nativity, property, education, and creed to its list of illegal criteria for the franchise. A congressional impasse ensued, as House Republicans argued that the Senate version would never be ratified by the states, and Senate Republicans held fast to the notion that the political-economic situation in the South demanded greater protection for the black man.[83]

At this crossroads Wendell Phillips stepped in. The Fifteenth Amendment, he argued, "calls for the most delicate handling." Though he no doubt shared the concerns of the Senate Republicans, in a striking departure from form, he endorsed the House version of the amendment, which, he argued, covered "all the ground that the people are ready to occupy." After a lifetime of agitation—of keeping several steps ahead of public opinion—Phillips now called for "political prudence" and warned against asking for too much.[84]

Phillips's response was not the incongruity it appeared to be. As he astutely noted, the "formative hours"—the time during which the "national purpose" grew and ripened rapidly—were at an end. "Our *day* is fast slipping away," he wrote just months after the congressional impasse. "Once let public thought float off from the great issue of the war, and it will take perhaps more than a generation to bring it back again." Republicans accepted Phillips's analysis. If the great moral agitator believed that this was all the nation could accept, then surely it was. The House version of the Fifteenth Amendment passed Congress and was adopted in 1870.[85]

With the passage of the Fifteenth Amendment, the American Anti-Slavery Society finally disbanded. Dickinson took to the lyceum circuit, speaking on behalf of labor and women. Determined to expand the egalitarian sphere of the nation, she became a founding member of the National Woman Suffrage Association, which campaigned for a federal amendment to extend the franchise to women.[86]

As he had before the war, Douglass held to his faith in the Republican Party as the vehicle for the realization of his vision. He worked until his death within the party, striving to keep it true to its early radical principles. As the years wore on this became an uphill battle. "The earth appears to be gradually crumbling away beneath its foundations," he wrote in 1871, as the Republican Party faced a mounting challenge from the Democrats and appeared to be abandoning its Civil War tenets. By 1880, he acknowledged that the Fourteenth and Fifteenth Amendments were "virtually nullified," and "the old master class . . . triumphant." Still, to the very end of his life, Douglass continued in his belief that "the native land of the American Negro is America," and that if only the nation were to "try justice . . . the problem will be solved."[87]

Phillips channeled his postwar energies into the labor movement. But the limits of the nation's willingness to ameliorate its racial inequalities had taken its toll. Speaking before the AASS as the organization prepared to disband, he recognized the abolitionists' accomplishment: "The American Anti-Slavery Association, for thirty years, with straining oars . . . has at last reached the level of the nation's frigate. We don't disband; she takes us on board. We have no constitution under which to exist. The Constitution of the United States has absorbed it all." But if much of what Phillips had wanted had come to pass, it was in form only; the essence of his idealized nation had never materialized. Unable to hide his disillusionment, he added: "I am no longer proud, as I once was, of the flag or the name of an American. I am no longer proud of the Declaration of Independence. . . . I still do not read it with any national pride."[88]

6

Abraham Lincoln and
the Construction of
National Patriotism

Students of nationalism have long argued that the most effective nation-building is, in essence, a synthetic process. Nations may be invented, but the loyalties and ideologies that define them are never truly novel. As David Potter writes, "National loyalty flourishes not by challenging and overpowering all other loyalties, but by subsuming them all in a mutually supportive relation to one another." Similarly, successful nationalisms do not introduce alien ideologies; rather, they recast particular or parochial concerns in terms coextensive with the nation.[1]

Such was the case in the Civil War North: the campaigns that appear to have been most welcomed and accepted by the people drew on or transformed existing loyalties and ideologies. The Union's nation-builders tapped into a repository of nineteenth-century values, traditions, and ideals, including notions of Christian charity, sacrifice, and redemption; ideas of liberal self-interest and republican virtue; local and partisan identities; free labor tenets; the longing for "self and freedom"; a profound faith in the founding fathers; and a providential view of history. The transcendent nationalism that developed during the war was a product of the dialogue—and at times the struggle—between these disparate voices.

If Civil War ideas of patriotism and nation were diverse and at times conflicting, it was the extraordinary accomplishment of Abraham Lincoln to construct a composite national loyalty—one which drew from nearly all the elements in the Union's patriotic repertoire. Uniquely suited for such a task—as Phillips Brooks, Philadelphia Episcopal minister and Lincoln eulogist, noted, "If ever there was a man who was a part of the time and country he lived in, this was he . . . Abraham Lincoln was the type-man of the country"—Lincoln became the preeminent author of a new national patriotism. The nation he described offered Americans a meaningful history and was a vehicle for the realization of self and freedom. His national state was strong but beneficent, bestowing economic well-being and guaranteeing liberty to its people. His patriotism served self-interest but demanded sacrifice; was partisan while seemingly above party; required vigilant citizenship yet commanded obedience.[2]

But Lincoln's contribution to the construction of a transcendent nationalism went beyond recapitulation. Convinced that the tenets contained in the Declaration of Independence rendered the United States the "last best hope of mankind," he infused his synthesis with a profound ideological significance. Lincoln set out to restore the notion of American identity as rooted in an idea. Yet one of his most lasting contributions lay in his death, which provided the nation with a missing "organic" element.[3]

It was as the nation's president that Lincoln promulgated his notions of patriotism and national identity. But the presidency in 1861 was not, as it was by the time Theodore Roosevelt occupied the White House, a "bully pulpit." Candidates in Lincoln's time did not campaign, and presidents did not make frequent speeches to the public. Nevertheless, Lincoln took full advantage of the opportunities he did have to set his ideas before the people. These ideas were widely circulated: as he himself noted, "Everything I say . . . goes into print." In his inaugurals, annual addresses to Congress, published replies to letters, public appearances, and responses to serenades, Lincoln articulated his vision of the nation and patriotism.[4]

LINCOLN'S PATRIOTIC SYNTHESIS

Like almost all antebellum Americans, Lincoln saw and appreciated the material benefits that the Union had bestowed on its citizens. He frequently spoke in terms of the prosperity of the Union: its vast mineral and timber resources, abundant harvests, steady population growth, and expanding industry. This prosperity Lincoln deemed a natural product of the North's free labor system. As Gabor Borrit argues, for Lincoln liberty meant, at least in part, an economic liberty—the freedom to enjoy the fruits of one's own labor, and thereby, by dint of hard work and discipline, improve one's condition. Similarly, equality implied that all men—black or white—were equal in their right to that freedom. Hence the "leading object" of the government was "to elevate the condition of men—to lift artificial weights from all shoulders—to clear paths of laudable pursuit for all—to afford all, an unfettered start, and a fair chance, in the race of life." As Lincoln repeatedly emphasized, these were economic *and* moral imperatives: this was the "just, and generous, and prosperous system, which open[ed] the way to all." Much of Lincoln's pre-war rhetoric concerned slavery's threat to this "right to rise."[5]

The Union, then, was precious in part because it offered its residents both bountiful land and a moral political-economic system that paved the way to the acquisition of those bounties. Moreover, as the wartime national state expanded, Lincoln, like Cooke, worked to redefine Americans' relationship with that state: he presented the state itself as an active economic benefactor. After all, as he reminded Americans in his address to the Special Session of Congress in July 1861, the national government had created the states to begin with. It had purchased the territories that had given many of them rise, it had paid to "relieve" them of Indian tribes, it had even assumed their debts. Lincoln supported the continuing growth of this active, beneficent state when he supported the Thirty-seventh Congress in its unprecedented expansion of national power in economic legislation. He offered the South and the border states the benefits of this generous state every time he offered them compensation for their slaves or offered to buy their cotton. And since "we have been mistaken all our lives if we do not know whites as well as blacks look to their self-interest," Lincoln's state offered blacks freedom if they fought, and rich, productive coal mines in Central America if they agreed to abandon their homes at the end of the fight.[6]

Lincoln never stopped offering Northerners this vision of a prosperous nation-state guaranteeing the right to rise; nor did he cease his appeals to Americans' economic self-interest. As late as February 1865, he entertained the notion of distributing $400 million among the Southern states who agreed to abandon slavery and ratify the Thirteenth Amendment. But free labor, though clearly serving self-interest, was also a moral order; and a government bound to its principles could not operate effectively if its members did not think beyond self-interest. As the war progressed, Lincoln began to question both the attention Northerners paid to material prosperity and the self-congratulatory tone they assumed in its celebration. In March 1863, as he proclaimed a day of fasting, he sounded a note to which he would return repeatedly in the last two years of the war. Americans, he observed, had been "the recipients of the choicest bounties of Heaven. We have been preserved, these many years, in peace and prosperity. We have grown in numbers, wealth and power, as no other nation has ever grown." But, he cautioned, "we have forgotten God . . . and we have vainly imagined, in the deceitfulness of our hearts, that all these blessings were produced by some superior wisdom and virtue of our own. Intoxicated with unbroken success, we have become too self-sufficient to feel the necessity of redeeming and preserving grace, too proud to pray to the God that made us."[7]

Believing that unbridled materialism and pride had contributed to Civil War, Lincoln urged Northerners to humble themselves before God, in hopes that the nation's suffering would lead it to God's redemptive grace. This theme of suffering, sacrifice, and redemption, so pervasive in the Sanitary Fairs, appeared more frequently in Lincoln's rhetoric as the war progressed. Because they undertook the most profound of sacrifices, the Union soldiers were never far from its center. Lincoln frequently thanked the soldiers, who were "endeavoring to purchase with their blood and their lives the future happiness and prosperity of this country." Like the Sanitary Fairs, Lincoln juxtaposed the sacrifice of the soldiers with that rendered by other Americans—including his own—and found all others' wanting. "Say what you will," he told a Philadelphia crowd in June 1864, "after all the most is due to the soldier, who takes his life in his hands and goes to fight the battles of his country." If the soldiers did not waver in their support of the Union, by what right did those who had given less? "Do they not have the hardest of it? Who should quail while they do not?" Addressing a regiment of one-legged soldiers, he pronounced his own words inadequate to the occasion. As the *National Intelligencer* later reported, he said there was no need for a speech from him, for "the men upon their crutches were orators; their very appearance spoke louder than tongues."[8]

For Lincoln, the blood sacrifice of the soldiers defined the highest type of patriotism. But though no civilian contribution could compare, there was, he assured Northerners, "enough yet before us requiring all loyal men and patriots to perform their share of the labor." Lincoln often called on his countrymen to "sink all personal considerations" in a united effort to save the Union. The contributions of the Sanitary Commission and the Sanitary Fairs received high praise, as did those of the Christian Commission—a philanthropic relief organization—and Civil War nurses. In one of his least attractive moments, the president even called on a visiting deputation of African-Americans to emulate the sacrifices for both country and race made by the revolutionaries by emigrating to Central America.[9]

One of the most important sacrifices that Lincoln believed a patriot could make was that of party. Like the Republicans who formed the Union Party,

Lincoln repeatedly urged Northerners to rise "far above personal and parti-
zan politics" and rally behind the administration. Those who did, he deemed
"eminently patriotic." To those who did not, he expressed his keen dis-
appointment. Responding in a public message to a letter from Erastus Corning and the Albany Democrats, Lincoln noted, "I can not overlook the fact
that the meeting . . . preferred to designate themselves 'democrats' rather
than 'American citizens.'" This designation—clearly, Lincoln felt, a conscious
choice—was troubling, for "in this time of national peril I would have preferred to meet you upon a level one step higher than any party platform. . . .
I am sure that from such more elevated position, we could do better battle
for the country we all love, than we possibly can from those lower ones, where
from the force of habit, the prejudices of the past, and selfish hopes of the
future, we are sure to expend much of our ingenuity and strength, in finding fault with, and aiming blows at each other." A patriot in Lincoln's eyes
left party behind and focused on the life of the nation.[10]

But leaving party behind was an ill-defined assignment. Lincoln did not
suggest, as did many Republicans, that there could be no patriotism outside
the Republican (or Union) Party. And he did not, as historians for generations charged, freely arrest any man or woman who dissented from his wartime policy. As Mark E. Neely, Jr., has shown, the majority of Northern
civilians arrested under Lincoln's suspension of the writ of habeas corpus
were suspected deserters or draft evaders. Lincoln did, however, call upon
loyal men and women to withhold their criticisms of the national government
in its time of peril. Moreover, in his public response to the Corning letter's
criticism of the arrest of Clement Vallandigham, he suggested that even
silence might not be enough. In language reminiscent of the Union Leagues,
he asserted that true patriots would make their allegiance clear and without
qualification. "The man who stands by and says nothing, when the peril of
his government is discussed, can not be misunderstood. If not hindered, he
is sure to help the enemy. Much more, if he talks ambiguously—talks for his
country with 'buts' and 'ifs' and 'ands.'"[11]

Lincoln could sound like Jay Cooke, the Sanitary Fairs, Republican par-
tisans, and even the Union Leagues. His rhetoric drew on the themes that
suffused Northern political culture both because he was a product of that
culture and because he made conscious efforts to remain close to the people.
But Lincoln did not invoke those themes unmodified. Self-interest in his view
did not, as it did for Cooke, by definition produce the public good; nor did
sacrifice independent of a specific moral cause necessarily represent virtue.

Similarly, though Lincoln was a partisan—in spite of his no party pleas, for example, he used patronage in a traditional manner—his Republicanism never existed outside the context of the nation he believed it would save. Moreover, though he discouraged dissent, Lincoln did not demand obedience to country for the sake of an abstract state: as John Schaar has pointed out, Lincoln's patriotism was less the civil religion of Rousseau—designed to create a mysticism around the state *solely* in order to cultivate obedience—than a reverence for and commitment to a "city on a hill." In short, the sacrifice and obedience that Lincoln demanded were for the perpetuation of a moral order that offered generous rewards to ordinary people. At the heart of Lincoln's image of patriotism was his conception of the American nation.[12]

ABRAHAM LINCOLN AND THE "LAST BEST HOPE"

Lincoln had a profound vision of the republic he believed Americans had inherited from the founding fathers, a vision that found its roots in the Declaration of Independence. The founders had rejected monarchy and hierarchy, asserting the right to consent of the governed and the fundamental equality of all men. As Gary Wills points out, because the founders had challenged the divine right of kings in terms of equality, they had established as the governing principle of the nation a maxim which slavery by definition contradicted. Lincoln believed that the founders understood this contradiction. Knowing slavery to be a "cancer" on the body politic, they had established equality as a *proposition:* a moral imperative asserted within the context of the existence of slavery, with a promise to the future for the decline of slavery and the expansion of freedom.[13]

The ideas about political democracy and economic equality contained in the Declaration formed the basis of American national identity. They defined Lincoln's own sense of political self—as he told a crowd gathered at Independence Hall in February 1861, "I have never had a feeling politically that did not spring from the sentiments embodied in the Declaration of Independence"—as well as providing the foundation for a shared identity among a diverse people. Americans, he noted, were not linked by blood: there were

> among us perhaps half our people who . . . have come from Europe—German, Irish, French and Scandinavian . . . if they look back through this history to trace their connection with [the founding] days by blood, they find they have none, they cannot carry themselves back into that glorious epoch and make themselves feel that they are part of us, but when they look through

that old Declaration of Independence they find that those old men say that "We hold these truths to be self-evident, that all men are created equal" and then they feel that the moral sentiment taught in that day evidences their relation to those men, that it is the father of all moral principle in them, and that they have a right to claim it as though they were blood of the blood, and flesh of the flesh, of the men who wrote that Declaration, and so they are. That is the electric cord in that Declaration that links the hearts of patriotic and liberty-loving men together, that will link those patriot hearts as long as the love of freedom exists in the minds of men throughout the world.[14]

The centrality of the Declaration of Independence to Lincoln's notion of American national identity is evocative of Wendell Phillips's nationalism. Indeed, like Phillips, Lincoln regularly asserted his belief that a Union without liberty was not worth saving. Struggling to work out his own understanding of the relationship between ideals of liberty and equality and the value of the Union, he termed the assertions of the Declaration an "apple of gold," the Union a "frame of silver," designed to "*adorn* and *preserve* it. The *picture* was made for the apple—*not* the apple for the picture." His version of the Union marked a sharp contrast to that of Union League intellectuals like Edward Everett Hale, who celebrated the nation as a transcendent entity, seemingly independent of any specific moral or political meaning. In February 1861, Lincoln told the New Jersey Senate that as a boy he had been inspired by the story of the Revolutionary battle at Trenton: "The crossing of the river; the contest with the Hessians; the great hardships endured at that time . . . I recollect thinking then, . . . that there must have been something more than common that those men struggled for . . . something even more than National Independence; that something that held out a great promise to all the people of the world to all time to come." The Declaration, he told a crowd at Independence Hall a few days following, had given "liberty, not alone to the people of this country, but hope to the world for all future time." And if the country could not be saved without giving up its defining principle, "I was about to say that I would rather be assassinated on this spot than to surrender it."[15]

But unlike Phillips, who, when faced with a Union that did not in fact represent liberty, called for disunion, Lincoln could never separate his hopes for freedom from his belief in the Union. The United States represented a fragile experiment in republican government; a challenge to hereditary privilege and the divine right of kings. The Union was not just one vehicle for the realization of freedom and equality, it was the *only* available vehicle. Though its progress might remain slow, Lincoln could not surrender the Union, because to do so would be to surrender the notion of self-rule, the "last best, hope of mankind."[16]

Even an imperfect equality, then, was better than none. If for Phillips, the true meaning of America had been established in 1776, that meaning had been betrayed by 1787, with the Constitution's sanction of slavery. Since Lincoln understood the founders' assertions of liberty and equality as propositions toward which Americans must strive, the nation could remain true to the ideals of the Declaration so long as it moved toward, not away from, those ideals. In this analysis, it was the Kansas-Nebraska Act, with its revocation of the Missouri Compromise, which had betrayed the ideals promulgated in the Declaration. Slavery must be contained and the territories guaranteed to freedom; then the Union would be placed back on the track to liberty and equality. Hence, from the outset of the war, Lincoln insisted that the war was not a war for emancipation, but for the restoration of Union and, with it, hope for the ultimate realization of freedom for all.[17]

Lincoln's unique amalgam of idealism and Unionism lent an additional dimension to his notion of patriotism. As a legacy of the fathers, an experiment in popular government, and a proposition for equality, Americans' Revolutionary inheritance devolved tremendous responsibilities upon the people. As he told the Special Session of Congress in July 1861, the government of the fathers was an experiment. "Two points in it, our people have already settled—the successful establishing and the successful administering of it." To the Civil War generation had been handed the third: "its successful maintenance against a formidable (internal) attempt to overthrow it." It was a weighty obligation, to be carried out in the tradition of the fathers and for the benefit of generations yet unborn. "There is more involved in this contest than is realized by everyone," he told an Ohio Regiment returning home in August 1864. "There is involved in this struggle the question whether your children and my children shall enjoy the privileges we have enjoyed. . . . When you return to your homes, rise up to the height of a generation worthy of a free government."[18]

An attachment to the Union marked one important difference between Lincoln's understanding of the nation and patriotism and that of Wendell Phillips. Lincoln's acceptance of the temporary existence of slavery marked another. Though he often expressed both his abhorrence of slavery and his *"personal* wish that all men everywhere could be free," Lincoln's notion of American identity was nonetheless circumscribed by race. He was, as Frederick Douglass said, "preeminently the white man's president." The most dramatic statement of this appeared in an address he delivered to a committee of African-Americans who visited him in August 1862, an address published in the *New York Tribune* on the fifteenth of that month. "You and we are different races," he asserted:

> We have between us a broader difference than exists between almost any other two races. Whether it is right or wrong I need not discuss, but this physical difference is a great disadvantage to us both, as I think your race suffer very greatly, many of them by living among us, while ours suffer from your presence. . . . I need not recount to you the effects upon white men, growing out of the institution of Slavery. I believe in its general evil effects on the white race. . . . But for your race among us there could not be war. . . . It is better for us both, therefore, to be separated.

Lincoln proposed colonization in Central America, where "to your colored race they have no objection."[19]

What is particularly striking about this passage is that Lincoln did not consider the possibility that blacks might feel, like the Germans, Irish, French, and Scandinavians who lacked blood connections to the founders, that they had an organic connection to the nation by virtue of *their* belief in the Declaration of Independence. In fact, he made clear that, in his view, the popular government of the United States had been founded primarily for whites when he pointed out that George Washington, who "himself endured greater physical hardships than if he had remained a British subject," was yet a "happy man, because he was engaged in benefiting his race." Lincoln urged the committee to emulate Washington by undertaking the hardships of emigration: "For the sake of *your* race, you should sacrifice something of your present comfort." Lincoln actively supported compensated emancipation with colonization until January 1863.[20]

But with the Emancipation Proclamation, Lincoln's ideas about the role of race in American national identity began to change. The Proclamation authorized the enrollment of African-American troops, and tens of thousands of blacks were mustered into service. In July 1863, Colonel Robert Gould Shaw led the Fifty-fourth Massachusetts Colored Infantry into battle at Fort Wagner. Like the white soldiers Lincoln so admired, black troops heroically vindicated their loyalty to the ideals of the Union. Inspired by their unflinching performance, Lincoln—who in September 1862 had expressed fears that African-Americans would make poor soldiers, as "in a few weeks the arms would be in the hands of the rebels"—began to suggest that their fidelity to the cause had earned them a place in the nation. In August 1863, he wrote a public letter to James C. Conkling, president of the Springfield branch of the Union League. Peace, he predicted, would soon come to the land, and "it will then have been proved that, among free men, there can be no successful appeal from the ballot to the bullet; and that they who take such appeal are sure to lose their case, and pay the cost. And then, there will be some black men who can remember that, with silent tongue and clenched teeth, and steady eye, and well-poised bayonet, *they have helped mankind on to this great consummation;* while I fear there will be some white ones, unable to forget that, with malignant heart, and deceitful speech, they have strove to hinder it."[21]

Surely blacks who had fought for the ideals that defined America would make better citizens than whites who had betrayed those ideals. In March 1864 Lincoln wrote to Governor Michael Hahn of Louisiana about the franchise. He suggested, "for your private consideration, whether some of the colored people may not be let in—as, for instance, the very intelligent, and especially those who have fought gallantly in our ranks." Black suffrage might, Lincoln noted, "help, in some trying time to come, to keep the jewel of liberty in the family of freedom." In April 1865, he publicly endorsed limited Negro suffrage. Though Lincoln's commitment to a race-inclusive nation never approached either Phillips's or Douglass's—note the very tentative nature of his suggestion to Hahn, which was, he wrote, "only a suggestion, not to the public, but to you alone"—by the end of the war it was clear that for Lincoln, devotion to the Union's ideals and, more important, a willingness to fight for those ideals, could eclipse race in defining national identity.[22]

Concomitant with the shift in Lincoln's understanding of nationality came a change in his view of the war itself. In September 1862, a Chicago Christian delegation had presented Lincoln with an Emancipation Memorial, arguing that the war was the nation's "just punishment" for the high crime of slavery. It was the conviction of the Christian community of Chicago that God now willed the North to free the slaves. Lincoln was not yet ready to embrace this position, at least in public. He reminded the delegation that proponents of widely varying views had approached him with equal certainty that they alone represented God's will. Surely, he argued, if God wished His will known, He would reveal it to Lincoln himself, "for unless I am more deceived in myself than I often am, it is my earnest desire to know the will of Providence in this matter." He suggested that the struggle for constitutional government was sufficient as a grand moral cause: "This is a fundamental idea, going down about as deep as anything."[23]

But the course of the war dictated that this view give way. Moved by the carnage of battles like Shiloh and Gettysburg, by the "weight of responsibility" for those deaths as well as for the executions he had sanctioned, and by the courage of the black soldiers, Lincoln began to search for the war's higher meaning. Increasingly he spoke of God's will, both as the elusive aim of a quest for understanding and as the moral imperative of war. Like Frederick Douglass, he adopted an apocalyptic view of the struggle, wherein the war was both God's punishment for the sin of slavery and a prophetic revelation of His wish that America embrace "a new birth of freedom."[24]

Lincoln's apocalyptic language reflected a broader Northern phenomenon. Since the mid–seventeenth century, Americans had held as a faith the notion that they were God's chosen people; that America was the new Israel. This belief in a sacred national covenant had offered a framework of understanding for political events throughout American history. Set before the nations of the world as an archetype of democracy, America was to lead the way to a new era of liberty and equality. Like Winthrop's city on the hill, the United States need only maintain its distinctive virtues to preserve its historic purpose and maintain God's favor.[25]

But during the Civil War, many Americans began to fear that their role as a divinely ordained democratic model was in jeopardy. Led by the Northern clergy, they proclaimed that the widespread suffering the war had delivered was in fact divine retribution for the sin of slavery. In this interpretation, the war was both punishment and crusade: the Union troops who fought valiantly to purge the nation of its sin against God were hastening the coming of the Kingdom of the Lord. Though few took this position in the early months of the struggle, by war's end, Americans across the North believed with Julia Ward Howe that with each Union victory, "His truth is marching on."[26]

Lincoln's public embrace of a providential interpretation of the war became evident as early as the Gettysburg Address, as his rhetoric began to acquire a distinctly millennial quality. Issuing a charge to loyal Americans, Lincoln told his audience that the war ushered in a new chapter in American history: after 250 years of toil by bondsmen, the United States was to become a nation without slavery. What were the ethics—what did it mean to be a patriot—as Americans struggled toward the new order? Here, and more profoundly, in the Second Inaugural, Lincoln refined his notion of American patriotism in accordance with his new providentialism. If the legacy of the fathers had heretofore demanded the *maintenance* of American liberty and equality, the war now dictated their extension. No words, he told the crowd gathered at the new national graveyard in Gettysburg on November 19, 1863, could dedicate the memorial:

> It is for us, the living, rather, to be dedicated here to the unfinished work which they who fought here have thus far so nobly advanced . . . that from these honored dead we take increased devotion to that cause for which they gave the last full measure of devotion—that we here highly resolve that these dead shall not have died in vain—that this nation, under God, shall have a new birth of freedom—and that government of the people, by the people, for the people, shall not perish from the earth.[27]

Calling for the immortality of American democracy, Lincoln suggested that the immortality of the nation-state was essential to its survival.

But could a nation whose prosperity and democratic identity had for so long been informed by slavery sincerely reverse course? The increased devotion Lincoln called for could not, he argued in the Second Inaugural, take place without repentance. The North and South were both responsible for slavery, and if God willed that the war "continue, until all the wealth piled up by the bond-man's two hundred and fifty years of unrequited toil shall be sunk, and until every drop of blood drawn with the lash, shall be paid with another drawn with the sword, as was said three thousand years ago, so still it must be said, 'the judgments of the Lord, are true and righteous altogether.'" As a people and as a nation, Americans had sinned, and acknowledgment of these sins would lay the groundwork for a new understanding of national identity: less self-righteous, more forgiving, yet with a renewed dedication to the ideals of liberty and equality: "With malice toward none; with charity for all; with firmness in the right, as God gives us to see the right, let us strive on to finish the work we are in."

By the end of the war, the patriotism that Lincoln articulated was both chastened and self-critical. As he wrote to Thurlow Weed eleven days after the inauguration, "Men are not flattered by being shown that there has been a difference of purpose between the Almighty and them. To deny it, . . . is to deny that there is a God governing the world. It is a truth which I thought needed to be told; and as whatever humiliation there is in it, falls most directly on myself, I thought others might afford for me to tell it."[28]

"A NEW IMPULSE OF PATRIOTISM FOR HIS SAKE"

The Civil War ended with the surrender of General Robert E. Lee to General Ulysses S. Grant at a courthouse in Appomattox on April 9, 1865. On April 14—Good Friday—the president attended Ford's Theater with his wife and was assassinated by actor John Wilkes Booth.

Americans mourned President Lincoln as they had mourned no public figure in their history. Businesses and schools closed; men and women wept openly in the streets. Buildings and homes were decorated with black muslin, rosettes, and flags flown at half-mast. In the poorer parts of New York, according to George T. Strong, "people who could afford to do no more have generally displayed at least a little twenty-five cent flag with a little scrap of crape annexed." Across the North, in churches and schoolhouses, people held memorial services and town meetings to proclaim their grief. In editorials and eulogies, essays and poems, they strove to understand and give meaning to Lincoln's death. As they did, they revisited many of the themes about patriotism and the nation that had informed their wartime thinking.[29]

Almost universally, Northerners blamed the South for the murder of their president. Though Booth had pulled the trigger, they argued, his actions were the culmination of four years of rebel treachery. The *New York Times* published a dispatch from Secretary of War Stanton suggesting that the assassination had been approved in Richmond. Reflecting the partisan prejudices of the North, Copperheads were also accused, both of having participated directly in the plot—the *Washington Star* claimed that members of the Knights of the Golden Circle were implicated—and of wielding influence, even if inadvertently. One cartoon featured a drawing of George Bickley, founder of the Knights of the Golden Circle, under the heading "Theory"; a picture of the assassin, John Wilkes Booth, under the heading "Practice," and a picture of the martyred president on a tombstone under the heading "Effect."[30]

If the crime was not the work of a few individuals, neither was the target a single man. Eulogists argued that the murder of the president was in fact an attack on the Union. As Henry Ward Beecher told his Brooklyn parishioners, "This blow was aimed at the life of the Government and the Nation. . . .

It was the President who was killed. It was national life, breathing freedom and meaning beneficence, that was sought." Yet again, argued a pastor in Philadelphia, the South had attempted to destroy "law and liberty; government and freedom."[31]

And yet again, the South had failed. Like the attack on Fort Sumter, the assassination had worked to rally the people behind the nation. As Strong reported in his diary, the people's reaction was "very much like that of four years ago. . . . This atrocity has invigorated national feeling in the same way, almost in the same degree." The Union had emerged from Lincoln's murder with a renewed strength and spirit. Though there were numerous instances of violence against those who dared dissent from the consensus of bereavement, on the whole, order prevailed. There were no riots; no mutinies; businesses did not collapse; the public credit was not damaged. And for this, Northerners expressed tremendous pride. "Such an act would probably overthrow the throne of any European power today," the *New York Times* asserted. "But it will not inaugurate anarchy here." Ironically, the attack on the nation had only served to vindicate it. The nation had "dissolved—but in tears only," said the Reverend Beecher. "It stands, four-square, more solidly than any pyramid in Egypt. . . . God I think has said, by the voice of this event, to all nations of the earth, 'Republican liberty, based upon true Christianity, is firm as the foundation of the globe.'"[32]

The idea that Lincoln's death proclaimed the final realization of the nation was expressed in both religious and secular terms. Contemporaries drew parallels between the president and Moses, who, like Lincoln, had labored for the salvation of his people, liberated a race from bondage, only to perish before he glimpsed the promised land. Others described Lincoln as a Christ figure who had given his life for the sins of the nation. "It would really seem . . . that this tragedy almost parallels that of the Son of God," said General James A. Garfield, "who died saying, 'Father forgive them, they know not what they do.'"[33]

Other Northerners placed Lincoln in the tradition of the founding fathers. Charles Sumner argued that Lincoln had completed the task begun by Washington. His death was "the sacrificial consecration of those primal truths embodied in the birthday Declaration of the Republic, which he had so often vindicated, and for which he had announced his willingness to die." His sacrifice, which personified for Americans the sacrifices of all the martyred soldiers, supplied the nation with a much-needed emotional cement. As a speaker before the American Historical Society averred, "Before we were bound by the memories of our fathers—now the blood of the martyred president binds us."[34]

Lincoln's eulogists also struggled to plumb the meaning of his patriotism. Here they were faced with a fundamental tension, for Lincoln's patriotism contained contradictions that were compounded by his death. He had called for a humility that would lead to forgiveness and charity, yet at the same time asserted the necessity of "firmness in the right." As the process of Reconstruction would show—in fact as it already had shown—and as contemporaries at the time suggested, both were not necessarily possible. Radical Republicans had criticized Lincoln's Ten Percent Plan as far too lenient, his "Quarrel-not" policy as inherently unrealistic. They warned of the dangers of empowering a wealthy class that would no doubt find it in its interest to perpetuate some form of indentured servitude. Like Phillips, many Northerners questioned the value of a freedom unaccompanied by state protection on some level, and wondered whether Lincoln's policy of charity would not undermine the ideals of liberty to which he was also committed.[35]

Some eulogists resolved this tension by arguing that God had allowed Lincoln to be killed because the situation demanded a sterner hand, or to spare him the pain of witnessing a harsh Reconstruction. Speaking in Springfield, Illinois, at the interment of the president, Matthew Simpson told his listeners that Lincoln, "though he fell by an assassin, still fell under the permissive hand of God." Lincoln had completed the "work for which God had sent him," and angels had been "sent to shield him from one moment of pain or suffering." Americans must now go forward in "painful duty." Simpson suggested that Lincoln's charge of mercy be carried out by extending "arms of forgiveness" to the "deluded masses," but not to the leaders of the rebellion, to whom he promised "speedy and certain punishment," even death. Standing by Lincoln's coffin, he vowed to "carry forward the policy which he so nobly began . . . eradicate every vestige of human slavery . . . crush every form of rebellion, and to stand by the flag which God has given us."[36]

For some Northerners, Lincoln's murder had itself absolved the North of any obligation to show mercy to the South. Herman Melville suggested this position in his poem "The Martyr." Lincoln had been killed "in his prime of clemency and calm":

> They have killed him, the Forgiver—
> The Avenger takes his place,
> The Avenger wisely stern,

Who in righteousness shall do
What the heavens call him to,
And the parricides remand; . . .
For they killed him in his kindness,
In their madness and their blindness,
And his blood is on their hand. . . .
Beware the People Weeping
When they bare the iron hand.

Melville suggested his ambivalence about abandoning the charge to mercy, both in his warning to "Beware the People Weeping" and in his later confession of a desire to "withdraw or modify [the poem], . . . lest in presenting . . . the passions and epithets of Civil War, I might be contributing to a bitterness which every sensible American must wish at an end." Nonetheless, many Americans shared the feeling that with Lincoln's assassination, the South had surrendered any right to clemency. "Yesterday we were with the late President, for lenity . . . and conciliatory kindness," wrote the *Chicago Tribune,* two days after Lincoln's death, "today we are with the people for justice."[37]

For many, however, the tensions inherent in Lincoln's patriotism were swept away by the emotional power of his martyrdom. In death, Lincoln became a symbol of the entire North, not just of a single party or section. Democrats and Republicans alike spoke in vague terms about rededication to the mission for which Lincoln had given his life, about devotion to the nation-state that had been sanctified by his sacrifice. George Bancroft, a Democrat who had freely criticized Lincoln in his lifetime, told Americans to turn their grief into action, "in the assertion of the policy to which he fell a sacrifice." And Henry Ward Beecher, also a critic of the living Lincoln, predicted that Americans would experience a "new impulse of patriotism for his sake, and will guard with zeal the whole country which he loved so well. . . . I swear to you an emulation of his justice, his moderation and his mercy."[38]

No event contributed more to the making of Lincoln as a national symbol than his funeral, an extraordinary event that lasted fourteen days and took place across seven states. It was, as historian Merrill Peterson has claimed, "the grandest funeral spectacle in the history of the world." Three days following Lincoln's death, his body, dressed in the suit that he had worn for his first inauguration, was placed in the State Room in the White House for public viewing. An estimated twenty-five hundred men and women filed past the open casket in the eight hours it was on display. One day later, the casket was placed in a hearse and borne through the streets of Washington. The long, slow funeral procession was led by a contingent of black troops recently returned from the front. The military units were followed by carriages bearing the cabinet, members of the Union Leagues, workingmen's societies, and a variety of other mourners. Thousands of African-American mourners brought up the rear.[39]

On Friday, April 21, Lincoln's casket was placed in a railway car for the seventeen-hundred-mile journey to Springfield, Illinois, its final resting place. Slowly the funeral train made its way first North, then West, stopping at major cities to allow for viewing of the body. In drenching rain and in brilliant sunshine, the multitudes turned out to honor the martyred president. Elaborate arches of evergreen stretched across the tracks. Bands played funeral dirges; choruses sang mournful hymns; and ministers, priests, and rabbis delivered eulogies. In elaborate processionals, horse-drawn carriages carried the body past buildings draped in black to local state houses, city halls, or courthouses for display.[40]

Over time the displays grew more elaborate, as, in a phenomenon reminiscent of the Sanitary Fairs, hosting cities sought to outdo one another in their devotion to their fallen hero. In Cleveland and Columbus, the body was housed in Chinese pagodas; in Indianapolis the catafalque was made of black velvet and gold stars. By the time the train reached Chicago, a bust of Lincoln topped an arch carried over the casket, and thirty-six high school girls dressed in white walked beside Lincoln's casket, sprinkling flowers. As Lloyd Lewis remarked over fifty years later, the funeral had become "half-circus, half heartbreak."[41]

As Lincoln's corpse lay atop its bier in each of the hosting cities, thousands of men, women, and children stood for hours in lines that stretched for miles, waiting to view the body. At night, when the viewing ended, hundreds were left in line, and farmers who had driven in from the surrounding countryside camped out overnight, resuming their wait in the morning. After several days, the president's face grew discolored and sunken, and the casket was closed. Still, the crowds kept coming. In the villages and towns where the train did not stop, tableaux were erected along the hillsides, torch-bearing mourners lined the tracks, and bonfires lit up the night. Passengers on the train described seeing farmers in the fields drop their plows, doff their hats, and bow their heads as the train bearing the martyred president, symbol of the nation, passed by. All told, one and a half million Americans viewed his body, while an estimated seven million saw the coffin. On May 3, twenty

By the time Lincoln's funeral train reached Chicago, tributes to the nation's martyred president had grown increasingly elaborate. In Chicago, a figure of Lincoln topped the arch carried over his casket, and thirty-six high school girls dressed in white walked alongside the casket, sprinkling flowers. (Lincoln's funeral procession. Courtesy Illinois State Historical Library.)

days after Lincoln's assassination, the train reached its final destination, and the president was buried in Oak Ridge Cemetery.[42]

On April 14, 1879, the fourteenth anniversary of the assassination of Abraham Lincoln, Walt Whitman delivered a lecture in New York City on the subject of the president's death. Lincoln had, the poet noted, strung "the principal points and personages of the period, like beads, upon the single string of his career." Indeed, as we have seen, Lincoln was the embodiment of much that defined the Civil War North. His vision was a powerful synthesis of the ideas of his time, elevated to a higher plane by its infusion with his own distinct moral and ideological understandings. As in life, so in death, Lincoln reflected the prevailing themes of his time. As Northerners struggled to understand his assassination, they brought to that understanding partisan prejudices and local loyalties, as well as larger ideas about American history and the founding fathers, sacrifice and redemption, and organic nationhood.[43]

It was the last of these—the relationship between Lincoln's death and the nation's organic life—that especially moved Whitman. While he recognized Lincoln's manifold contributions to the nation, he believed that the president's most powerful legacy had not been immediately apparent, but had come "subtly and invisibly afterward." A "heroic-eminent death" such as Lincoln's provided a nation with its essential organic element, for

> then there is a cement to the whole people, subtler, more underlying than any constitution, . . . namely, the cement of a death identified thoroughly with that people, at its head, and for its sake. Strange, (is it not) that battles, martyrs, agonies, blood, even assassination, should so condense—perhaps only really, lastingly condense—a Nationality.[44]

Conclusion

At seven o'clock in the morning on May 23, 1865, a crowd that would reach an estimated two hundred thousand people began lining Washington's Pennsylvania Avenue. They had come from hundreds of miles away—from New York, from Massachusetts, from Maryland—arriving in carriages and standing-room-only railway cars, cramming the city's hotels and boarding houses. As the morning progressed, they thronged the balconies, roofs, sidewalks, and doorsteps along the avenue; some even sat atop lampposts.[1]

Washington, D.C., was still a city in mourning—black crepe marked the homes and offices of many of its residents. But on this day, the city was clearly bedecked for a celebration. Government buildings sported blue and white bunting; arches of flowers lined the streets. And the city's American flags, for the first time since Lincoln's assassination, were flying at full mast.[2]

At nine o'clock the crack of a signal gun sounded the beginning of the event the throng awaited: a Grand Review of the Union's victorious armies. For the next six hours, and for another six hours on the following day, 150,000 members of Meade's Army of the Potomac and Sherman's Western Army—an assemblage stretching back twenty-five miles—marched sixty men abreast down Pennsylvania Avenue. Accompanied by bands playing "The Battle Hymn of the Republic," "When Johnny Comes Marching Home," and "Tramp, Tramp, Tramp, the Boys Are Marching," under banners acclaiming them the "pride of the Nation," the troops paraded from the Capitol, past the Treasury Building, and to the White House, where a viewing stand housing President Andrew Johnson, his cabinet members, and select military officers had been constructed. Marching lockstep past the president, while eager spectators watched and cheered, waved flags, and threw flowers, the North's armies proceeded down the avenue and into Georgetown.[3]

As Americans at the time did not hesitate to point out, Northerners had never seen anything like the Grand Review. It was, as one journalist described it, "the greatest military pageant ever witnessed on this American continent." Observers marveled at the uniformity: a sea of blue soldiers, marching in "cadence-step." "The column was compact," General Sherman declared in his memoirs, "and the glittering muskets looked like a solid mass of steel, moving with the regularity of a pendulum." The symbolism was unmistakable: a far cry from the ragtag collection of local boys who had presented themselves to their states for service in 1861, this disciplined, orderly army, now marching in synchrony down the streets of the country's capital, represented the new American nation. As historian Wilfred M. McClay writes, "That river of blue was a visual confirmation of a sea change, the emblem of a powerful new political order whose authority would emanate increasingly from Washington."[4]

The Grand Review was, as journalists at the time understood, "a grand national pageant": a celebration of a reunified nation. But understood as symbolism, the review possesses another important facet. In his study of the Grand Army of the Republic, Stuart McConnell suggests that those accounts of the march that focus narrowly on discipline and uniformity do not tell the entire story. In fact, the march contained "anomalies." The unending sea of blue that witnesses described had "gaps"—gaps that created delays between units of up to thirty minutes. And though Meade's Army may have marched with precision in their regulation blue uniforms, Sherman's Army presented a bit differently. Their uniforms were "a cross between the regulation blue and the Southern grey," and they sported guns of every variety. They laughed and chatted and bowed to their admirers, and straggling alongside many of them were goats and chickens and raccoons—plunder from Sherman's March to the Sea.[5]

Perhaps most significantly, there were no black regiments represented in either Meade's or Sherman's Armies. The marching white troops were occasionally accompanied by captured slaves or by black pick-and-shovel brigades, but the nearly 180,000 black troops who saw action in the war—men who might claim as much credit for the Union's victory as the white soldiers present—were nowhere to be seen. Though viewed as an emblem of a nation reborn, the review's racial exclusion was disturbingly reminiscent of the old Union.[6]

If the Grand Review was a symbol of the new nation, then, what kind of nation did it represent? And how was loyalty to this new nation defined? Just as the review highlighted the nation's new centralizing tendencies, its new sense of discipline and rigor, so it also spoke to the nation's fundamental ambivalence about these changes. Just as it presaged a new order, so it also suggested the limits of that order. As symbolism, the Grand Review foreshadowed the uneven trajectory that this newly defined nation-state and American national identity and patriotism would follow.[7]

In retrospect, anyone comparing the United States government before and immediately after the Civil War would conclude, with Randolph Bourne, that "war is essentially the health of the state." The war had profound centralizing effects on the nation's politics and economics: it gave rise, in effect, to the modern American nation-state.[8]

The war also fostered a metamorphosis in American national identity. It introduced Northerners to new ways of thinking about the national government, while transfiguring old ways. It increased public consciousness of the nation and redefined Americans' relationship with and obligations to their federal government.

The Civil Rights Act of 1866 began the process of codifying some of those changes, establishing for the first time in American history the criteria for and rights of American citizenship. In 1868, the Fourteenth Amendment encoded the principles of the Civil Rights Act into the Constitution: *all* persons "born or naturalized in the United States, and subject to the jurisdiction thereof" were to be citizens of the United States. Thus, if the Thirteenth Amendment had guaranteed blacks that they would never again be slaves, the Fourteenth Amendment established that they were, contrary to the Supreme Court's pronouncement only eleven years earlier, citizens of the United States. Slavery in the United States would, from that point on, be unimaginable. The Fourteenth Amendment also dramatically altered both the relationship between individual citizens and the national state, and the meaning of national citizenship. It conferred upon the federal government the power to protect Americans from infringements by the various states of their individual rights, and declared for the first time that all citizens of the United States were entitled to equal protection of the law. In 1870, the Fifteenth Amendment assured blacks that one right the federal government would protect against abridgement was the right to the suffrage.[9]

But in the years following the Confederate surrender at Appomattox, the North's commitment to the egalitarian ideals embodied in the Civil War amendments receded. The Ku Klux Klan unleashed a reign of terror throughout the South, destroying many of the political bases of Republican power. This violence, coupled with widespread corruption—both North and South—and the distractions of an industrializing economy spurred the North's retreat from Reconstruction. In the 1873 *Slaughterhouse* decision, the Supreme Court declared that the Fourteenth Amendment directed the federal government to protect only those individual rights guaranteed by national, not state, citizenship, circumscribing the amendment's egalitarian intent. Violence, discriminatory apportionment, and revised state election laws worked together to keep Southern blacks from the polls, effectively nullifying the Fifteenth Amendment. In 1877, as a part of a compromise to settle a disputed presidential election, Republicans agreed to return the South to home rule, and almost a century of discrimination against African-Americans ensued.[10]

The return of local control to the South marked both the end of Reconstruction and a halt to the expansion of the wartime state. As a new class of finance capitalists campaigned against Radical Reconstruction and centralized government, laissez-faire economics were revived: during the 1870s, for example, the Civil War income tax was abolished. The nation's new bureaucracy, created as a response to wartime exigencies, contracted, and a more permanent expansion of the federal government's administrative capacities would not develop until the turn of the century. The forceful, assertive presidency of Lincoln gave way to a series of chief executives who owed their power to party elites and were deeply entangled in patronage battles. Local interests reasserted themselves; party politics lost its ideological edge.[11]

As the wartime state receded, some Civil War constructions of nation and loyalty also faded or assumed new forms. Recent literature on postwar patriotism has shown how reconciliation between North and South took place at the cost of abolitionist notions of American identity. Like the Sanitary Fairs, postwar military ceremonies such as battlefield commemorations and veterans' reunions focused public attention on the soldiers' heroism and sacrifice, independent of the cause—or side—for which they fought. Southerners who had shown a willingness to fight and die for the slave Confederacy became heroes in the nation's eyes, patriots on a par with those Northern soldiers who had died for freedom. The notion of equal sacrifice was immortalized in the numerous monuments erected in the late nineteenth and early twentieth centuries: in Chicago's Oakwood Cemetery, for example, a monument was erected to honor the thousands of Confederate soldiers who had died in the Camp Douglas prison. Such monuments became a part of the nation's history and tradition, shaping a national identity that included, even honored, the South. The newfound fraternity of "the Blue and the Grey" did not, however, welcome blacks: segregation in veterans' organizations was widespread. Thus, as Southern whites were received back into the heart of the national polity, blacks were forced onto its margins.[12]

So too were women. When the Sanitary Fairs called on Americans to sacrifice for their country, they pointed not only to soldiers, but to the women of the North as models of patriotic loyalty. After the war, patriotic culture continued to be shaped by women: for example, during the 1890s, the Women's Relief Corps campaigned for popular observance of Memorial Day, a national holiday designed to honor the Civil War dead. Yet ironically, by focusing almost exclusively on the valor of the soldiers, these women contributed to what historian Cecilia O'Leary calls a "male warrior" patriotism. This form of patriotism esteemed military valor above all else, and so minimized the contributions and sacrifices of women and other noncombatants.[13]

The postwar years also witnessed the decline of support for Phillips's idea that in America, true patriotism demands discussion and debate about the meaning of democracy. As American patriotic culture became dominated by military symbols, it seemed to many that patriotism implied a military-like respect for and obedience to the state. Indeed, the organic patriotism promulgated by the Union League enjoyed a brief period of popularity—albeit largely among intellectuals—in the years following the war. This form of patriotism reached its apotheosis in Theodore Roosevelt, who fused unquestioning loyalty to a nativist nation with masculine heroics, both in his presidency and in the 100 percent Americanism of World War I.[14]

Yet, as historian Merle Curti argues, Roosevelt exemplified but one conception of American identity and patriotism. Many of his contemporaries posited alternative understandings: Edward Bellamy's 1888 utopian novel *Looking Backward* envisioned an active national state committed to distributing the wealth of the nation equally among all its inhabitants, regardless of race or sex. Bellamy christened his version of socialism "Nationalism," and the success of his book sparked the nationwide formation of "Nationalist Clubs." Edward's cousin, Francis Bellamy, wrote what would become the nation's official Pledge of Allegiance. Like Edward, Francis was a socialist, and he entertained the notion of incorporating the slogan of the French Revolution—"Liberty, Equality, Fraternity"—into the pledge. In the end he deemed the phrase too much for Americans, and substituted "with liberty and justice for all." For these men, patriotism entailed not unquestioning obedience to an abstract nation-state, but a commitment to the principles that nation-state embodied.[15]

Clearly, postwar conceptions of American identity and loyalty remained fluid. As historian Morton Keller asserts, "The tensions of the earlier period—between individualism and social order, localism and centralism, laissez-faire and the active state, broad and restrictive views of American citizenship—continued to be prime determinants of public life." With so much at stake, successive generations of Americans would contest anew the meaning of the nation and of patriotic loyalty.[16]

But if the Civil War had not settled the issue of American national identity and loyalty, the nation had nonetheless turned a critical corner on its path toward cultural and ideological nationhood. Localism, self-interest, and partisan identity had long troubled American nationalists. Civil War nation-builders yoked these conventions directly to the nation and to the federal government. Ultimately, these parochial traditions helped form the foundation of a preeminent national loyalty—one that could override all other public, and at times, even private, obligations.

The war also witnessed the redefinition of the relationship between individual Americans and the national state. Though suspicions of centralized government would continue to play a prominent role in the American political dialogue, the nation-building campaigns of the Civil War recast that dialogue. In these campaigns, the national state was portrayed as an indispensable agent of the public interest, its benefits to individual Americans overshadowing its threats. The national state was a source of economic well-being; it offered protection from the financial incursions of states and localities; it was the foundation of both personal and political freedom. Thus Civil War nationalists offered an extraordinary demonstration of the notion that a strong, active government need not be an enemy to individual well-being, but might instead be the mechanism by which freedom and prosperity could be achieved.[17]

The new conception of the nation-state went beyond its value as an instrument. Observing American patriotism in 1835, Tocqueville had noted the absence of an "instinctive, disinterested, and undefinable feeling." As recently as 1854, George T. Strong had lamented the nation's lack of a "record . . . of Americanism." Civil War constructions of national identity and patriotism formed the foundation of Tocqueville's "feeling"; of Strong's "record." The Sanitary Fairs' depiction of American history and tradition; their presentation of a rich, meaningful national life; the Union Leagues' assurances that national loyalty would bring social prestige; the publication societies' promise that identification with the nation offered the sole route to "self and freedom," even the rituals and incantations of the smaller, partisan Union Leagues—all of these worked to envelop the nation-state in a mystical aura, beginning a process whereby Americans could lay claim to a transcendent nationalism. Lincoln's death offered, in Whitman's words, a "cement" to this new nationalism. The United States had become a "proper nation," and never again would the concept of this nation be called into question.[18]

Many of these new constructions survived in some form well after the war itself had ended. The numerous calls for national history and art museums that punctuated the Sanitary Fairs persisted and were ultimately realized. Beginning with the founding of the Metropolitan Museum of Art in 1869, a museum movement flowered in the United States: the following ten years witnessed the appearance of the Museum of Fine Arts in Boston, the Pennsylvania Museum of Art, the Art Institute of Chicago, and the American Museum of Natural History. Metropolitan Union Leagues persist to this day, continuing to function as elite gentlemen's clubs, cultivating a nationalist upper or upper-middle class. The organic patriotism they promulgated enjoyed a brief period of popularity in the postwar years, then faded. But it left a lasting legacy in Hale's "The Man Without a Country," which enjoyed numerous reprints and is still assigned in schools. As recently as 1991, a man convicted of "insult to the Flag" was sentenced to write an essay on Hale's story. Though the theoretical moorings of organic notions of patriotism may not appeal to Americans, the implications of those notions persist. Many Americans believe that their country is central to their identity, and associate loyalty to country with obedience to the national state. And Lincoln's martyrdom, endlessly fascinating to Americans, has become our national epic.[19]

Moreover, during the war the ideas which had for many years provided an unstable basis for American national identity were debated and refined. Prior to the war, many Americans had looked to the Constitution—with its promise to "secure the blessings of liberty"—as the embodiment of those ideas. But for Lincoln, it was the Declaration of Independence, with its notions of political democracy and moral equality, which formed the basis of American national identity. Over the course of the war, and most powerfully in the Gettysburg Address, Lincoln infused mainstream patriotic culture with those notions.[20]

If Lincoln worked to restore notions of freedom and equality to the ideological basis of American identity, it was the abolitionists' dedication to those ideals that helped ensure their enshrinement in the Constitution. Though the North's commitment to the enforcement of the Civil War amendments faded almost as quickly as it had appeared; though as many freedmen discovered, the postwar world offered a severely circumscribed freedom; the amendments themselves remained to serve as a touchstone for endless debates about equality, personal liberties, and the relationship between the individual and the national government.[21]

Finally, the abolitionists themselves stand as enduring models of patriotic activism. Civil Rights leaders of the 1960s looked to them for inspiration; even today, they provide a template for movements that press America to live up to its stated ideals. Though the meaning of patriotism may have narrowed over the years—though ideas of obedience, of unquestioning support, particularly in times of war, may temporarily eclipse older notions of loyalty—the abolitionists remind us that loyalty to nation can be expressed through questioning, prodding, even dissent. More important, if American national identity is today composed not only of ideas, but of sentiment, rituals, history, and tradition, the abolitionists remind us that its finest aspects remain those original principles of freedom and equality. Their Civil War vision of American identity represents an enduring challenge: in Wendell Phillips's words, "In my nationality, there is but one idea—the harmonious and equal mingling of all races. . . . I would leave no stone unturned until . . . the flag shall float over nothing but freedom."[22]

Notes

Introduction

1. Edward Everett Hale, *The Man Without a Country* (Boston, 1893) (reprint), p. 23.

2. For quote see Hale, *The Man Without a Country*, p. 23.

3. Hale, *The Man Without a Country*, p. 88.

4. Anthony D. Smith, *Nationalist Movements* (New York, 1977), writes, "Nationalism holds that . . . the only genuine identity is a national one, and every man, be he peasant or worker, merchant or intellectual, can only rediscover self and freedom through that new collective identity." Cited in Wilbur Zelinsky, *Nation into State: The Shifting Symbolic Foundations of American Nationalism* (Chapel Hill, 1988), p. 6; Rev. Joseph Fransioli, "Patriotism, A Christian Virtue: A Sermon Preached . . . at St. Peter's (Catholic) Church, Brooklyn, July 26th, 1863," New York Loyal Publication Society (NYLPS) Pamphlet #24, *Pamphlets Issued by the New York Loyal Publication Society* (New York: The Society, 1864).

5. John R. Adams, *Edward Everett Hale* (Boston, 1977), p. 27; Jean Holloway, *Edward Everett Hale* (Austin, 1956), p. 139. Hale's story was reprinted in 1887, 1888, and 1889, and a special Spanish War edition was published in 1898. In 1888 the *New York Times* expressed hope that Hale's story would be read "over and over again" (December 9, 1888), while in 1902, the *Nation* took a dimmer view: "Though it has received a fresh certificate of beneficence from President Roosevelt, there are some who look upon it as the primer of jingoism." *Nation*, (April 17, 1902).

6. Ralph Waldo Emerson, *The Journals and Miscellaneous Notebooks of Ralph Waldo Emerson*, Ralph H. Orth, ed. (Cambridge, Mass., 1982); Horace Bushnell, cited in Merle Curti, *Roots of American Loyalty* (New York, 1946), p. 171.

7. Allan Nevins, *The War for the Union*, vols. 1–4 (New York, 1959–1971); Nevins, "A Major Result of the Civil War," *Civil War History* 5 (September 1959): 237–250; James M. McPherson, *Battle Cry of Freedom* (New York: 1988); George M. Fredrickson, *The Inner Civil War: Northern Intellectuals and the Crisis of the Union* (New York, 1965); Phillip Shaw Paludan, *"A People's Contest": The Union and the Civil War 1861–1865* (New York, 1988); Merle Curti, *Roots of American Loyalty;* McPherson, *Battle Cry of Freedom*, p. 859; Garry Wills, *Lincoln at Gettysburg: The Words That Remade America* (New York, 1992), p. 145.

Many books also describe the war's centralizing effects on the nation's politics and economics. See, for example, Nevins, *The War for the Union*, vols. 1–4 (New York: 1959–1971); McPherson, *Battle Cry of Freedom*; Paludan, *"A People's Contest"*; William B. Hesseltine, *Lincoln and the War Governors* (New York, 1955); Richard Franklin Bensel, *Yankee Leviathan: The Origins of Central State Authority in America, 1859–1877* (Cambridge, 1990); Bray Hammond, *Sovereignty and an Empty Purse: Banks and Politics in the Civil War* (Princeton, 1970); Heather Richardson, *The Greatest Nation of the Earth* (Cambridge, Mass., 1997).

   8. Many historians have examined individual aspects of this phenomenon. See Fredrickson, *The Inner Civil War*; Jeanie Attie, *Patriotic Toil: Northern Women and the American Civil War* (Ithaca, 1998); David Blight, *Frederick Douglass' Civil War: Keeping Faith in Jubilee* (Baton Rouge, 1989); James McPherson, *The Struggle for Equality: Abolitionists and the Negro in the Civil War and Reconstruction* (Princeton, 1964); George Winston Smith, "Generative Forces of Union Propaganda: A Study of Civil War Pressure Groups" (Ph.D. dissertation, University of Wisconsin, 1940); T. Harry Williams, *Lincoln and the Radicals* (Madison, 1960); Hans Trefousse, *The Radical Republicans: Lincoln's Vanguard for Racial Justice* (New York: 1969); Frank Klement, *Dark Lanterns: Secret Political Societies, Conspiracies, and Treason Trials in the Civil War* (Baton Rouge, 1984); Guy James Gibson, "Lincoln's League: The Union League Movement During the Civil War" (Ph.D. dissertation, University of Illinois, 1957); Clement Mario Silvestro, "None But Patriots: The Union Leagues in Civil War and Reconstruction" (Ph.D. dissertation, University of Wisconsin, 1959).

   Students of American history who focus on the growth of American nationalism have examined that phenomenon from a number of perspectives, including the evolution of a nationalist ideology, the growth of institutions, and the creation of national images and symbols. These works tend to focus on the years preceding or following the war; some note that the war served as a defining moment for American national identity, but fail to explore that notion at any length. See Paul C. Nagel, *One Nation Indivisible: The Union in American Thought* (New York, 1964); Major Wilson, *Space, Time and Freedom: The Quest for American Nationality* (Westport, Conn., 1974); Peter Dobkin Hall, *The Organization of American Culture, 1700–1900* (New York, 1982); Zelinsky, *Nation into State*; Cecilia O'Leary, *To Die For: The Paradox of American Patriotism* (Princeton, 1999). Two books by American historians that include a discussion of the impact of the war itself on national identity are Curti, *Roots of American Loyalty*, which devotes a chapter to the role of the Civil War in the cultivation of a sense of sacrifice among Americans, and Yehoshua Arieli, *Individualism and Nationalism in American Ideology* (Baltimore, 1964), which examines the tension and interaction between American ideas of individualism and a growing nationalism in the period from 1776 through 1865. Arieli finds that as a product of the war, "concepts of individualism and of a 'free society' became organic parts of a new national consciousness."

9. Abraham Lincoln, *The Collected Works of Abraham Lincoln*, vol. 7, Roy P. Basler, ed. (New Brunswick, 1953), p. 23.

10. Heinrich von Treitschke, cited in David Potter, *The South and the Sectional Conflict* (Baton Rouge, 1968), p. 56.

11. Benedict Anderson, *Imagined Communities: Reflections on the Origins and Spread of Nationalism* (London, 1983), pp. 15–16; E. J. Hobsbawm, *Nations and Nationalism Since 1780: Programme, Myth, Reality* (Cambridge, 1990), p. 9; E. J. Hobsbawm and Terence Ranger, eds., *The Invention of Tradition* (Cambridge, 1983), esp. pp. 1–14.

12. The few studies of nationalism that do examine the United States agree that American nationalism is defined, at bottom, by an "idea." Both Hans Kohn, whose 1944 work *The Idea of Nationalism* reflected the concern of the World War II generation with distinguishing "good" from "bad" nationalism, and Liah Greenfeld (*Nationalism: Five Roads to Modernity* [1992]), whose categories of "civic" versus "ethnic" nationalism hint at a more contemporary concern with the same problem, argue that the Civil War played an important part in the realization of the American idea, and therefore in the crystallization of American nationalism. But neither author examines the *experience* of the war for its contribution to that nationalism. Hans Kohn, *The Idea of Nationalism* (New York, 1944), pp. 263–325; Kohn, *American Nationalism: An Interpretive Essay* (New York, 1957); Liah Greenfeld, *Nationalism: Five Roads to Modernity* (Cambridge, Mass., 1992). Greenfeld argues that the North's victory settled the question of the geopolitical referent for the American national ideas of individual liberty and consent of the governed. While this is true, American national identity was tentative on many other levels, not the least of which concerned the allegiance Americans owed their national government and the role that the national state was to play in the lives of individual Americans. This question was addressed during the war itself.

A multidimensional approach to nation-building has been fruitfully applied to Britain. See, for example, Raphael Samuel, ed., *Patriotism: The Making and Unmaking of British National Identity*, vols. 1 and 2 (London, 1989); and Linda Colley, *Britons: Forging the Nation, 1707–1837* (New Haven, 1992).

13. Kohn, *American Nationalism*, pp. 3–36; Greenfeld, *Nationalism*, pp. 399–403; Bernard Bailyn, *The Origins of American Politics* (New York, 1967), pp. 3–58; Gordon S. Wood, *The Creation of the American Republic* (Chapel Hill, 1969).

14. Greenfeld, *Nationalism*, pp. 400–401, 412; Thomas Paine, cited in Eric Foner, *Tom Paine and Revolutionary America* (New York, 1976), p. 78; Gordon Wood, *The Radicalism of the American Revolution* (New York, 1992), p. 229.

15. Wood, *Radicalism*, describes the ways in which the democratic society of the nineteenth century was a product—unintended by many of the founders—of the radicalism of the Revolution. For contractual patriotism see Nagel, *One Nation Indivisible*, pp. 31–41; Curti, *Roots of American Loyalty*, p. 175; Fredrickson, *The Inner Civil War*, p. 132; Alexis de Tocqueville, *Democracy in America*, vol. 1, Phillips Bradley, ed. (New York, 1945), pp. 250–253.

16. For Democrats and the role of the state see Marvin Meyers, *The Jacksonian Persuasion* (Stanford, 1957); Jean H. Baker, *Affairs of Party: The Political Culture of Northern Democrats in the Mid–Nineteenth Century* (Ithaca, 1983), esp. pp. 143–146; and Joel Silbey, *A Respectable Minority: The Democratic Party in the Civil War Era, 1860–1868* (New York, 1977). For Whigs see Daniel Walker Howe, *The Political Culture of the American Whigs* (Chicago, 1979); and Merrill D. Peterson, *The Great Triumvirate: Webster, Clay, and Calhoun* (New York, 1987), pp. 68–84. For Republicans and support of the national state for the market revolution, see Eric Foner, *Free Soil, Free Labor, Free Men* (New York, 1970), pp. 186–225.

17. Robert Wiebe, *The Opening of American Society: From the Adoption of the Constitution to the Eve of Disunion* (New York, 1984), pp. 143–167 and 255–384, describes the "revolution in choices" which helped to shape this democratic and interest-oriented society. Wood, *Radicalism,* pp. 229–230, 325–347; Charles Sellers, *The Market Revolution: Jacksonian America, 1815–1846* (New York, 1991); Harry L. Watson, *Liberty and Power: The Politics of Jacksonian America* (New York, 1990), p. 252; Joyce Appleby, *Inheriting the Revolution: The First Generation of Americans* (Cambridge, Mass., 2000); Susan-Mary Grant, *North Over South: Northern Nationalism and American Identity in the Antebellum Era* (Lawrence, 2000).

18. Zelinsky, *Nation into State;* Nagel, *One Nation Indivisible;* Wilson, *Space, Time and Freedom;* Hall, *The Organization of American Culture.*

19. Nagel, *One Nation Indivisible,* pp. 69–103; Zelinsky, *Nation into State,* pp. 218–219; James H. Moorhead, *American Apocalypse: Yankee Protestants and the Civil War 1860–1869* (New Haven, 1978), pp. 1–22; Ruth Bloch, *Visionary Republic: Millennial Themes in American Thought, 1756–1800* (Cambridge, 1985); Eric Foner, *The Story of American Freedom* (New York, 1998), pp. 57–58; Wood, *Radicalism,* p. 117.

20. Michael Paul Rogin, *Subversive Genealogy: The Politics and Art of Herman Melville* (New York, 1983), pp. 71–74; Edward L. Widmer, *Young America: The Flowering of Democracy in New York City* (New York, 1999), pp. 27–124; Larzer Ziff, *Literary Democracy: The Declaration of Cultural Independence in America* (New York, 1982), pp. 300–301; Priscilla Wald, *Constituting Americans: Cultural Anxiety and Narrative Form* (Durham, 1995), pp. 106–171. For quote, see Herman Melville, "Hawthorne and His Mosses," in Jay Leyda, ed., *The Portable Melville* (New York, 1952), p. 409.

The literary version of the Young America movement was waning by the late 1840s; its fading coincided with the rise of the political Young America movement. Literary Young America did not share many of the ideas of the expansionist political Young America. See Widmer, *Young America,* for the most recent treatment of this multifaceted movement. John L. O'Sullivan, cited in Sellers, *The Market Revolution,* pp. 422–423.

21. Rogers M. Smith, *Civic Ideals: Conflicting Visions of Citizenship in U.S. History* (New Haven, 1997), pp. 1–39, 197–242; Widmer, *Young America,* pp. 51–52; Foner, *Story of American Freedom,* pp. 77–78, 86.

22. For the effect of the War of 1812 and the Mexican War on American nationalism, see Curti, *Roots of American Loyalty,* pp. 16–29, 152–156; and David Potter, *The Impending Crisis: 1848–1861* (New York, 1976), pp. 12–14. For the North's reaction to the attack on Fort Sumter, see McPherson, *Battle Cry of Freedom,* pp. 274–275. Hobsbawm, *Nations and Nationalism,* p. 83, discusses the effect of universal suffrage on nation-building.

23. On war as a state-building activity, see Charles Tilly, ed., *The Formation of National States in Western Europe* (Princeton, 1975), pp. 74–75.

24. Frank L. Klement, *The Copperheads in the Middlewest* (Chicago, 1960); McPherson, *Battle Cry of Freedom,* pp. 493–494, 590–625, 760–762; Frank L. Klement, *The Limits of Dissent: Clement L. Vallandigham and the Civil War* (Lexington, 1970); Clement L Vallandigham, "The Great Civil War in America," Frank Friedel, ed., *Union Pamphlets of the Civil War,* vol. 2 (Cambridge, Mass., 1967), p. 738.

25. Iver Bernstein, *The New York City Draft Riots: Their Significance for American Society and Politics in the Age of the Civil War* (New York, 1990); Nevins, *The War for the Union,* vol. 3, pp. 126–127; Grace Palladino, *Another Civil War: Labor, Capital and the State in the Anthracite Regions of Pennsylvania, 1840–1868* (Urbana, 1990), pp. 95–117; Lincoln in Basler, *The Collected Works,* vol. 7, p. 514.

26. Lincoln in Basler, *Complete Works,* vol. 5, p. 537; James M. McPherson, *For Cause and Comrades: Why Men Fought in the Civil War* (New York, 1997), p. 100.

27. For Confederate soldiers' notions of liberty, see McPherson, *For Cause and Comrades,* pp. 20–21, 104–107. For quote see Richard W. Simpson to Caroline Miller, September 20, 1861, as cited in McPherson, *For Cause and Comrades,* p. 21. For more on Confederate nationalism, see Drew Gilpin Faust, *The Creation of Confederate Nationalism: Ideology and Identity in the Civil War South* (Baton Rouge, 1988). Fredrickson, *Inner Civil War,* p. 132.

28. Baker, *Affairs of Party,* pp. 150–158; Silbey, *Respectable Minority,* pp. 57, 69, 73–80; Irving H. Bartlett, *Wendell Phillips: Brahmin Radical* (Boston, 1961), p. 119. For quotes see Clement L. Vallandigham, cited in Silbey, *Respectable Minority,* p. 103; Wendell Phillips, *Speeches, Lectures, and Letters* (Boston, 1902), pp. 419–420.

29. Mellon, cited in Curti, *Roots of American Loyalty,* p. 161; Curti, *Roots of American Loyalty,* pp. 160–162.

30. Nagel, *One Nation Indivisible,* pp. 69–103; Zelinsky, *Nation into State,* pp. 218–219.

31. Alexis de Tocqueville, *Democracy in America,* vol. 1, pp. 250–251; George T. Strong in Allan Nevins and Milton Halsey Thomas, eds., *The Diary of George Templeton Strong,* vol. 2, November 8, 1854 (New York, 1952). For the tendency of antebellum Americans to focus on the present and reject tradition and history, see Michael Kammen, *Mystic Chords of Memory: The Transformation of Tradition in American Culture* (New York, 1991), pp. 40–61.

32. Lee in Nevins, *War for the Union,* vol. 1, p. 107; Curti, *Roots of American Loyalty,* p. 159.

33. Wiebe, *Opening of American Society,* pp. 354–355; Bancroft in Curti, *Roots of American Loyalty,* p. 159; Zelinsky, *Nation into State,* p. 218.

34. Similarly, each of the chapters in this study explores one strand of Civil War nationalism; but not all strands of Civil War nationalism are the focus of an entire chapter. Religion, for example, played a large role in sustaining patriotic motivation throughout the war, as several earlier works have documented. In this study, religion is examined chiefly as a constituent element of other constructions of the nation. For religion and the Civil War, see Moorhead, *American Apocalypse;* Randall M. Miller, Harry S. Stout, and Charles Reagan Wilson, eds., *Religion and the American Civil War* (New York, 1998). For religion, see also Paludan, "*A People's Contest,*" pp. 339–374. In Miller et al., see in particular George M. Fredrickson, "The Coming of the Lord: The Northern Protestant Clergy and the Civil War Crisis," pp. 110–130.

35. Hobsbawm, *Nations and Nationalism,* p. 11.

36. de Tocqueville, *Democracy in America,* vol. 1, pp. 250–251; vol. 2, p. 106.

1. "A Union Love Feast"

1. *Chicago Tribune,* October 28, 1863; Mrs. A. H. Hoge, *The Boys in Blue, or Heroes of the Rank and File* (New York, 1867), pp. 334–337.

2. Hoge, *Boys in Blue,* p. 338; *The Sanitary Reporter* (Louisville, United States Sanitary Commission), vol. 1, no. 13, November 15, 1863; *History of the North-West Soldiers' Fair, Held in Chicago, Last Week of October and First Week of November* (Chicago, n.d.), p. 17; Hoge, *Boys in Blue,* pp. 339–340; *Chicago Tribune,* October 28, 1863.

3. Mary A. Livermore, *My Story of the War: A Woman's Narrative of Four Years Personal Experience* (New York, 1889; reprint, New York, 1972), p. 433; *History of the North-Western Soldiers' Fair,* pp. 23, 31; Hoge, *Boys in Blue,* p. 357; Abraham Lincoln to Ladies having in Charge of the Northwestern Fair, October 26, 1863, in Basler, *Collected Works,* vol. 6, p. 539.

Thomas B. Bryan purchased Lincoln's manuscript for three thousand dollars and donated it to the Chicago Soldiers Home. Thousands of dollars were raised for the home from the sale of lithographed copies. In 1871, the manuscript was destroyed in the Chicago fire. See Basler, *Collected Works,* vol. 6, p. 30, footnote.

4. Livermore, *My Story of the War,* p. 437.

5. Three hundred works of art were loaned from Chicago homes alone. Livermore, *My Story of the War,* pp. 441–442; *History of the North-Western Soldiers' Fair,* pp. 32–34; *Sanitary Reporter,* vol. 13, p. 102.

6. Livermore, *My Story of the War,* pp. 430–434; *History of the North-Western Soldiers' Fair,* pp. 26–27.

7. *History of the North-Western Soldiers' Fair*, pp. 35–38.

8. Livermore, *My Story of the War*, p. 455; *Chicago Tribune*, October 28, 1863.

9. William Y. Thompson, "Sanitary Fairs of the Civil War," *Civil War History* 4 (March 1958): 64; Livermore, *My Story of the War*, pp. 410–411; Papers of the United States Sanitary Commission (USSCP), Box 1006. "Sanitary Fairs" is a somewhat confusing category. Though the first large-scale fair to benefit the soldiers was in fact sponsored, if somewhat belatedly and certainly half-heartedly, by the Sanitary Commission, of the numerous fairs that followed some were sponsored by the Sanitary Commission, others by the Christian Commission. The Fair records examined in this chapter are almost entirely from Sanitary Commission fairs. Nonetheless, this is not an important distinction for our purposes: those fairs with recorded histories seem to have followed much the same form as the original, though of course some variation existed. The fair phenomenon in general directed the energies of much of the Northern populace toward the construction of large-scale fairs that paid tribute to the soldiers and celebrated the nation.

10. Attie, *Patriotic Toil*. Attie argues that the fairs were a sign of women reasserting older charitable methods to reclaim regional control over soldier relief, and that as a result, they accommodated local identities.

11. I am borrowing the phrase "see themselves" from Lawrence Goodwyn, who uses it to describe an important step in the creation of the movement culture of the Populists in his book, *Democratic Promise: The Populist Moment in America* (New York, 1976). Though Goodwyn describes an intricate process which is not applicable to the Sanitary Fairs, it is nonetheless a useful concept for understanding the fairs and the construction of national identity. The idea of "imagined communities" is drawn from Anderson's *Imagined Communities*.

12. W. Dennison to Great Western Fair Commission, in United States Sanitary Commission, ed., *History of the Great Western Sanitary Fair* (Cincinnati, 1864), p. 159; Ella L. Gibson to Great Western Fair Commission, *History of the Great Western Sanitary Fair*, p. 128. For the trend toward legislative and institutional change, see Lori Ginzberg, *Women and the Work of Benevolence: Morality, Politics, and Class in the Nineteenth-Century United States* (New Haven, 1990). Ginzberg argues that though the trend was well under way by the 1850s, the Sanitary Fairs were for the most part organized by an "older generation of benevolent workers" (see p. 167).

Merle Curti discusses the role that the Civil War played in injecting the notion of sacrifice into American patriotism. See Curti, *Roots of American Loyalty*, pp. 144–172.

13. Strong, *Diary*, vol. 2, p. 197.

14. Attie, *Patriotic Toil*, pp. 198–199.

15. Livermore, *My Story of the War*, p. 411. For other expressions of desire that the fairs help create a national sentiment, see Edgar Conkling to *Cincinnati Times* in *History of the Great Western Sanitary Fair*, pp. 36–37; J. R. Lowell,

in ibid., pp. 183–184; *Record of the Metropolitan Fair, Held in Aid of the United States Sanitary Commission* (New York, 1867), pp. 2–5; General W. S. Rosecrans, circular for the Mississippi Valley Fair, February 5, 1864, in Sanitary Commission Papers (SCP), Box 1006; Hoge, *Boys in Blue,* p. 332.

16. Fredrickson, *Inner Civil War,* p. 98. For various interpretations of the Sanitary Commission and its work, see William Quentin Maxwell, *Lincoln's Fifth Wheel: The Political History of the United States Sanitary Commission* (New York, 1956); Charles J. Stillé, *The History of the United States Sanitary Commission* (New York, 1868); Attie, *Patriotic Toil;* and Judith Ann Giesberg, *Civil War Sisterhood: The United States Sanitary Commission and Women's Politics in Transition* (Boston, 2000). In September 1861, the WCRA, originally an autonomous female-led organization, was transformed into a branch of the Commission. See Attie, *Patriotic Toil,* pp. 82–86.

17. Henry W. Bellows, *Historical Sketch of the Union League Club of New York: Its Origin, Organization, and Work, 1863–1869* (New York, 1879), p. 6; Fredrickson, *Inner Civil War,* pp. 98–112; Bellows to Cyrus A. Bartol, April 12, 1861, and August 9, 1861, in Fredrickson, *Inner Civil War,* p. 103.

18. Bellows to Edgar Conkling, *History of the Great Western Sanitary Fair,* p. 144; Bellows, *Union League,* pp. 6–7; *Statement of the Object and Methods of the Sanitary Commission,* U.S. Sanitary Commission Document 69 (Boston, 1863), pp. 55–56, in Fredrickson, *Inner Civil War,* pp. 103–104.

19. Strong, *Diary,* pp. 411–412; Olmsted in a public letter to women in 1862, quoted in Jeanie Attie, "Warwork and the Crisis of Domesticity in the North," Catherine Clinton and Nina Silber, eds., *Divided Houses: Gender and the Civil War* (New York, 1992), p. 250; ibid., p. 250.

20. Attie, *Patriotic Toil,* pp. 98–108; Ginzberg, *Women and the Work of Benevolence,* p. 153; Helen Smith to Louisa Lee Schuyler, in Ginzberg, *Women and the Work of Benevolence,* p. 153.

21. Livermore, *My Story of the War,* p. 411; Maria Lydig Daly, *Diary of a Union Lady, 1861–1865,* Harold E. Hammond, ed. (New York, 1962), p. 286; Bloor quoted in Thompson, "Sanitary Fairs of the Civil War," p. 56.

22. *History of the North-Western Soldiers' Fair,* p. 5.

23. Alvin Robert Kantor and Marjorie Sered Kantor, *Sanitary Fairs: A Philatelic and Historical Study of Civil War Benevolences* (Glencoe, Ill., 1992), p. 154; Thompson, "Sanitary Fairs of the Civil War," p. 64.

Larger cities hosting fairs included Cincinnati, Boston, Brooklyn and Long Island, Manhattan, Philadelphia, St. Louis, Baltimore, Cleveland, and Washington, D.C. Fairs were also held at Pittsburgh, Dayton, Dubuque, Kalamazoo, Michigan; Burlington, Iowa; Taylorsville, California; Springfield, Massachusetts; Chelsea, Massachusetts; Carlisle, Pennsylvania; New Castle and Damiroscatta, Maine; Bridgeport, Connecticut; Stamford, Connecticut; South Adams, Massachusetts; and Wheeling, Virginia. Fairs were particularly popular in New York: Albany, Poughkeepsie, Yonkers, Flushing, Schuyler, Elmira, Buffalo, Warwick, Irvington, and Hornellsville were each home to one.

24. Livermore, *My Story of the War,* p. 412; *Record of the Metropolitan Fair,* pp. 224–226; Patricia West, "Clio at Home: Historic House Museums and the History of Women" (Ph.D. dissertation, State University of New York at Binghamton, 1988), pp. 30–41; Attie, *Patriotic Toil,* pp. 198–219; Strong, *Diary,* pp. 412–413; Stillé, *Memorial of the Great Central Fair,* pp. 24–25; Kantor and Kantor, *Sanitary Fairs,* p. 116; *History of the Great Western Sanitary Fair,* pp. 44–46, 565–566; *Report of the Duchess County and Poughkeepsie Sanitary Fair,* p. 9.

25. Ginzberg suggests that, in spite of the rhetoric of separate spheres, with the exception of public speaking, women performed almost all of the various jobs in most of the benevolent organizations they served, including fundraising, teaching, and administration. See Ginzberg, *Women and the Work of Benevolence,* pp. 36–66.

26. Ginzberg, *Women and the Work of Benevolence,* p. 37; Linus Pierpont Brockett and Mary C. Vaughn, *Women's Work in the Civil War: A Record of Heroism, Patriotism, and Patience* (Philadelphia, 1867), pp. 70, 527–580, 596–597; Attie, *Patriotic Toil,* pp. 38–44; Ginzberg, *Women and the Work of Benevolence,* pp. 149–150; *Sanitary Reporter* (Louisville), vol. 1, no. 19, February 15, 1864, p. 150. While these societies were frequently inspired by sermons and rooted within a congregation, over time increasing numbers of benevolent societies existed outside the purview of church congregations, and a sprawling network of nondenominational associations spread across the North. Gradually, those societies began to associate with one another, and, according to a recent historian of female benevolence in the United States, by the mid–nineteenth century they "operated as a coherent financial network within a given city or town." See Ginzberg, *Women and the Work of Benevolence,* p. 48; Glenna Matthews, *The Rise of Public Woman: Woman's Power and Woman's Place in the United States, 1630–1970* (New York, 1992), p. 116.

27. Ginzberg, *Women and the Work of Benevolence,* pp. 44–45; Attie, *Patriotic Toil,* pp. 153–157; Sarah E. Morris to Mrs. C. J. Moore, Sec. of Women's Pennsylvania Branch USSC, October 1863, USSCP B571.

28. *A Record of the Metropolitan Fair,* p. 23. Curious sentimental items abounded, including a pair of earrings made from the buttons of General Rosecrans's coat and a bracelet made from the tree under which Grant and Pemberton consummated the surrender of Vicksburg. See *History of the Great Western Fair,* pp. 276, 360–361.

I have drawn this general description of the Sanitary Fairs from primary and secondary records of fairs in Chicago, Cincinnati, Boston, Brooklyn and Long Island, Manhattan, Philadelphia, Pittsburgh, St. Louis, Baltimore, Cleveland, Albany, Poughkeepsie, Stamford, Conn., and Springfield, Mass.

29. *Baltimore American,* April 19, 1864; *History of the Brooklyn and Long Island Fair,* p. 28, *A Record of the Metropolitan Fair,* p. 119; "Rough Hints" in Ibid., pp. 2–5; Kantor and Kantor, *Sanitary Fairs,* p. 154; *St. Louis Daily Mission Democrat,* June 9, 1864; J. Matthew Gallman, "Voluntarism in Wartime: Philadelphia's Great Central Fair," Maris A. Vinovskis, ed., *Toward a Social*

History of the American Civil War: Exploratory Essays (New York, 1990), p. 105; Thompson, "Sanitary Fairs of the Civil War," p. 64. These amounts include only the fairs that kept records. Jeanie Attie has suggested that the Metropolitan fair attempted to limit admission to the more affluent classes.

30. USSC Secretary J. Foster Jenkins in Attie, *Patriotic Toil*, p. 215; Thompson, "Sanitary Fairs of the Civil War," pp. 56–57; WCRA circular, cited in Brockett, *Women's Work in the Civil War*, p. 535. Attie argues that these complaints were disingenuous.

31. "A Lady" to *Cincinnati Times*, October 31, 1863, *History of the Great Western Sanitary Fair*, p. 44; Thompson, "Sanitary Fairs of the Civil War," p. 55; Stillé, *Memorial of the Great Central Fair*, p. 15; *History of the Brooklyn and Long Island Fair, February 22, 1864* (Brooklyn, 1864), pp. 5–7, 166; ibid., pp. 81–82. See also ibid., p. 166; Walter Dickson, ed., *St. Andrews Society of Albany Memorial of the Great Sanitary Fair, Held in the City of Albany, New York, February and March, 1864* (Albany, 1864), p. 67; Gallman, "Voluntarism in Wartime," pp. 104, 107; *Report of the Duchess County and Poughkeepsie Sanitary Fair Held at Sanitary Hall in the City of Poughkeepsie, from March 15, 1864 to March 19, 1864* (Poughkeepsie, 1864), p. 15; *Record of the Metropolitan Fair*, p. 223; Hoge, *Boys in Blue*, p. 333; *History of the Great Western Sanitary Fair*, pp. 564–567.

The competition that characterized the Sanitary Fairs was informed in part by local loyalties and pride; but equally influential was an economically driven civic boosterism. Throughout much of the nineteenth century, cities across the nation sought to stimulate local economies and vied with one another to become commercial centers. While this competition included struggles over such central components of economic growth as trade routes, it also manifested as the drive to cultivate a city's or town's cultural or social reputation. In this form, civic boosterism focused on cultural institutions such as philharmonic societies, mercantile libraries, historic societies, and, as fair mania got under way, Sanitary Fairs. On economic civic boosterism, see Dennis R. Judd and Todd Swanstrom, *City Politics: Private Power and Public Policy* (New York, 1994), pp. 25–27; Richard C. Wade, *The Urban Frontier: The Rise of the Western Cities, 1790–1830* (Chicago, 1959), p. 103.

32. Stillé, *Memorial of the Great Central Fair*, p. 117; USSCP Box 1004; *The Press*, June 8, 1864; *New York Daily Tribune*, April 5, 1864; *Record of the Metropolitan Fair*, pp. 99, 223; *St. Andrews Society*, p. 81; *Canteen*, in USSCP, Box 1011; *Report of the Duchess County and Poughkeepsie Sanitary Fair*, p. 15. See also *History of the Great Western Sanitary Fair*, pp. 483–484; *History of the Brooklyn and Long Island Fair*, p. 24; Hoge, *Boys in Blue*, p. 333; *Sanitary Reporter*, November 15, vol. 1, no. 13, 1863.

33. USSCP B1003; *History of the North-Western Soldiers' Fair*, pp. 24–25; *A Record of the Metropolitan Fair*, p. 152; *Sanitary Reporter*, vol. 1, no. 19, February 15, 1864, p. 150; *Baltimore American*, April 19, 1864; *St. Andrews Society of Albany*, p. 34; USSCP B1019.

34. *Missouri Daily Mission Democrat*, April 13, 1864.

35. Attie discusses the appeal that the fairs held for the women whose labor the commission wished to control. Attie, *Patriotic Toil*, pp. 218–219.

36. *Daily Missouri Democrat*, April 11, 1864, May 5, 1864; For daily bulletins, see ibid., April and May; *Record of the Metropolitan Fair*, pp. 9–10.

37. *Record of the Metropolitan Fair*, p. 16; Strong, *Diary*, p. 422; *Report of the Duchess County and Poughkeepsie Fair*, p. 10; *Record of the Metropolitan Fair*, pp. 211–212; *Daily Mission Democrat*, April 13, 1864; *History of the Great Western Sanitary Fair*, pp. 489, 493.

38. *History of the Northwest Fair*, p. 10; *History of the Great Western Sanitary Fair*, p. 96; *Record of the Metropolitan Fair*, p. 13; *History of the Great Western Sanitary Fair*, pp. 47–49, 92; Gallman, "Voluntarism in Wartime," p. 101; *A Record of the Metropolitan Fair*, pp. 14–16; *History of the Great Western Sanitary Fair*, pp. 92–93; Stillé, *Memorial of the Great Central Fair*, pp. 19–24, 43–44; Gallman, "Voluntarism in Wartime," p. 99; Kantor and Kantor, *Sanitary Fairs*, p. 122.

Special provisions were made for children: in Chicago, the papers carried an announcement of the formation of an "Army of the American Eagle," a military-style club wherein boys and girls could obtain rank through the sale of oil-painted pictures of an American eagle. Circulars were sent to schools, asking that the children donate their "spending money . . . giving the most healthful exercise to their benevolent and patriotic feelings. To every child, the thought—'I did something for the soldiers who were crushing the Great Rebellion,' will afford an inspiring recollection to the end of life." Individual children donated their prized toy soldiers, dolls, or meager savings to the fair. USSCP B999; Circular, USSCP B1006; see also Circular, USSCP B1001; *History of the Great Western Sanitary Fair*, pp. 47–49, 89–90.

39. *Record of the Metropolitan Fair*, p. 31; *Baltimore American*, April 19, 1864; USSCP B1003; Stillé, *Memorial of the Great Central Fair*, pp. 26–31; Hoge, *Boys in Blue*, p. 346.

40. *Report of the Duchess County and Poughkeepsie Fair*, p. 12; *Daily Missouri Democrat*, June 6, 1864; Stillé, *Memorial of the Great Central Fair*, pp. 42–43; *Record of the Metropolitan Fair*, pp. 96, 120; *History of the Brooklyn and Long Island Fair*, p. 76; *History of the Great Western Sanitary Fair*, pp. 228–333; Kantor and Kantor, *Sanitary Fairs*, p. 11; Elizabeth Stillinger, *The Antiquers* (New York, 1980), p. 9.

41. Gallman, "Voluntarism in Wartime," pp. 99, 104; *Record of the Metropolitan Fair*, pp. 126, 129–130; "Rough Hints" in *A Record of the Metropolitan Fair*, pp. 2–5; *New York Tribune*, April 7, 1864.

Nathaniel Hawthorne expressed disgruntlement about the fairs and the war they sought to support when he was asked to contribute a holograph. In contrast to the inspiring texts his fellow writers contributed, the selection Hawthorne chose to copy was from a short story he had written years before about the folly of reformers' hopes. See Daniel Aaron, *The Unwritten War: American Writers and the Civil War* (New York, 1973), pp. 42–43.

42. *St. Louis Daily Mission Democrat,* May 28, 1864; Daly, *Diary of a Union Lady,* p. 287; Gallman, "Voluntarism in Wartime," p. 104.

43. Sarah Edwards Henshaw, *Our Branch and Its Tributaries* (Chicago, 1868), pp. 216–217; *Chicago Tribune,* October 28, 1863. See also Gallman, "Voluntarism in Wartime," p. 104.

44. Anderson, *Imagined Communities,* p. 6.

45. Cited in Curti, *Roots of American Loyalty,* pp. 160–161.

46. Bellows in Fredrickson, *Inner Civil War,* p. 103; Strong in Fredrickson, *Inner Civil War,* p. 103. Commission leaders also wanted Americans to experience suffering to improve the national character, which they felt had been weakened by prosperity.

47. Lewis O. Saum, *The Popular Mood of Pre–Civil War America* (Westport, 1980), pp. 3–75.

48. Ginzberg, *Women and the Work of Benevolence,* pp. 11–25; Sarah Hale in Ginzberg, *Women and the Work of Benevolence,* p. 14; on women's sphere and reform activities, see also Nancy F. Cott, *The Bonds of Womanhood: "Woman's Sphere" in New England* (New Haven, 1977), esp. pp. 63–100, 126–159; Mary P. Ryan, *Cradle of the Middle Class: The Family in Oneida County, New York, 1790–1865* (New York, 1981); and Nancy A. Hewitt, *Women's Activism and Social Change: Rochester, New York, 1822–1872* (Ithaca, 1984).

49. Ginzberg, *Women and the Work of Benevolence,* p. 14; Buckminister in Cott, *Bonds of Womanhood,* p. 148. Though many women were discontented with the bonds this ideology imposed, most recognized the power the ideology held for them and worked within those bonds. See Hewitt, *Women's Activism,* p. 39. For Republican motherhood, see Mary Beth Norton, *Liberty's Daughters: The Revolutionary Experience of American Women, 1750–1800* (Boston, 1980); and Linda Kerber, *Women of the Republic: Intellect and Ideology in Revolutionary America* (Chapel Hill, 1980).

50. *Statement of the Object and Methods of the Sanitary Commission,* U.S. Sanitary Commission Document 69 (Boston, 1863), pp. 55–56, in Fredrickson, *Inner Civil War,* pp. 103–104. This shift and its class origins and implications are the thesis of Ginzberg's *Women and the Work of Benevolence.* Glenna Matthews disagrees with Ginzberg's assessment of the forties and fifties, arguing that the Civil War witnessed the apogee of benevolence based on the model of female superiority. See Matthews, *Rise of Public Woman,* pp. 10, 120–146.

51. For this "older generation" of benevolent workers, see Ginzberg, *Women and the Work of Benevolence,* p. 167.

52. Circular, USSCP Box 1001; *Voice of the Fair,* 5–31, USSCP B1019; *History of the Great Western Sanitary Fair,* pp. 81, 93. See also Hoge, *Boys in Blue,* pp. 344, 355; USSCP B1006; Stillé, *Memorial of the Great Central Fair,* pp. 30–31; *Record of the Metropolitan Fair,* p. 44; *History of the Great Western Sanitary Fair,* pp. 68, 85, 110, 137, 138–139; Circular USSCP B1006; USSCP B1019; *Voice of the Fair,* May 31, 1864; *Baltimore American,* April 19, 1864.

53. *Cincinnati Gazette,* December 22, 1863, cited in *History of the Great Western Sanitary Fair,* pp. 254–255; USSCP B1006.

54. *History of the Great Western Sanitary Fair,* pp. 254–255, 369–402; Livermore, *My Story of the War,* p. 451.

55. Curtin, quoted in Stillé, *Memorial of the Great Central Fair,* pp. 30–31.

56. *Baltimore American,* April 19, 1864. See also circular for the Great Western Fair Nursery Stock committee in *History of the Great Western Sanitary Fair,* p. 85; Letter to Fair Secretary, *History of the Great Western Sanitary Fair,* pp. 138–139; Circular, Committee on Hardware, USSCP B1006; *Record of the Metropolitan Fair,* pp. 134–135; Stillé, *Memorial of the Great Central Fair,* pp. 18–19; Inaugural Address, ibid., pp. 30–31; Hoge, *Boys in Blue,* p. 344.

57. Thomas B. Bryan, in *Chicago Tribune,* October 28, 1864; *Report of the Duchess County and Poughkeepsie Fair,* p. 9; "The Ladies and the Sanitary Fair," *Missouri Daily Mission Democrat,* April 12, 1864; *History of the Great Western Sanitary Fair,* pp. 246–247.

58. *History of the Great Western Sanitary Fair,* p. 245; *Record of the Metropolitan Fair,* p. 225. *History of the Great Western Sanitary Fair,* pp. 47, 138–139.

59. *History of the Great Western Sanitary Fair,* pp. 478–479.

60. Kantor and Kantor, *Sanitary Fairs,* p. 275; *History of the Great Western Sanitary Fair,* p. 275; Lincoln in Basler, *Collected Works,* vol. 7, pp. 396–397; Stillé, *Memorial of the Great Central Fair,* p. 10.

61. Kammen, *Mystic Chords of Memory,* pp. 40–61; Strong, *Diary,* November 8, 1854.

62. T. R. Adam, *The Museum and Popular Culture* (New York, 1939), pp. 5–13; Laurence Vail Coleman, *The Museum in America: A Critical Study* (Washington, 1939), pp. 6–14; Thomas Bender, *New York Intellect: A History of Intellectual Life in New York City from 1750 to the Beginnings of Our Own Time* (New York, 1987), pp. 46–47; Gary Kulik, "Designing the Past: History Museum Exhibitions from Peale to the Present," Warren Leon and Roy Rosenzweig, eds., *History Museums in the United States: A Critical Assessment* (Urbana, 1989), pp. 3–4; Michael Wallace, "Visiting the Past: History Museums in the United States," in Susan Porter Benson, Stephen Brier, and Roy Rosenzweig, eds., *Presenting the Past: Essays on History and the Public* (Philadelphia, 1986), pp. 137–161; Paul Marshall Rea, *The Museum and the Community: A Study of Social Laws and Consequences* (Lancaster, 1932), pp. 8–9; Neil Harris, *Humbug: The Art of P. T. Barnum* (Boston, 1973), pp. 33, 172–173. On placing the fairs in historical context, I am grateful for numerous conversations with Patricia West.

63. Coleman, *Museum in America,* pp. 14–15; Neil Harris, *The Artist in American Society: The Formative Years, 1790–1860* (New York, 1966), pp. 122, 146–160, 300–312.

64. *Record of the Metropolitan Fair,* pp. 112–113; *History of the Great Western Sanitary Fair,* pp. 467–472.

65. Daly, *Diary of a Union Lady*, p. 286; USSCP B1003; *New York Herald*, April 4, 1864; *The (Philadelphia) Press*, June 8, 1864, in USSCP B1004.

66. *History of the Great Western Sanitary Fair*, pp. 403–404; *Record of the Metropolitan Fair*, p. 99; Stillé, *Memorial of the Great Central Fair*, p. 117. See also USSCP B1003; *New York Herald*, April 4, 1864.

67. Stillé, *Memorial of the Great Central Fair*, p. 117; Livermore, *My Story of the War*, p. 442; Stillé, *Memorial of the Great Central Fair*, p. 117. On the need for a national museum, see *New York Daily Tribune*, April 5, 1864; *The Philadelphia Press*, June 8, 1864; *Record of the Metropolitan Fair*, pp. 39–41; and *Memorial of the Great Central Fair*, p. 117.

68. Kammen, *Mystic Chords of Memory*, p. 47.

69. USSCP B1006; Stillinger, *The Antiquers*, pp. 8–9; *History of the Great Western Sanitary Fair*, pp. 360–361; *Record of the Metropolitan Fair*, p. 73; *Report of the Duchess County and Poughkeepsie Fair*, p. 11; *Record of the Metropolitan Fair*, pp. 35–36.

70. USSCP B1004; *Baltimore American*, April 19, 1864, and April 30, 1864; USSCP B998; *Report of the Duchess County and Poughkeepsie Fair*, pp. 11, 73–75; USSCP B1019; *Record of the Metropolitan Fair*, pp. 183–185; Stillinger, *The Antiquers*, pp. 9, 15; Strong, *Diary*, pp. 426–427; USSCP B1019; *Voice of the Fair*, June 1, 1865, in USSCP B1019. For more on fairs' period rooms, see *History of the Brooklyn and Long Island Fair*, pp. 73–79; *Record of the Metropolitan Fair*, pp. 119, 182–183; *Memorial of the Great Central Fair*, pp. 100–103; Daly, *Diary of a Union Lady*, p. 287; "The Knickerbocker Kitchen," in *New York Daily Tribune*, April 5, 1864. Stillinger argues that, although previous histories of period rooms have suggested that they originated at the Philadelphia centennial, they in fact originated in the Civil War Sanitary Fairs.

71. Kulik, "Designing the Past," p. 13; *New York Tribune*, April 6, 1864; *A Record of the Metropolitan Fair*, p. 183. See also USSCP 998.

72. *History of the Brooklyn and Long Island Fairs*, p. 75. Once again, in the period rooms the service of refined women reinforced the theme of sacrifice for country—as the *Baltimore American* wrote in its evaluation of the Baltimore fair's colonial kitchen, "We should learn from the New England Kitchen, that in personal effort, in renewed simplicity of life, in self-denial and honored duty, lies the secret of the strength that is to sustain us in our present great struggle." *Baltimore American*, April 30, 1864.

2. Let the Nation Be Your Bank

1. Jay Cooke's Memoir, in Jay Cooke and Company Collection, Baker Library, Harvard Business School, pp. 2, 82.

2. Such references are scattered throughout Cooke's Memoir; see, for example, pp. 43, 75, 127.

3. Harriet Larson, *Jay Cooke: Private Banker* (Cambridge, Mass., 1936),

p. 148; Ellis Paxson Oberholtzer, *Jay Cooke: Financier of the Civil War,* vol. 1 (Philadelphia, 1907), p. 577; Matthew Josephson, *The Robber Barons: The Great American Capitalists, 1861–1901* (New York, 1934), p. 57; *Constitutional Union,* n.d., cited in Oberholtzer, *Jay Cooke,* p. 483.

4. For a discussion of the role of self-interest and nationalism, see Potter, "The Historian's Use of Nationalism and Vice-Versa," *The South and the Sectional Conflict,* pp. 34–83. For the nation as a source of economic well-being, see Hans Kohn, *The Idea of Nationalism: A Study of Its Origins and Background* (New York, 1944).

5. Bray Hammond, *Sovereignty and an Empty Purse: Banks and Politics in the Civil War Era* (Princeton, 1970), pp. 37–38; "Report of the Secretary of the Treasury," *Congressional Globe,* 37th Congress, 1st Session, July 4, 1861, Appendix. For a recent treatment of Civil War finances, see Richardson, *The Greatest Nation of the Earth.*

6. Paul Studenski and Herman E. Kroos, *Financial History of the United States* (New York, 1952), pp. 123, 159; Nevins, *War for the Union,* p. 382.

7. "Report of the Secretary of the Treasury," *Congressional Globe,* 37th Congress, 1st session, July 4, 1861, Appendix; Frederick J. Blue, *Salmon P. Chase: A Life in Politics* (Kent, Ohio, 1987), pp. 129–133; John Niven, ed., *The Salmon P. Chase Papers,* vol. 1 (Kent, Ohio, 1993), "Introduction," xxxv–xxxvi; Hammond, *Sovereignty and an Empty Purse,* pp. 73–105.

8. Hammond, *Sovereignty and an Empty Purse,* pp. 40–41.

9. Blue, *Salmon P. Chase,* pp. 143–144, 157; Studenski and Kroos, *Financial History of the United States,* p. 127; Hammond, *Sovereignty and an Empty Purse,* pp. 26–34.

10. "Report of the Secretary of the Treasury," *Congressional Globe,* 37th Congress, 1st Session, July 4, 1861, Appendix; Hammond, *Sovereignty and an Empty Purse,* p. 43. In his report to Congress, Chase argued that the war was a "contest for national existence and the sovereignty of the people" and it was therefore fitting that an appeal be made first to "the people themselves." By offering the loan in denominations as low as fifty dollars, to be paid for in as many as ten installments, at a liberal rate of interest, Chase hoped that it would be possible to "transmute the burden into a benefit," inspiring "satisfaction and hopes of profit rather than annoyance and fears of loss."

This was not the federal government's first attempt at a popular loan: in 1813, the Treasury Department offered a $16 million loan to the public in denominations as low as one hundred dollars. The loan did not sell. (Larson, *Jay Cooke,* p. 24.)

11. For the specie requirements of the independent treasury act and its impact on Civil War finance, see Hammond, *Sovereignty and an Empty Purse,* esp. pp. 18–26.

12. Hammond, *Sovereignty and an Empty Purse,* pp. 26, 76–77; Robert T. Patterson, "Government Finance on the Eve of the Civil War," *Journal of Economic History* 12 (1952): 35–44; George Harrington, "Finances of the War 1861–1865, Extracts from the Forthcoming Work Entitled Personal Recollections and

Official Experiences," in Historical Society of Pennsylvania (HSP), Jay Cooke Manuscript Papers, p. 26; Oberholtzer, *Jay Cooke*, p. 162; McPherson, *Battle Cry of Freedom*, p. 9; Larson, *Jay Cooke*, p. 119; *Boston Daily Adviser*, September 11, 1861, cited in Hammond, *Sovereignty and an Empty Purse*, p. 109. The Cooke Papers in HSP contain scrapbooks with flyers and clippings.

13. Hammond, *Sovereignty and an Empty Purse*, pp. 150–159.

14. Blue, *Salmon P. Chase*, pp. 150–157; Hammond, *Sovereignty and an Empty Purse*, pp. 159–235, 264–265.

15. Blue, *Salmon P. Chase*, pp. 150–151; Hammond, *Sovereignty and an Empty Purse*, pp. 159–235. The revenue act and the bank bill were passed in July 1862 and February 1863, respectively.

16. Chase in Larson, *Jay Cooke*, p. 117; Harrington, "Finances of the War 1861–1865," pp. 12–13.

17. HSP Harrington, "Finances of the War 1861–1865," pp. 12–13; Salmon P. Chase (SC) to Jay Cooke (JC), October 23, 1862, in Salmon P. Chase Papers: Microfilm Edition (University Publications, Bethesda, Md.), John Niven, ed. All correspondence between Chase and Cooke is from the Chase Papers.

18. HSP, Jay Cooke Manuscript Papers, JC to Henry David Cooke (HC), March 1, 1861; HSP, Eleutheros Cooke to JC, March 25, 1861. Cooke lost many of his financial assets in the Bank Panic of 1857. For Cooke and the Bank Panic, see Larson, *Jay Cooke*, pp. 77–85.

19. Oberholtzer, *Jay Cooke*, p. 134; Richardson, *Greatest Nation of the Earth*, pp. 31–64. SC to JC, September 4, 1861; for Cooke's methods and reports of progress, see JC to SC: September 6, 7, 10, 11, 1862, October 19, 1862; SC to JC, March 7, 1862; HSP, JC to HDC, March 4, 1862.

20. HSP, JC to HDC, March 4, 1862; JC to SC, March 6, 1862. For early examples of this advice, see JC to SC: December 27, 1861, January 18, 1862, March 6, 1862, March 22, 1862, April 11, 1862, June 28, 1862, July 2, 1862, August 7, 1862, October 14, 1862.

21. JC to SC, March 22, 1862; JC to SC, July 12, 1861. For the establishment of Cooke's Washington firm, see Larson, *Jay Cooke*, p. 113.

22. JC to SC, January 18, 1862; JC to SC, January 31, 1862.

23. For examples of Cooke's and Chase's early social relationship, see JC to SC: October 24, 1861, January 31, 1862, April 26, 1862, June 28, 1862, September 22, 1862, and SC to JC: November 21, 1861, December 16, 1861, December 24, 1861, October 24, 1862, December 20, 1862. For early financial transactions between the two men, see JC to SC: February 8, 1862, March 10, 1862, April 15, 1862, April 26, 1862, July 5, 1862, August 7, 1862, October 14, 1862, and SC to JC: February 7, 1862, March 7, 1862, April 16, 1862, May 3, 1862, May 31, 1862, June 2, 1863, June 17, 1862, August 8, 1862. For the quote see JC to SC, February 8, 1862.

24. HSP, HC to JC, June 12, 1862.

25. SC to JC, October 23, 1862; HSP, Cooke's circular to his agents and sub-agents, November 7, 1862. The U.S. Treasury and designated depositories would

also handle the loan. The $830 million seven-thirty loan consisted of short-term bonds redeemable before three years, in denominations not less than ten dollars, earning 7.3 percent interest. (Larson, *Jay Cooke,* pp. 116, 165.) The seven-thirty campaign was for the most part merely an elaboration of the five-twenty campaign; for that reason they will be discussed together, though significant differences will be noted.

26. SC to JC, October 23, 1862; JC to SC, October 25, 1862.

27. HSP, Jay Cooke Manuscript Papers, *Bunett, Drake and Co.'s Reporter and Register of Counterfeit Bank Notes* (Boston, 1864); Larson, *Jay Cooke,* pp. 123–126; Oberholtzer, *Jay Cooke,* p. 222; HSP, Undated Circular to 7–30 Agents; HSP, *Lane Express,* March 18, 1863; HSP, *New York Tribune,* March 21, 1865; HSP, *Philadelphia Inquirer,* March 24, 1865.

28. JC to SC, November 12, 1862; JC to SC, December 8, 1862; JC to SC, September 18, 1863; HSP, Albert Van Couss to JC, February 11, 1865; HSP, Isaac H. Steeves to JC, February 11, 1865; HSP, Julian Brewer to JC, February 12, 1865; HSP, HC to JC, September 14, 1863; Larsen, pp. 123–126, 166–168; Oberholtzer, *Jay Cooke,* p. 82; HSP—Scrapbook, Circular Letter to Agents, n.d.; HSP, Postmaster Gen. Alex W. Randall to JC, n.d.; Extracts from agents' letters in JC to SC, November 12, 1862.

29. Larson, *Jay Cooke,* pp. 125–126; Thomas C. Cochran, *Frontiers of Change: Early Industrialism in America* (New York, 1981), p. 105; John F. Stover, "Railroads," in Eric Foner and John A. Garraty, *The Reader's Companion to American History* (Boston, 1991), p. 907.

30. Larson, *Jay Cooke,* p. 127; HSP—scrapbook, Circular Letter to Agents, July 1, 1863; HSP—scrapbook, Circular letter to Seven Thirty Agents, n.d.

31. HSP, Harrington, "Finances of the War," p. 13; HSP, Isaac H. Stevens to JC, February 11, 1865; JC to SC, October 25, 1862. Cooke also used the newspapers to set forth Chase's national policies. As he explained in his memoir, with "a vast number of agents traveling through the country . . . expending vast sums with the newspaper of the country for advertizements, We felt that we had a right to claim their columns in [which] to set forth the merits of the [National Banking] system," Cooke Memoir, p. 87.

32. HSP, HC to JC, September 11, 1863; HSP, HC to JC, October 29, 1863; Harrington, "Finances of the War," p. 13; HSP, John Wills to JC, February 15, 1863.

33. HSP, Fisk and Hatch to JC, August 18, 1863; Oberholtzer, *Jay Cooke,* pp. 581–582. See also SC to JC, September 4, 1863; JC to SC, September 7, 1863; HSP, Fisk and Hatch to JC, August 15, 1863.

34. HSP, Jay Cooke Scrapbook contains numerous clippings listing the day's subscribers or the daily totals by region.

35. HSP, Paul Jagode and F. L. Loes to JC, October 31, 1863.

36. JC to SC, April 22, 1864; HSP, JC to HC, March 4, 1862.

37. C. B. Macpherson, *The Political Theory of Possessive Individualism: Hobbes to Locke* (Oxford, 1962), p. 3.

38. Joyce Appleby, *Liberalism and Republicanism in the Historical Imagination* (Cambridge, 1992), p. 42; Foner, *Tom Paine,* p. 153.

39. Smith, cited in Foner, *Tom Paine,* p. 153.

40. HSP, unlabeled clipping, May 7, 1863; *Christian Secretary,* Hartford, November 7, 1862; see also HSP, seven-thirty circular, "Interesting Questions and Answers Relative to the 7-30 U.S. Loan."

41. JC to SC, September 10, 1861; JC to SC, September 7, 1861.

42. HSP, "The Best Way to Put Money Out at Interest," Circular. In another ad, Cooke described the advantages of compounded interest over the hoarding of gold. HSP, *Danville Democrat,* April 24, 1863.

43. JC to SC, October 25, 1863.

44. HSP, *Fitzgerald City Stern,* April 18, 1863; HSP, *Burlington Sentinel,* April 29, 1865 (this appeared widely); HSP, "Supplement to Imlay and Bucknell's Bank Note Reporter," December 5, 1862; HSP, *Weekly Tribune* (Middletown, Pa.), April 8, 1863.

45. HSP, *Delaware Gazette,* April 17, 1863; HSP, *Delaware County America and Media Advertiser,* Media, Pa., February 22, 1865; Seven-Thirty Poster advertising night agencies in Oberholtzer, *Jay Cooke,* p. 585.

46. HSP, *Christian Secretary,* Hartford, February 15, 1864; Seven-Thirty Poster in Oberholtzer, *Jay Cooke,* p. 585.

47. HSP, *Union County Herald,* March 4, 1865.

48. HSP, *Buffalo Express,* February 13, 1865; HSP, *Galena Gazette,* February 15, 1865. See also HSP, *Delaware County America and Media Advertiser,* Media, Pa., February 22, 1865.

49. HSP, *City Item,* February 11, 1865; HSP, *Phoenix,* February 18, 1865; HSP, *Fitzgerald City Stern,* April 18, 1863; Circular, "The Best Way to Put Out Money at Interest," cited in Oberholtzer, *Jay Cooke,* p. 245. See also *Hollidaysburg Register,* March 25, 1863, cited in Oberholtzer, *Jay Cooke,* p. 247.

50. HSP, *Boston Traveler,* February 7, 1865.

51. HSP, *Eastern Express,* May 13, 1863; HSP, *Allentown Democrat,* April 24, 1863.

52. HSP, Unlabeled clipping, May 7, 1863; HSP, *Republican,* March 14, 1865.

53. HSP, *Fitzgerald City Stern,* April 18, 1863; HSP, *Fitzgerald City Stern,* n.d.

54. Oberholtzer, *Jay Cooke,* p. 253; for Ohio quote see HSP, *Philadelphia Inquirer,* April 8, 1863.

55. JC to SC, December 8, 1862; Oberholtzer, *Jay Cooke,* p. 253; Larson, *Jay Cooke,* pp. 145–148; HSP, Five-Twenty circular, n.d. For supply problems, see: JC to SC April 23, 1863; HSP, JC to HC, May 28, 1863; HSP, HC to JC, April 14, 1863; Oberholtzer, *Jay Cooke,* p. 577.

56. HSP, *Philadelphia Press,* April 28, 1863; HSP, *New York Tribune,* March 21, 1865; HSP, Circular, n.d.; W. T. Page to JC, April 28, 1863, cited in Oberholtzer, *Jay Cooke,* p. 250. An unlabeled clipping in the Cooke Scrapbook broke down the sales for May 15, 1863, as follows: New York and New Jersey: 959,000/ Boston: 440,000/ Rhode Island: 100,000/ Pennsylvania: 61,000/ Washington, D.C.:

33,000/ Baltimore: 23,000/ Kentucky: 27,000/ Missouri: 9,000/ Indiana and Illinois: 17,000.

57. JC to SC, November 17, 1863; Larson, *Jay Cooke,* p. 167; *New York Tribune,* n.d., in Oberholtzer, *Jay Cooke,* pp. 585–587; "Who Are the Bondholders?" *The Nation,* February 6, 1868; Undated manuscript containing excerpts from letters, cited in Larson, *Jay Cooke,* p. 174.

58. The idea of the nation as a perceived source of economic well-being is discussed in Kohn, *The Idea of Nationalism,* p. 17. The role of self-interest in the creation of a patriotic nationalism is discussed in Potter, *The South and the Sectional Conflict,* pp. 54–56; and in Curti, *Roots of American Loyalty,* pp. 92–121. Both Peter Parish, *The American Civil War* (New York, 1975), pp. 359–360; and Paludan, *"A People's Contest,"* pp. 115–117, mention Cooke's campaign as helping link the interests of individual citizens with that of the nation.

59. For the economic nationalism of Carey and Webster, see Curti, *Roots of American Loyalty,* pp. 109–112.

60. HSP, S. Davis to JC, June 3, 1863; HSP, *Lane Express,* March 18, 1865; HSP, *Philadelphia Press,* April 31, 1863. See also Paludan, *"A People's Contest,"* p. 117. For an argument that tax and banking legislation also worked to this end, see Richardson, *The Greatest Nation of the Earth,* pp. 66–138, 255.

61. Larson, *Jay Cooke,* pp. 151, 161; Blue, *Salmon P. Chase,* p. 155; McPherson, *Battle Cry of Freedom,* p. 443; *Congressional Globe,* March 11, 1864, pp. 1046–1047.

62. Cooke established that he saw the potential profits inherent in this practice early on; see JC to SC, September 7, 1861, and JC to SC March 6, 1862.

63. JC to SC, September 7, 1861; SC to JC, September 10, 1861; SC to JC, March 22, 1862, SC to JC, April 26, 1862 (two letters, both written that day). Cooke used the money from the three-year bonds to redeem certificates, which he apparently could not profitably redeem on the terms proposed by Chase. Chase suggested that if he was informed of such situations in the future, he would send Cooke separate sums to carry on this redemption.

64. HSP, HC to JC, May 13, 1862; HSP, HC to JC, November 12, 1862; HSP, HC to JC, December 22, 1862. Unmoved, the Philadelphia banker continued to allow the proceeds of the bond drives to sit in his own account as well as those of his agents. The latter practice was particularly galling to Henry, who feared that the agents would lend on stock margins and generate a loss. "I would rather forego the profits arising from the interest in the balances in hands of agents, than to run the risk you are running," he wrote. (HDC to JC, May 26, 1863.) Chase chastised Cooke for many other reasons, including sloppy accounting and failing to accept financial responsibility for the acts of his agents. See SC to JC, April 23, 1862; SC to JC July 29, 1863.

65. SC to JC, November 13, 1862; SC to JC, April 26, 1862; HSP, HC to JC, November 12, 1862.

66. *Congressional Globe,* December 22, 1862, p. 167; HSP, HC to JC, June 1, 1863; *New York World,* May 20, 1863, in Oberholtzer, *Jay Cooke,* p. 260; *Congressional Globe,* March 11, 1864, p. 1,046.

67. HSP, HC to JC, May 14, 1863; SC to JC, December 23, 1862; SC to JC, June 1, 1863; HSP, HC to JC, June 24, 1863; HSP, HC to JC, June 29, 1863.

68. Larson, *Jay Cooke*, pp. 161–165, 173; Oberholtzer, *Jay Cooke*, pp. 560–562.

69. Josephson, *The Robber Barons*, p. 57; Larson, *Jay Cooke*, pp. 399–415.

70. Cooke Memoir, p. 75.

71. HSP, Unlabeled clipping, May 7, 1863.

3. "From Democracy to Loyalty"

1. For quotes see George W. Julian, "The Rebellion—The Mistakes of the Past—The Duty of the Present," Speech Before the House of Representatives, February 18, 1863, *Speeches on Political Questions* (New York, 1872), pp. 194–196; Clement L. Vallandigham, "Loyalty," *Speeches, Arguments, Addresses, and Letters of Clement L. Vallandigham* (New York, 1864), p. 558.

2. Baker, *Affairs of Party*, p. 22; Jabez Hammond, *History of Political Parties in the State of New York*, vol. 2 (Syracuse, 1852), p. 53.

3. Julian, *Speeches*, p. 195.

4. Clement Vallandigham, "The Great Civil War in America," *Speeches*, pp. 418–454; Klement, *The Limits of Dissent*, p. 125.

5. Oliver P. Morton, "Message to the General Assembly, April 25, 1861," in William M. French, ed., *Life, Speeches, State Papers and Public Services of Governor Oliver P. Morton* (Indianapolis, n.d.), p. 150. On the Union Party, see William A. Dunning, "The Second Birth of the Republican Party," *American Historical Review* 16 (1910–1911): 56–63; Dunning takes Union Party founders completely at their word, claiming that with the founding of the Union Party, the Republican Party effectively disappeared. Gary Lee Cardwell, "The Rise of the Stalwarts and the Transformation of Illinois Republican Politics, 1860–1880" (Ph.D. dissertation, University of Virginia, 1976), pp. 37–90, argues that in Illinois, the Union Party was "simply the most auspicious beginning of a more gradual transformation" toward a conservative Republicanism. Michael F. Holt, "Abraham Lincoln and the Politics of Union," *Political Parties and American Political Development: From the Age of Jackson to the Age of Lincoln* (Baton Rouge, 1992), pp. 322–353. Holt proposes that the Union Party was the project of Abraham Lincoln but acknowledges the absence of a "smoking gun."

6. Silbey, *Respectable Minority;* Baker, *Affairs of Party;* Paludan, *"A People's Contest";* Cincinnati Daily Gazette, April 3, 1863.

7. Alexis de Tocqueville, *Democracy in America*, vol. 1 (New York, 1961), p. 293.

8. *Indianapolis Daily Journal*, June 13, 1862.

9. Watson, *Liberty and Power*, pp. 233–234; Joel Silbey, *The American Political Nation, 1838–1893* (Stanford, 1991), pp. 33–45; Robert H. Wiebe, *Self-Rule: A Cultural History of American Democracy* (Chicago, 1995), pp. 66–68; Ronald P. Formisano, *The Transformation of Political Culture: Massachusetts*

Parties, 1790s–1840s (New York, 1983), pp. 311–312; William E. Gienapp, *The Origins of the Republican Party, 1852–1856* (New York, 1987), p. 6.

10. Harry L. Watson, *Jacksonian Politics and Community Conflict: The Emergence of the Second Party System in Cumberland County North Carolina* (Baton Rouge, 1981), pp. 151–197, 167, 196; Zelinsky, *Nation Into State*, pp. 77–78; Weibe, *Self-Rule*, p. 72.

11. For the political culture of the Democrats, see Meyers, *The Jacksonian Persuasion;* Baker, *Affairs of Party.* For Whig culture and ideology, see Howe, *Political Culture of the American Whigs;* and Merrill D. Peterson, *The Great Triumvirate: Webster, Clay, and Calhoun* (New York, 1987), pp. 68–84. For the political culture of Republicans, see Foner, *Free Soil, Free Labor, Free Men.*

12. Silbey, *American Political Nation,* p. 161; Greeley, cited in Howe, *Political Culture of the American Whigs,* p. 35; Democrats cited in Silbey, *American Political Nation,* p. 94.

13. Michael Wallace, "Changing Concepts of Party in the United States: New York in 1815–1828," *American Historical Review* 74 (December 1968): 471–474; Richard Hofstadter, *The Idea of a Party System: The Rise of Legitimate Opposition in the United States, 1780–1840* (Berkeley, 1969), pp. 12–13; Ronald P. Formisano, *The Birth of Mass Political Parties: Michigan, 1827–1861* (Princeton, 1971), p. 77; Silbey, *American Political Nation,* p. 126.

As the newer, less established party, Whigs occasionally employed antipartyism in their attempts to undermine the devotion of Democratic Party followers. For similar reasons, Republicans followed suit. See Watson, *Jacksonian Politics,* pp. 203–204; Silbey, *American Political Nation,* pp. 90–91, 126. Jean Baker describes three "images" of party co-existing at midcentury, characterized by the work of George Bancroft, Martin Van Buren, and Samuel Cox. See Baker, *Affairs of Party,* pp. 108–140.

14. Hammond, *History of Political Parties,* p. 53.

15. *Indianapolis Daily Journal,* April 16, 1861; Douglas, cited in McPherson, *Battle Cry of Freedom,* p. 274; Douglas, cited in George H. Porter, *Ohio Politics During the Civil War Period* (New York, 1911), p. 87.

16. *Chicago Tribune,* January 29, 1861, through March 25, 1862; Klement, *Copperheads,* p. 27; Kenneth Stampp, *Indiana Politics During the Civil War* (Bloomington, 1949), pp. 176–180.

17. William B. Hesseltine, *Lincoln and the War Governors* (New York, 1955), pp. 35–46; Foner, *Free Soil, Free Labor, Free Men,* pp. 107–109; Klement, *Copperheads,* p. 14; Stampp, *Indiana Politics,* pp. 1–7. Economic struggles also contributed to the highly charged nature of midwestern politics. While all three states at midcentury were mostly agricultural, the market revolution had made inroads into the economy and society of each state. As was the case in much of the country, politics prior to the breakdown of the second party system often focused on the conflict between agrarian and industrial ways of life. This conflict assumed an unusually explicit form within these states. Moreover, though the issues that informed the second party system were overshadowed by questions of slavery

and Union in the years preceding the war, such economic issues as the tariff and taxes continued to be potent in Illinois, Indiana, and Ohio, particularly for Democratic spokesmen for midwestern sectionalism.

18. Klement, *Copperheads,* pp. 3–5.

19. *Chicago Tribune,* January 7, 1862, through March 25, 1862; Charles A. Church, *The History of the Republican Party in Illinois 1854–1912* (Rockford, 1912), pp. 86–88; Robert P. Howard, *A History of the Prairie State* (Grand Rapids, 1972), pp. 305–307. Klement, *Copperheads,* pp. 27, 142–145. Quote is from *Chicago Tribune,* January 29, 1862.

20. Howard, *History of the Prairie State,* pp. 310–312; Church, *History of the Republican Party,* pp. 89–92; Klement, *Copperheads,* pp. 58–65.

21. Hesseltine, *Lincoln and the War Governors,* p. 240; Stampp, *Indiana Politics,* pp. 156–185.

22. Porter, *Ohio Politics,* pp. 73–199; Klement, *Limits of Dissent,* pp. 229–256.

23. Foner, *Free Soil, Free Labor, Free Men,* p. 107; Sidney David Brummer, *Political History of New York State During the Period of the Civil War* (New York, 1967), pp. 17–32; Iver Bernstein, *The New York City Draft Riots: Their Significance for American Society and Politics in the Age of the Civil War* (New York, 1990), pp. 8–10, 126–127.

24. Bernstein, *New York City Draft Riots,* pp. 9–10; Sven Beckert, "The Making of New York City's Bourgeoisie, 1850–1886" (Ph.D. dissertation, Columbia University, 1995), p. 31; McPherson, *Battle Cry of Freedom,* p. 609.

25. Brummer, *Political History of New York State,* pp. 152–154, 179–200.

26. Hesseltine, *Lincoln and the War Governors,* pp. 281–282; Brummer, *Political History of New York State,* pp. 255–256, 261–262; Seymour, in Charles Z. Lincoln, ed., *Messages from the Governors* (Albany, 1909), pp. 445–483, esp. pp. 462, 466.

27. Brummer, *Political History of New York State,* pp. 265–271.

28. Cardwell, "The Rise of the Stalwarts," pp. 2–3; Stampp, *Indiana Politics,* p. 4; Porter, *Ohio Politics,* pp. 16–17. For the challenges faced by the Democratic Party during the war, see Silbey, *Respectable Minority.*

In Illinois, Democratic control was less secure than it appeared: Democrats controlled only 1 percent more of the electorate than did the Whigs in the elections of 1848 and 1852. In Indiana, except for 1836 and 1840, when Harrison was the Whig candidate, Democrats carried Indiana in every presidential election until 1860. See Cardwell, "The Rise of the Stalwarts"; and Stampp, *Indiana Politics.*

It is true that sectionalism, while a cornerstone of midwestern politics, did not readily translate into partisan politics. But during the war, the Republican Party was effectively an instrument of nationalization. In the Midwest, this left Democrats to argue that the war was producing a Whig state dedicated to the interests of New England intellectual, business, and industrial leaders. This appeal was more common early in the war. For the sectional nature of midwestern wartime politics, see Stampp, *Indiana Politics;* and Klement, *Copperheads.*

29. Hesseltine, *Lincoln and the War Governors,* p. 74; Stephen L. Hanson, *The Making of the Third Party System, Voters and Parties in Illinois, 1850–1876* (Ann Arbor, 1980), pp. 89; 140–141; William E. Gienapp, "Politics Seem to Enter into Everything," Stephen E. Maizlish and John J. Kushma, eds., *Essays on American Antebellum Politics, 1840–1860* (College Station, 1982), pp. 47–49.

30. Foner, *Free Soil, Free Labor, Free Men,* pp. 103–115; Trefousse, *Radical Republicans,* pp. 5–20.

31. Foner, *Free Soil, Free Labor, Free Men,* pp. 103–148; Trefousse, *Radical Republicans,* pp. 168–170; Julian, *Speeches,* pp. 196, 195.

32. Wade, *Congressional Globe,* 37th Congress, 2nd Session, p. 1737; Sister Mary Karl George, R.S.M., *Zachariah Chandler: A Political Biography* (East Lansing, 1969), p. 95.

33. William Whatley Pierson, "The Committee on the Conduct of the Civil War," *American Historical Review* 23 (April 1918): 550–576; Williams, *Lincoln and the Radicals* (Madison, 1960); Hans L. Trefousse, "The Joint Committee on the Conduct of the War: A Reassessment," *Civil War History* 10 (1964): 5–19; *New York Tribune,* May 1, 1862; April 6, 1863.

The newest study of the Joint Committee, Bruce Tap, *Over Lincoln's Shoulder: The Committee on the Conduct of the War* (Lawrence, 1998), argues that committee members were generally unqualified to intervene in military matters and that the committee had an "uneven" effect on the North's war effort.

34. T. Harry Williams, *Lincoln and His Generals* (New York, 1952), pp. 24–178; Williams, *Lincoln and the Radicals;* Trefousse, *The Radical Republicans,* pp. 168–202; *New York Tribune,* April 6, 1863; Chandler, cited in George, *Zachariah Chandler,* p. 101. See also Tap, *Over Lincoln's Shoulder,* pp. 101–166.

35. Cited in Porter, *Ohio Politics,* p. 180.

36. Holt, *Political Parties and American Political Development,* pp. 338–339; Hans L. Trefousse, "The Republican Party, 1854–1864," Arthur M. Schlesinger, Jr., ed., *History of U.S. Political Parties,* vol. 2 (New York, 1973), p. 1,168; Dunning, "Second Birth of the Republican Party," pp. 56–63.

37. Porter, *Ohio Politics,* p. 86; *Ohio State Journal,* August 13, 1861, cited in Porter, *Ohio Politics,* p. 86.

38. Cardwell, "The Rise of the Stalwarts," pp. 42, 64–68, 89; Stampp, *Indiana Politics,* pp. 94–95, 133–134; Brummer, *Political History of New York State,* pp. 151–178, 218. Klement, *Copperheads,* p. 208. Though radicals in several states objected to the idea of a Union Party, in New York, where factionalism in the Republican Party was widespread, the decision to form a Union Party was more heatedly contested. See Brummer, *Political History of New York State,* pp. 191–194.

Cardwell says 11.5 percent of Republicans were "Egyptians" in 1860, compared to 13.1 percent in 1862 and 11.5 percent in 1860. The Union Party may have been more successful in states with significant Southern populations. In *The Civil War Party System: The Case of Massachusetts* (Chapel Hill, 1984), Dale Baum argues that the Union Party in Massachusetts was a "total failure" as a political tactic (pp. 70–71). It is difficult to determine much beyond this, as I could find no information on precisely how many Democrats voted for the Union Party.

39. Morton, quoted in *Indiana Indianapolis Daily State Sentinel*, September 5, 1862; George Dawson, Committee on Resolutions, quoted in *Albany Evening Journal*, July 16, 1862; *Cincinnati Daily Gazette*, July 15, 1863.

40. *Indianapolis Daily Journal*, June 18, 1862.

41. Stephen Douglas's call for unity was at the masthead of the *Indianapolis Daily Journal* through the summer and fall of 1861. *Cincinnati Daily Gazette*, October 11, 1862; *Indianapolis Daily Journal*, August 27, 1861; *New York Tribune*, April 29, 1863; Elbert B. Smith, *Francis Preston Blair* (New York, 1980), p. 222; *Cincinnati Daily Gazette*, September 18, 1863; September 8, 1863; July 11, 1863; and April 6, 1863.

As Smith points out, "Enlisting Andrew Jackson into the Republican party of Charles Francis Adams, Sumner" was "a remarkable feat of grave danger to the Democratic party, and only Blair could have done it" (p. 222).

42. Hughes, cited in *Indianapolis Daily Journal*, June 13, 1862; *Cincinnati Daily Gazette*, October 8, 1863; *Albany Evening Journal*, January 4, 1864.

43. *Indianapolis Daily Journal*, June 19, 1862, June 21, 1862.

44. Morton, in *Brevier Legislative Reports*, pp. 12–15; *Indianapolis Daily Journal*, June 13, 1862. Morton's plea to rise above "these paltry considerations" was issued during a legislative session where relief for farmers was hotly debated.

45. *New York Tribune*, April 10, 1861; *Cincinnati Daily Gazette*, October 11, 1862.

46. *Cincinnati Daily Gazette*, July 13, 1863; *Indianapolis Daily Journal*, May 7, 1862; *Cincinnati Daily Gazette*, September 15, 1863, July 18, 1863; *Indianapolis Daily Journal*, May 2, 1862.

47. *Cincinnati Daily Gazette*, April 7, 1863; *Indianapolis Daily Journal*, May 12, 1862; "Minute Book, Board of Publication of the Union League of Philadelphia," September 10, 13, 1863, cited in Maxwell Whiteman, *Gentlemen in Crisis: The First Century of the Union League of Philadelphia, 1862–1962* (Philadelphia, 1975), p. 80.

48. Frank Klement, *Limits of Dissent*, p. 96; *Cincinnati Daily Gazette*, October 3, 1863.

49. *Cincinnati Daily Gazette*, April 4, 1863, March 29, 1861, April 6, 1863.

50. According to Frank Klement (*Copperheads*, pp. 138–139), the first exposé of the Knights of the Golden Circle for Republican purposes stemmed from a partisan conflict in Marion, Ohio.

51. Frank Klement has written at length about the secret societies alleged to exist during the Civil War. These various publications include *The Copperheads in the Middle West; Dark Lanterns: Secret Political Societies, Conspiracies, and Treason Trials in the Civil War* (Baton Rouge, 1984); "Carrington

and the Golden Circle Legend in Indiana during the Civil War," *Indiana Magazine of History* 61 (1965): 31–52; and "Copperhead Secret Societies in Illinois During the Civil War," *Journal of the Illinois State Historical Society* 48 (1955): 152–180.

52. Klement, "Carrington," p. 33.

53. For the Sons of Liberty and the Order of the American Knights, see Klement, *Copperheads*, pp. 165–168, and Klement, *Dark Lanterns*, pp. 64–135. For Republican investigations and the limited evidence they procured, see, for example, Klement, *Copperheads*, pp. 175–187; and "Carrington," pp. 37, 40.

54. *Chicago Tribune*, August 15, 1863, June 5, 1862; *Report of the Judge Advocate General, on the 'Order of the American Knights', or 'Sons of Liberty'* ... *Washington, 1864*, in Frank Freidel, ed., *Union Pamphlets of the Civil War, 1861–1865*, vol. 2 (Cambridge,1967), p. 1047; U.S. National Union Club, *KGC: An Authentic Exposition of the Origins, Objects, and Secret Work of the Organization Known as the Knights of the Golden Circle* (Louisville, 1862), pp. 10–11. Holt states in his report that membership may more realistically be in the five hundred thousand range, with a state-by-state breakdown as follows: Indiana, 75–125,000; Illinois, 100–140,000; Ohio, 80–108,000; Kentucky, 40–70,000; Missouri, 20–40,000; Michigan and New York, 20,000.

55. *Chicago Tribune*, February 11, 1862; *KGC: An Authentic Exposition*, pp. 10–11.

56. McPherson, *Battle Cry of Freedom*, p. 596; *Buckeye State*, October 20, 1862, cited in Klement, *Limits of Dissent*, p. 113; Pamphlet, Klement, *Limits of Dissent*, pp. 110, 113; *Cincinnati Daily Gazette*, April 6, 1863.

57. Klement, *Limits of Dissent*, pp. 152–256.

58. Klement, *Limits of Dissent*, p. 272; Halstead cited in Klement, *Limits of Dissent*, p. 276; Greely in Klement, *Limits of Dissent*, p. 276. On enemies, see Murray Edelman, *Constructing the Political Spectacle* (Chicago, 1988), chap. 4.

59. William O. Stoddard, cited in Guy Gibson, "Lincoln's League," p. 21.

60. Silvestro, "None But Patriots," p. 14.

61. Silvestro, "None But Patriots," pp. 93–95.

62. Silvestro, "None But Patriots," pp. 27–30; "Proceedings," quoted in Silvestro, "None But Patriots," p. 27.

63. Silvestro, "None But Patriots," pp. 30–72, 96–97; Gibson, "Lincoln's League," p. 106. According to Gibson, a breakdown of delegates by state went as follows: Pennsylvania, 26; Ohio, 23; Illinois, 16; Indiana, 13; Iowa, 12; Michigan, 11; Massachusetts, 10; Wisconsin, 10; Maryland, 9; New York, 7; Washington, D.C., 7; Connecticut, 6; Vermont, 5; Minnesota, 4; Rhode Island, 4; Kansas, 3; Tennessee, 3; New Hampshire, 2.

64. Mark C. Carnes, *Secret Ritual and Manhood in Victorian America* (New Haven, 1989).

65. Silvestro, "None But Patriots," pp. 162–163; Gibson, "Lincoln's League," pp. 19–20. Quote is Stoddard, cited in Gibson, p. 19.

66. Silvestro, "None But Patriots," pp. 7, 102, 122–216.

67. See, for example, Silvestro, "None But Patriots," p. 101.

68. *Indianapolis Daily State Sentinel*, June 5, 1861; *Illinois State Register*, August 28, 1862; *Indianapolis Daily State Sentinel*, August 5, 1862, August 27, 1862. See also *Albany Argus*, August 8, 1861.

69. *New York World*, September 23, 1862.

70. *Indianapolis Daily State Sentinel*, July 30, 1862.

71. *New York World*, September 26, 1862.

72. *Illinois State Register*, October 14, 1862.

73. *Indianapolis Daily State Sentinel*, August 19, 1862; *Albany Atlas and Argus*, April 16, 1863.

74. *Indianapolis Daily State Sentinel*, August 10, 1861; July 20, 1861.

75. Thomas Paine, "African Slavery in America," Michael Foot and Isaac Kramnick, eds., *The Thomas Paine Reader* (New York, 1987), pp. 54–56; Foner, *Tom Paine*, p. 127.

76. *Indianapolis Daily State Sentinel*, July 13, 1861; *Albany Atlas and Argus*, April 16, 1863.

77. *Indianapolis Daily State Sentinel*, July 17, 1862; Klement, *Limits of Dissent*, p. 247; *Atlas and Argus*, February 3, 1865, in Silbey, *Respectable Minority*, p. 83. See also Silbey, *Respectable Minority*, pp. 81–84.

78. *Indianapolis Daily State Sentinel*, July 17, 1862; *New York World*, November 4, 1862; Silbey, *Respectable Minority*, p. 81; Bernstein, *New York City Draft Riots*, p. 78.

79. "The Lincoln Catechism, Wherein the Eccentricities and Beauties of Despotism Are Fully Set Forth: A Guide to the Presidential Election of 1864," Frank Freidel, ed., *Union Pamphlets of the Civil War 1861–1865* (Cambridge, 1967), pp. 981–1015; Vallandigham, *Speeches*, p. 414. See also *New York World*, November 4, 1862.

80. Bernstein, *New York City Draft Riots*, pp. 9–10; Beckert, "The Making of New York City's Bourgeoisie," p. 31; McPherson, *Battle Cry of Freedom*, p. 609; Brummer, *Political History of New York State*, pp. 27–30; Seymour, cited in McPherson, *Battle Cry of Freedom*, p. 609.

81. McPherson, *Battle Cry of Freedom*, pp. 600–602.

82. Bernstein, *New York City Draft Riots*, pp. 12–14.

83. Bernstein, *New York City Draft Riots*, pp. 17–42.

84. *Albany Evening Journal*, July 17, 1863; September 10, 1863, October 9, 1863; *New York Tribune*, July 17, 1863, October 10, 1863. See also Brummer, *Political History of New York State*, pp. 321–323.

Democratic papers, on the other hand, blamed Republicans for the riots: the *New York World* asked if "the insensate men at Washington" might at last realize that "Defiance of Law in the rulers breeds Defiance of Law in the people." *New York World*, July 14, 1863.

85. McPherson, *Battle Cry of Freedom*, p. 687.

86. Philip Shaw Paludan, *The Presidency of Abraham Lincoln* (Lawrence, 1994), p. 283.

87. Klement, *Copperheads,* pp. 170–241; *Report of the Judge Advocate General,* in Freidel, *Union Pamphlets,* pp. 200–212; William O. Stoddard, cited in Gibson, "Lincoln's League," p. 21.

88. McPherson, *Battle Cry of Freedom,* pp. 760–806; Paludan, *Presidency of Abraham Lincoln,* pp. 289–290.

4. "A Profound National Devotion"

1. Adams, *Edward Everett Hale,* p. 1; Holloway, *Edward Everett Hale,* pp. 11–18, 50–51.

2. Holloway, *Edward Everett Hale,* pp. 11–18, 50–51.

3. According to Frank Klement, the elite Union Leagues had "more spontaneity and less calculation, less partisanship and more social emphasis." *Dark Lanterns,* p. 42. Charles Eliot Norton to G. W. Curtis, February 26, 1863, in *Letters of Charles Eliot Norton,* Sara Norton and M. A. DeWolfe Howe, eds. (Boston, 1913); Will Irwin, Earl Chapin May, and Joseph Hotchkiss, *A History of the Union League Club of New York City* (New York, 1952), p. 19.

4. Robert Dahl, *Who Governs? Democracy and Power in an American City* (New Haven, 1961); Sam Bass Warner, *The Private City: Philadelphia in Three Periods of Its Growth* (Philadelphia, 1968); Frederic Cople Jahar, *The Urban Establishment: Upper Strata in Boston, New York, Charleston, Chicago, and Los Angeles* (Urbana, 1982); and Amy Bridges, *A City in the Republic: Antebellum New York and the Origins of Machine Politics* (New York, 1984), present different versions of this phenomenon. On gentry rule, see Dahl, *Who Governs?* pp. 11–24; Warner, *The Private City,* pp. 3–21; Jahar, *Urban Establishment,* pp. 1–13; Bridges, *A City in the Republic,* pp. 70–73.

5. Alexis de Tocqueville writes of the abandonment by the wealthy of public positions in *Democracy in America,* vol. 1 (New York, 1945), pp. 186–187. See also Dahl, *Who Governs?* pp. 16–24; Warner, *The Private City,* pp. 85–86; Bridges, *A City in the Republic,* pp. 126–128.

6. Bridges, *A City in the Republic,* pp. 126–145; for quotes, see pp. 131, 134.

7. William Dusinberre, *Civil War Issues in Philadelphia, 1856–1865* (Philadelphia, 1965), pp. 19–23; J. Robert Mendte, *The Union League of Philadelphia: 125 Years* (Devon, 1987), p. 39; Bernstein, *New York City Draft Riots,* p. 149; Oscar Handlin, *Boston's Immigrants* (Cambridge, 1959), pp. 76, 186–206; Howard Mumford Jones, "Boston in the Civil War," in *The Many Voices of Boston: A Historical Anthology, 1630–1975,* ed. Howard Mumford Jones and Bessie Zaban Jones (Boston, 1975), pp. 268–269.

8. Whiteman, *Gentlemen in Crisis,* pp. 5–6; Dusinberre, *Civil War Issues,* p. 113; Beckert, "The Making of New York City's Bourgeoisie," pp. 119–204; Bernstein, *New York City Draft Riots,* pp. 125–161; Jahar, *Urban Establishment,* pp. 55–56; Daniel Walker Howe, *The Unitarian Conscience: Harvard Moral Philosophy, 1805–1861* (Cambridge, 1970), p. 295.

9. Whiteman, *Gentlemen in Crisis*, pp. 15–16; George Parsons Lathrop, *History of the Union League of Philadelphia, From Its Origin and Foundation to the Year 1882* (Philadelphia, 1884), pp. 26–27; Gibson, "Lincoln's League," p. 79.

10. Whiteman, *Gentlemen in Crisis*, pp. 5–6; Kenneth M. Stampp, *And The War Came: The North and the Secession Crisis* (Baton Rouge, 1950), pp. 123–125; Foner, *Free Soil, Free Labor, Free Men*, pp. 186–187.

11. *Philadelphian North American and United States Gazette*, April 9, 1861; April 11, 1861; April 16, 1861.

12. Lathrop, *History of the Union League of Philadelphia*, pp. 15–18; Whiteman, *Gentlemen in Crisis*, p. 14; George Boker, cited in Lathrop, *History of the Union League of Philadelphia*, p. 27; Union League of Philadelphia, *Chronicle of the Union League of Philadelphia, 1862–1902* (Philadelphia, 1902), pp. 32–33.

13. *Address by the Union League of Philadelphia to Citizens of Pennsylvania, in favor of the Re-Election of Abraham Lincoln* (Philadelphia: October, 1864), Manuscript Papers Union League of Philadelphia (MSS, ULP); "Articles of Association of the Union Club," cited in *Chronicle of the Union League of Philadelphia*, pp. 52–53; M. A. DeWolfe-Howe to George Boker, February 17, 1863, MSS ULP; Original draft of "Articles of Association of the Union League of Philadelphia," MSS, ULP; Statement, "Union League Of Philadelphia," MSS, ULP.

14. George Boker, *First Annual Report of the Board of Directors of the Union League of Philadelphia* (Philadelphia, 1863), pp. 12–13; Whiteman, *Gentlemen in Crisis*, p. 28; Lathrop, *History of the Union League of Philadelphia*, pp. 28–31; Whiteman, *Gentlemen in Crisis*, p. 20. Shortly into the life of the Philadelphia Union Club, a motion was made to enlarge the club into a league, open to more than the original fifty-five members. The Philadelphia Union Club formed the nucleus of—and continued to exist as an autonomous unit within—what ultimately became the Union League of Philadelphia.

15. Beckert, "The Making of New York City's Bourgeoisie," pp. 166–167; Bernstein, *New York City Draft Riots*, pp. 132–148.

16. Beckert, "The Making of New York City's Bourgeoisie," pp. 119–204; Bernstein, *New York City Draft Riots*, pp. 148–161; Fredrickson, *Inner Civil War*, pp. 23–35, 98–112; Bellows, *Union League*, p. 6. See also Attie, *Patriotic Toil*, pp. 51–86. For conflicts between Belmont and Olmsted's circle prior to the war, see Roy Rosenzweig and Elizabeth Blackmar, *The Park and the People: A History of Central Park* (New York, 1992), pp. 143–145, 218, 184.

17. Frederick Law Olmsted to Oliver Wolcott Gibbs, November 5, 1862, in Jane Turner Censer, *The Papers of Frederick Law Olmsted*, vol. 4 (Baltimore, 1986).

18. FLO to OWG, November 5, 1862. C. Wright Mills argues the power of urban clubs both to socialize new members to the ways of the elite and to clarify class lines when they have become blurred. See Mills, *The Power Elite* (New York, 1956), pp. 47–70.

Olmsted's concern about young wealthy men with no clear place in American society was echoed in Hale's "The Man Without a Country." Hale's narrator was sympathetic to Nolan, in spite of the unpatriotic outburst which cost him his country, because Nolan had been raised in the West on a plantation where Spanish officers or French merchants were considered the finest company; he had been tutored by hired Englishmen and had spent his recreational time in Vera Cruz or in Texas. "In a word," said Hale, "to him United States was scarcely a reality." Hale, *The Man Without a Country*, p. 24.

19. FLO to OWG, November 5, 1862.

20. Strong, *Diary*, pp. 302–303, 307; Beckert, "The Making of New York City's Bourgeoisie," pp. 133–204; for N.Y. Chamber of Commerce quote, see Beckert, "The Making of New York City's Bourgeoisie," p. 161.

21. Bellows, *Union League*, pp. 6, 50; Strong, *Diary*, pp. 302–303, 307.

22. "Report of Executive Committee," Bellows, *Union League*, pp. 19–21; Strong, *Diary*, p. 307; Bellows, *Union League*, p. 53; Irwin, *History of the Union League Club*, pp. 27–28.

23. Strong, *Diary*, p. 319.

24. Daniel Walker Howe, *Unitarian Conscience*, pp. 140–141; Jahar, *Urban Establishment*, pp. 55–56.

25. S. Lothrop Thorndike, *A Brief Sketch of the History of the Union Club of Boston* (Boston, 1893), p. 6; Gibson, "Lincoln's League," pp. 79–81.

26. Thorndike, *A Brief Sketch*, p. 7; S. Lothrop Thorndike, *The Past Members of the Union Club of Boston* (Boston, 1893).

27. Oliver Wendell Holmes to John Murray Forbes, February 5, 1863, in Sarah Forbes Hughes, ed., *Reminiscences of John Murray Forbes* (Boston, 1902).

28. Edwin P. Whipple, cited in Lathrop, *History of the Union League of Philadelphia*, p. 42. Whiteman, *Gentlemen in Crisis*, p. 26, 66; Irwin, *History of the Union League Club*, p. 24; Thorndike, *Past Members;* Strong, *Diary*, p. 319.

29. Bellows, *Union League*, pp. 53–84; Lathrop, *History of the Union League Club of Philadelphia*, pp. 45–63, 70–81; *First Annual Report of the Board of Directors of the Union League*, pp. 3–9. For pamphlets, see below.

Alone among the elite Leagues, the Boston Club never moved much beyond its early function as a social club serving to unite the city's Unionist factions— its Cotton and Conscience Whigs, its manufacturers and its abolitionists. It did, however, sustain an alliance and share its leadership and membership with the New England Loyal Publication Society, discussed below.

30. Beckert, "The Making of New York City's Bourgeoisie," pp. 119–204.

31. Lathrop, *History of the Union League of Philadelphia*, pp. 75–81.

32. Irwin, *History of the Union League Club*, pp. 30–37; Bellows, *Union League*, pp. 56–57; Bernstein, *New York City Draft Riots*, pp. 65–68.

33. Irwin, *History of the Union League Club*, pp. 30–37; Bellows, *Union League*, pp. 56–57; Bernstein, *New York City Draft Riots*, pp. 65–68; *Address to the 20th Regiment, U.S. Colored Troops on the Occasion of the Presentation of a Stand of Colors By the Ladies, March 5, 1864*, in Bellows, *Union League*, p. 187.

34. Iver Bernstein makes this last point: "For conservatives, the message of the parade down Broadway was clear: entry into the upper reaches of loyal

'society' would now be predicated on willingness to embrace emancipation and attendant changes in the status of free black people." Bernstein, *New York City Draft Riots,* p. 67. The very act of welcoming blacks into the Union fold, however, was in part designed to define other prescriptions. The message of these parades for the working classes will be examined below.

35. Jahar, *Urban Establishment,* p. 43; Kermit Vanderbilt, *Charles Eliot Norton: Apostle of Culture in a Democracy* (Cambridge, Mass., 1959), p. 1; Charles Eliot Norton, *Considerations on Some Recent Social Theories* (Boston, 1853), cited in Vanderbilt, *Charles Eliot Norton,* pp. 44, 30; Strong, *Diary,* p. 272. See also Francis Lieber, *Miscellaneous Writings I,* 456–458, cited in Frank Friedel, *Francis Lieber: Nineteenth-Century Liberal* (Baton Rouge, 1947), p. 160. De Tocqueville writes of the elite's "hearty dislike of democratic institutions," *Democracy in America,* vol. 1, p. 187. See also Fredrickson, *Inner Civil War,* pp. 31–32.

36. Paludan, *"A People's Contest,"* p. 182; Arnold M. Shankman, *The Pennsylvania Antiwar Movement, 1861–1865* (Rutherford, 1980), p. 97.

37. Philip S. Foner, *History of the Labor Movement in the United States,* vol. 1 (New York, 1947), p. 339; David Montgomery, *Beyond Equality: Labor and the Radical Republicans, 1862–1872* (Urbana, 1981), pp. 96–97; Paludan, *"A People's Contest,"* p. 187; *Fincher's Trade Review,* June 20, 1863.

38. E. B. Ward to Henry C. Carey, December 26, 1862, in Edward Carey Gardiner Collection, Historical Society of Pennsylvania; JMF to William Pitt Fessenden, January 29, 1863, in Forbes, *Reminiscences;* Thomas C. Cochran, *Railroad Leaders 1845–1890: The Business Mind in Action* (New York, 1965), p. 180.

39. On the loyalty of labor, see Foner, *History of the Labor Movement,* pp. 331–337; and Montgomery, *Beyond Equality,* pp. 91–134.

40. *First Annual Report of the Board of Directors of the Union League of Philadelphia,* p. 6; *Minutes of the Union League of Philadelphia,* Feb. 17, 1863; Lathrop, *History of the Union League of Philadelphia,* p. 48; Whiteman, *Gentlemen in Crisis,* pp. 273–277.

41. Whiteman, *Gentlemen in Crisis,* p. 319; *Bylaws of the Board of Publication of the Union League of Philadelphia,* p. 2; *First Annual Report,* p. 6.

42. *Bylaws,* p. 3.

43. *Bylaws,* pp. 4–5; Whiteman, *Gentlemen in Crisis,* p. 33; Union League of Philadelphia, *Chronicle of the Union League of Philadelphia,* p. 106.

44. Whiteman, *Gentlemen in Crisis,* pp. 30–42; Clement Silvestro, "None But Patriots: The Union Leagues in the Civil War and Reconstruction" (Ph.D. dissertation, University of Wisconsin, 1959), p. 125; *First Annual Report,* p. 7.

45. Loyal Publication Society, *Report of Proceedings at the First Anniversary Meeting of the Loyal Publication Society* (N.Y.: The Society, 1864), pp. 8–21; Silvestro, "None But Patriots," p. 127; Freidel, *Lieber,* p. 346; Frank Freidel, "The Loyal Publication Society: A Pro-Union Propaganda Agency," *Mississippi Valley Historical Review* 17 (December 1939): 361, 359–363. See also Edith E. Ware, "Committees of Public Information 1863–1866," *Historical Outlook* 10 (Febru-

ary 1919): 65–66. As a result of the long gap between the discussions of a New York League and the formation of the league itself, the Loyal Publication Society actually predated the New York League. Both the New York and Boston Leagues appear to have been associated with, but were not necessarily direct products of, the Union Leagues.

46. Freidel, "The Loyal Publication Society," pp. 359–363; O. W. Smith to Samuel F. B. Morse, May 28, 1863, cited in Klement, *Dark Lanterns,* p. 56.

47. George Winston Smith, "Broadsides for Freedom: Civil War Propaganda in New England," *New England Quarterly* (September 1948): 292.

48. JMF to William Curtis Noyes, Sarah Forbes Hughes, ed., *Letters and Recollections of John Murray Forbes* (New York, 1981), pp. 324–327; New England Loyal Publication Society (NELPS) flyer in MSS, NELPS, Boston Public Library/ Rare Book Room; Charles Eliot Norton (CEN) to Lindsay Swift, Esq., n.d., MSS, NELPS; Silvestro, "None But Patriots," pp. 129–130; Smith, "Broadsides," p. 293–294. Because the Boston Union Club eschewed political activity, it was not *officially* associated with the New England Loyal Publication Society. But the NELPS became "a club within a club." Silvestro, "None But Patriots," p. 129.

49. *Dictionary of American Biography,* p. 507; Henry Greenleaf Pearson, *An American Railroad Builder: John Murray Forbes* (New York, 1911); JMF to CEN, March 18, 1863, MSS, NELPS. For a sampling of Forbes's input, see March 22, 1863; August 22, 1863; December 21, 1863; December 26, 1863; December 29, 1863; December 31, 1863; February 13, 1864; and June 17, 1864, all in MSS, NELPS.

50. Silvestro, "None But Patriots," p. 130; James B. Thayer to William E. Junior, Esq., MSS, NELPS, February 1, 1864.

In March of 1863, Secretary James Thayer began checking on the effectiveness of the broadsides: he sent out a questionnaire asking whether the recipient was printing the material and wished to continue receiving it. He asked if the editors had observed the material in other papers, and requested suggestions. This practice continued as long as the society functioned, though the questions changed: in January 1865, Thayer asked editors if the opinions carried in the broadsides were acceptable in their regions and inquired as to local views on black citizenship. Some responses were hostile: an editor from Warrenton, Missouri, stated that he never printed the broadsides, that he did not wish to continue receiving them, and for suggestions, offered "burn them." But on the whole, Thayer concluded that the broadsides were being used extensively: smaller Union Leagues wrote to say they had placed the broadsides in reading rooms, and Governor Morton of Indiana wrote to inform the society that he had set aside rooms for the storage of the broadsides NELPS questionnaires and responses in MSS, NELPS; Morton, Executive Department, State of Indiana to George Ward Nicholas, Esq., June 5, 1863 MSS NELPS.

51. Freidel, *Lieber,* p. 365; JMF to WCN, July 28, 1862, Hughes, *Letters and Recollections;* Union League of Philadelphia, *Chronicle of the Union League of Philadelphia,* p. 103.

Patriot Fires

52. NYLPS #11, "No Failure for the North"; Board of Publication of the Union
League of Philadelphia (BPULP) Pamphlet #4, MSS, ULP; and NYLPS #13,
"How a Free People Conduct a Long War"; BPULP #78, "The Nation's Success
and Gratitude"; BPULP #82, "The War For the Union, From Fort Sumter to
Atlanta." Quote is from BPULP #4.

53. NYLPS #9, "The Venom and the Antidote"; BPULP #50, "Counsel of a
Loyal Democrat." See also New England Loyal Publication Society (NELPS)
Clipping, March 13, 1863, MSS NELPS; NYLPS #4, "The Three Voices: Soldier, Farmer, and Poet, to the Copperhead"; NYLPS #5, "Voices From the Army";
and NYLPS #6, "Northern True Men and Southern Traitors."

54. BPULP #41, "The Nation's Sin and the Nation's Duty"; NYLPS #16, "No
Party Now, But All for Our Country"; JMF to WCN, August 12, 1862, in Hughes,
Letters and Recollections, p. 327; JMF to Samuel G. Ward, January 22, 1863, in
MSS, NELPS; NYLPS #63, "Letter on McClellan's Nomination"; NYLPS #65,
"Submissionists and Their Record"; NYLPS #66, "Coercion Completed, or Trea-
son Triumphant"; NYLPS #67, "Lincoln or McClellan"; BPULP #50, "A Few
Words for Honest Pennsylvania Democrats"; JMF to CEN, September 23, 1863,
in MSS, NELPS. See also NELPS #94, "Country Not Party"; NELPS #93, "The
Peace Democracy"; BPULP #90, "Address by the Union League Of Philadelphia
to Citizens of Pennsylvania, in Favor of the Re-election of Abraham Lincoln";
BPULP #13, "The Boot on the Other Leg, or Loyalty Before Part"; NELPS, October 1, 1863, "Spirit of True Democracy."

55. BPULP #12, "Our National Constitution: Its Adaptation to a State of War
or Insurrection"; BPULP #16, "The War Powers of the President and the Legislative Powers of Congress, in Relation to the Rebellion, Treason, and Slavery";
see also NYLPS #20, "Military Despotism! Suspension of the Habeas Corpus!
etc."; BPULP #33, "Decision of Judge Leavitt, of Ohio, in the Vallandigham
Habeas Corpus Case"; NYLPS #40, "The Conscription Act: A Series of Articles";
BPULP #30, "The Conscription"; NELPS, February 9, 1864, "The New Draft:
A Wise Measure"; BPULP #70, "Opinion of Judge Hare upon the Constitutionality of the Acts of Congress Declaring United States Notes Lawful Money and a
Legal Tender"; NELPS, October 15, 1864, "Commercial and Financial Strength
of the U.S."; NELPS, December 10, 1864, "How to Lessen the Burden of Taxation"; NYLPS #22, "Emancipation Is Peace"; NELPS, August 24, 1863, "A Few
of the Reasons for . . . a Black Army."

56. NELPS #47, "Letter from A Man of Business"; NELPS, January 28, 1863;
NELPS #80, "The Crisis and the Remedy"; NYLPS #80, "America For Free
Working Men"; NELPS #62, "Abolition—How It Will Affect the North"; NELPS
#95; NELPS, March 6, 1863, "The Question Fairly Stated"; NELPS #18, Sep-
tember 21, 1863. Quotes are from NELPS #47, "Letter from A Man of Business"; and NELPS #18, September 21, 1863.

57. NELPS #74, "Justice to the Blacks the Interest of the Nation"; NELPS
#150, December 29, 1863; NELPS, October 26, 1863; NYLPS #18, "Opinions
of the Early Presidents, and of the Fathers of the Republic, Upon Slavery, and

Upon Negroes as Men and Soldiers"; NYLPS #23, "Letter of Peter Cooper on Slave Emancipation"; BPULP #53, "Christianity and Emancipation, or the Teachings and the Influence of the Bible Against Slavery"; JMF to CEN, August 22, 1863, MSS, NELPS; NELPS, March 15, 1863, "Men of Color to Arms"; JMF to William Evans in Pearson, p. 109; JMF to WCN, August 12, 1862, in Hughes, *Letters and Recollections;* NELPS #156, January 16, 1864. Excerpts from Phillips's speeches appeared in NELPS, January 9, 1864; NELPS, February 18, 1864.

58. NYLPS #67, "Lincoln or McClellan: Appeal to the Germans in America"; BPULP #60, "The Irish Patriot—Daniel O'Connell's Legacy to Irish Americans." Many pamphlets were also printed in German; see NYLPS #19, "Einheit und Freiheit"; NYLPS #53, "How the War Commenced"; NYLPS #55, "Emancipated Slave and His Master"; NYLPS #59, "Lincoln or McClellan"; BPULP # 14, "The Loyalist's Ammunition."

59. NYLPS #45, "Finances and Resources of the United States"; see also NYLPS #48, "Resources of the United States"; NYLPS #54, "Our Burden and Our Strength"; BPULP # 37, "Debt and Resources of the United States"; BPULP #83, "The Commercial and Financial Strength of the United States"; BPULP #102, "The Commercial and Financial Strength of the United States brought up to the 1st of January, 1865"; JMF to CEN, March 22, 1863, in MSS, NELPS; NELPS #15; NELPS January 21, 1864; NELPS March 10, 1863; NELPS #91. See also WS Robinson to CEN, August 24, 1863, in MSS, NELPS.

60. JMF to CEN, March 22, 1863, MSS, NELPS; JMF to CEN, December 26, 1863, MSS, NELPS.

61. Foner, *Free Soil, Free Labor, Free Men,* p. 72; Foner, "The Meaning of Freedom in the Age of Emancipation," *Journal of American History* (September 1994): 453; Foner, *Free Soil, Free Labor, Free Men,* pp. 20, 27; Lieber in Freidel, *Lieber,* p. 60; Paludan, *"A People's Contest,"* p. 173.

62. JMF to CEN, March 22, 1863, MSS, NELPS.

63. NELPS #144; NELPS #139, NELPS #2. See also NELPS, September 27, 1862; NELPS, February 19, 1863; November 20, 1863.

64. NYLPS #14, "The Preservation of the Union, A National Economic Necessity"; NYLPS #80, "America for Free Working Men/ Mechanics, Farmers, and Laborers, Read!/ How Slavery Injures the Free Working Man/ The Free Working Man's Worst Enemy." See also BPULP #61, "Plantations for Slave Labor the Death of the Yeoman"; NYLPS #17, "The Cause of the War"; BPULP #89, "Proofs for Workingmen of the Monarchic and Aristocratic Designs of the Southern Conspirators and their Northern Allies."

65. Bellows cited in Strong, *Diary,* vol. 3, p. 178; Strong, *Diary,* vol. 3, p. 293; Bernstein, *New York City Draft Riots,* p. 57. As LeGrand B. Cannon argued, the undertaking also had consequences for the metropolis. It would "purge the city from the taint of that wicked, infamous, and inhuman riot of July" (cited in Bernstein, *The New York City Draft Riots,* p. 57).

66. NY LPS #7; NELPS #46.

67. BPULP #15, "Character and Results of the War: How to Prosecute It and How to End It"; NELPS, May 23, 1863; See also NYLPS #15, "Elements of Discord in Secessia."

68. Fredrickson, *Inner Civil War*, pp. 138, 130–165; see also Curti, *Roots of American Loyalty* (New York, 1946), pp. 172–199, and Hall, *Organization of American Culture*.

69. Curti, *Roots of American Loyalty*, pp. 173–181; Freidel, *Lieber*, p. 302; Bernard Edward Brown, *American Conservatives: The Political Thought of Francis Lieber and John W. Burgess* (New York, 1951), pp. 44–46; Freidel, *Lieber*, p. 303; Howe, *Unitarian Conscience*, pp. 125–131.

70. "American Political Ideas," *North American Review* 101 (October 1865); Alexander H. Bullock, *The Relations of the Educated Man with American Nationality: Address of Alexander H. Bullock, before the Literary Societies of Williams College, August 1, 1864* (Boston, 1864). For Bullock as a league member, see Thorndike, *Past Members*, p. 27.

71. Henry W. Bellows, *Unconditional Loyalty* (New York, 1863).

72. BPULP #41, "The Nation's Sin and the Nation's Duty."

73. Lieber, cited in Freidel, *Lieber*, p. 302; Brown, *American Conservatives*, pp. 44–45; Bullock, *Relations of the Educated Man*, my emphasis (for Bullock quote).

74. De Tocqueville, *Democracy in America*, p. 120.

75. Hale, "Introduction," *The Man Without a Country*, p. 12.

76. Adams, *Edward Everett Hale*, p. 8; Hale, "Introduction," pp. 4–5; Edward Everett Hale, *Memories of a Hundred Years*, vol. 2 (New York, 1902), pp. 217–218; William Sloane Kennedy, "Edward Everett Hale," *Century Illustrated Monthly Magazine* 29 (January 1885): 341.

77. Adams, *Edward Everett Hale*, p. 27; Nancy Esther James, "Realism in Romance: A Critical Study of the Short Stories of Edward Everett Hale" (Ph.D. dissertation, Pennsylvania State University, 1969), pp. 17, 178–185; Hale, "Introduction," pp. 9–12; Edward Everett Hale to Charles Hale, November 28, 1863, in Edward Everett Hale MSS; Holloway, *Edward Everett Hale*, pp. 136–137.

78. Holloway, *Edward Everett Hale*, pp. 135–136.

79. Edward Everett Hale, Introduction, "The Man Without a Country," *Outlook*, May 14, 1898, p. 116. Nolan's nickname "Plain Buttons" and its relation to the loss of identity are discussed in James, "Realism in Romance," pp. 17, 178–185.

5. "Until the Ideas of Massachusetts Kiss the Gulf of Mexico"

1. For a study of the abolitionists during the Civil War, see McPherson, *Struggle for Equality*.

2. McPherson, *Struggle for Equality*, pp. 117–120.

3. Frederick Douglass, *Life and Times of Frederick Douglass* (Hartford, 1881), pp. 357–359. For this description of the emancipation celebration at Tremont Temple, I have drawn from Benjamin Quarles, *The Negro in the Civil War* (Boston, 1953), chap. 8; William S. McFeely, *Frederick Douglass* (New York, 1991), p. 215; McPherson, *Struggle for Equality,* pp. 120–121; and Blight, *Frederick Douglass' Civil War,* p. 106.

4. Douglass, cited in McFeely, *Frederick Douglass,* p. 215; Douglass, *Life and Times,* p. 359.

5. For a general history of the abolitionists, see James Brewer Stewart, *Holy Warriors: The Abolitionists and American Slavery* (New York, 1976). For early roots in radical artisan, see Eric Foner, *Politics and Ideology in the Age of the Civil War* (New York, 1980), pp. 57–76; and John Jentz, "The Anti-Slavery Constituency in Jacksonian New York City," *Civil War History* 27 (1981): 101–122. For a focus on Theodore Weld and evangelism and an analysis of the introduction of antislavery into politics, see Gilbert Barnes, *The Anti-Slavery Impulse* (New York, 1933). For an examination of the role of Garrison, see Aileen Kraditor, *Means and Ends in American Abolitionism, 1834–1850* (New York, 1967).

6. McPherson, *Struggle for Equality,* pp. 47–51.

7. For Fremont's and Hunter's proclamations, see McPherson, *Battle Cry of Freedom,* pp. 352–354, 499. Abraham Lincoln to Horace Greeley, Aug. 22, 1962, Basler, *Collected Works,* vol. 5, pp. 388–389.

8. For the newfound popularity of the abolitionists, and the specific popularity of Phillips, Douglass, and Dickinson, see McPherson, *Struggle for Equality,* pp. 81–82; 128–132.

9. Gregory Clark and S. Michael Halloran, eds., *Oratorical Culture in Nineteenth-Century America: Transformations in the Theory and Practice of Rhetoric* (Carbondale, 1993), pp. 1–17; Willis D. Moreland and Erwin H. Goldenstein, *Pioneers in Adult Education* (Chicago, 1985), pp. 46–58; Giraud Chester, *Embattled Maiden: The Life of Anna Dickinson* (New York, 1951), p. 31.

10. Moreland and Goldenstein, *Pioneers in Adult Education,* pp. 35–51; Carl Bode, *The American Lyceum: Town Meeting of the Mind* (New York, 1956), pp. 8–18, 101, 131–182, 185–200, 201–223 (esp. 214). Quote is from Bernard K. Duffy and Halford R. Ryan, eds., *American Orators Before 1900: Critical Studies and Sources* (New York, 1987), p. xvi.

11. Bode, *American Lyceum,* pp. 247–248.

12. *Liberator,* December 20, 1850, cited in Bartlett, *Wendell Phillips,* p. 151; Bartlett, *Wendell Phillips,* p. 247; Richard Hofstadter, *The American Political Tradition* (New York, 1948), p. 154; J. O. A. Griffen to Butler, January 18, 1863, cited in Bartlett, *Wendell Phillips,* p. 260.

13. For major works on the life and career of Phillips, see James Brewer Stewart, *Wendell Phillips: Liberty's Hero* (Baton Rouge, 1986); Bartlett, *Wendell Phillips;* Hofstadter, *American Political Tradition,* pp. 137–163. According to Bartlett, Phillips passed the graves of his father, Otis, and Adams every day on his way to school. Bartlett, *Wendell Phillips,* p. 16.

14. *National Anti-Slavery Standard (NASS),* February 13, 1864; Wendell Phillips, *Speeches, Lectures and Letters,* vol. 1 (1863; reprint, Boston, 1902), pp. 35–54, esp. 46–48. See also Phillips, *Speeches,* vol. 1, p. 354; Phillips, *Speeches, Lectures and Letters,* 2d ser. (Boston, 1891), p. 21.

A potent force in American politics, public opinion was most notably informed by the pulpit and the press. But the church had become "but the servant of the broker and the kitchen of the factory"; newspapers, "agents of the banks and . . . slaveholders." Alternative voices were called for: "Outside of that press and that pulpit . . . there must be agitation." *NASS,* June 2, 1860; see also Phillips, *Speeches,* vol. 1, pp. 152–153, 225; Phillips, *Speeches,* 2d ser., pp. 252–275, esp. 267.

15. Phillips, *Speeches,* vol. 1, p. 110.

16. *NASS,* June 9, 1860; Phillips, cited in Oscar Sherwin, *Prophet of Liberty: The Life and Times of Wendell Phillips* (New York, 1958), p. 138; *NASS,* November 5, 1864; *NASS,* July 13, 1861.

For Phillips as an agitator, see Hofstadter, *American Political Tradition,* pp. 137–163. On the abolitionist as agitator, see Kraditor, *Means and Ends,* pp. 11–32. For the animosity Phillips's attitude evoked, see Stewart, *Wendell Phillips,* pp. 192–194, 212–215.

17. *NASS,* July 13, 1861; Phillips to Charles Sumner, March 24, 1866, cited in Eric Foner, *Reconstruction: America's Unfinished Revolution 1863–1867* (New York, 1988), p. 239. For the abolitionists' reaction to the attack on Fort Sumter, see McPherson, *Struggle for Equality,* pp. 46–49.

18. *NASS,* April 27, 1861; McPherson, *Struggle for Equality,* p. 50.

19. Phillips, *Speeches,* vol. 1, pp. 396–414.

20. *NASS* July 13, 1861; *NASS* July 11, 1863; Phillips, *Speeches,* vol. 1, p. 355; *NASS,* July 12, 1862; *NASS,* July 13, 1861. See also *NASS,* May 19, 1860; Phillips, *Speeches,* vol. 1, pp. 264–265.

21. *NASS,* July 13, 1861.

22. *NASS,* April 27, 1861; Phillips, *Speeches,* vol. 1, pp. 419–420. For Phillips's definition of the new egalitarian nation, see also *NASS,* May 17, 1862; January 17, 1863; February 21, 1863; February 13, 1863; December 10, 1864; Stewart, *Wendell Phillips,* pp. 209–242.

23. Phillips, *Speeches,* vol. 1, pp. 448–458, esp. p. 457.

24. Phillips, *Speeches,* vol. 1, p. 408; *NASS,* July 13, 1861.

25. Phillips, *Speeches,* vol. 1, p. 469.

26. Phillips, *Speeches,* vol. 1, p. 399; *NASS,* May 17, 1862; Phillips, *Speeches,* vol. 1, p. 411.

27. *NASS,* February 11, 1865; *NASS,* February 13, 1864.

28. *NASS,* August 16, 1864; *NASS,* May 17, 1862; *NASS,* December 10, 1864.

29. *NASS,* May 17, 1862.

30. *NASS,* December 10, 1864; *NASS,* January 17, 1863; *NASS,* December 10, 1864.

31. Phillips, *Speeches,* vol. 1, p. 397.

32. Phillips, *Speeches,* vol. 1, pp. 419–420, 464–467. Phillips found precedents for his understanding of loyalty in classical history. "Every public meeting in Athens was opened with a curse on anyone who should not speak what he really thought." In Egypt, it was believed that souls were required to utter the following oath before admission into heaven: "I have never defiled my conscience from fear or favor to my superiors." Phillips, *Speeches,* vol. 1, p. 398.

33. Phillips, *Speeches,* vol. 1, p. 398; Phillips, *Speeches,* vol. 1, pp. 230–231. See also *NASS,* June 2, 1860.

34. *NASS,* November 22, 1862.

35. *NASS,* January 17, 1863; January 12, 1863.

36. Phillips, *Speeches,* vol. 1, p. 423.

37. *NASS,* November 5, 1864. For Lincoln's 10 percent plan, see Foner, *Reconstruction,* pp. 35–37, 60–62. For the Wade-Davis Bill, see Foner, *Reconstruction,* pp. 60–62.

38. *NASS,* May 14, 1864. See also *NASS,* June 18, 1864.

39. Phillips, *Speeches,* vol. 1, pp. 464–467.

40. Douglass, *Life and Times,* pp. 196–263; McFeely, *Frederick Douglass,* pp. 3–103, quote, pp. 124–125; Blight, *Frederick Douglass' Civil War,* p. 2.

41. Frederick Douglass, *My Bondage and My Freedom* (New York, 1855), pp. 393–403; McFeely, *Frederick Douglass,* pp. 93–94, 108, 114, 146–154, 157, 169; Waldo E. Martin, Jr., *The Mind of Frederick Douglass* (Chapel Hill, 1984), pp. 79–81.

42. Martin, *The Mind of Frederick Douglass,* pp. 79–81; Leonard I. Sweet, *Black Images of America, 1784–1870* (New York, 1976), pp. 89–94; Vincent Harding, *There Is a River: The Black Struggle for Freedom in America* (1981; reprint, New York, 1983), pp. 186–189; H. Ford Douglas in Harding, *There Is a River,* p. 189. On Douglass and colonization/emigration efforts see Blight, *Frederick Douglass' Civil War,* pp. 122–147.

43. Harding, *There Is a River,* pp. xx–xxi; Ray, cited in Harding, *There Is a River,* p. 132.

44. For Douglass's view on Providence and the millennium see Blight, *Frederick Douglass' Civil War,* pp. 5–11, 101–121; Martin, *The Mind of Frederick Douglass,* pp. 173–174; Douglass, in Philip S. Foner, *The Life and Writings of Frederick Douglass,* vol. 3 (New York, 1952), p. 112. Douglass in Foner, *Life and Writings,* pp. 119–120, 323. For Douglass's view of what Martin calls a "composite American nationality," see Martin, *The Mind of Frederick Douglass,* pp. 197–224.

45. Blight, *Frederick Douglass' Civil War,* pp. 132–133.

46. For African-Americans' reaction to the Civil War, see Harding, *There Is a River,* pp. 219–241.

47. Douglass, in Foner, *Life and Writings,* pp. 114–117, 136–142, 246–248, 333; Martin, *The Mind of Frederick Douglass,* pp. 221–224. For quotes, see

Douglass, in Foner, *Life and Writings,* p. 197; Douglass, cited in Martin, *The Mind of Frederick Douglass,* p. 222.

48. Douglass, in Foner, *Life and Writings,* pp. 119–120, 98–99, 138–139, 99.

49. Douglass in Foner, *Life and Writings,* pp. 124–125, 116, 277, 293, 124–125, 259. For Douglass's notion of the war as apocalypse, see Blight, *Frederick Douglass' Civil War,* pp. 101–121.

50. Douglass in Foner, *Life and Writings,* pp. 223, 289, 153, 205, 213, 287, 284, 336. See also Blight, *Frederick Douglass' Civil War,* p. 153.

51. Douglass in Foner, *Life and Writings,* p. 224. Leonard I. Sweet discusses the recognition by blacks of the notion that "black participation in American history [was] an organic ingredient in the development of the nation." Sweet, *Black Images of America,* p. 44.

52. Douglass in Foner, *Life and Writings,* pp. 224–225; Sweet, *Black Images of America,* p. 161.

53. Douglass in Foner, *Life and Writings,* pp. 393–394. For the meaning of black troops to Douglass, see Martin, *The Mind of Frederick Douglass,* p. 53; Blight, *Frederick Douglass' Civil War,* pp. 148–174.

54. Douglass in Foner, *Life and Writings,* p. 94, 365; Martin, *The Mind of Frederick Douglass,* p. 53; Blight, *Frederick Douglass' Civil War,* pp. 148–174. According to Mary Berry, *Military Necessity and Civil Rights Policy: Black Citizenship and the Constitution, 1861–1868* (Port Washington, 1977), the notion that militia service led to citizenship, brought to the colonies by European settlers, concerned service in a state militia, not in the regular army. Service in the regular army, which was "collected from the stews and the brothels of the cities," had virtually no impact on one's future civic status. Thus, although blacks had in the past served the United States in emergencies, it had as a rule been in the army, and had not affected their citizenship status. The 1863 Conscription Act changed this assumption, as it marked the failure of the state militia system, replacing service in a state militia with "subjection to conscript service" as the "badge and moral consequence of citizenship."

55. Douglass in John W. Blassingame, ed., *The Frederick Douglass Papers,* ser. 1, vol. 3 (New Haven, 1985), p. 604. For discriminatory policies and reaction, see Dudley Taylor Cornish, *The Sable Arm: Negro Troops in the Union Army, 1861–1865* (New York, 1966), pp. 184–195; James M. McPherson, *The Negro's Civil War: How American Blacks Felt and Acted During the War for the Union* (New York, 1991), pp. 197–207; Ira Berlin, ed., *Freedom: A Documentary History of Emancipation,* ser. 2, *The Black Military Experience* (Cambridge, 1982), pp. 362–405; Joseph T. Glathaar, *Forged in Battle: The Civil War Alliance of Black Soldiers and White Officers* (New York, 1990), pp. 169–176.

56. Blight, *Frederick Douglass' Civil War,* pp. 167–169; McFeely, *Frederick Douglass,* 228; Foner, *Life and Writings,* pp. 34–35; Benjamin Quarles, *Lincoln and the Negro* (New York, 1962), pp. 172–175; Lincoln in Basler, *Collected Works,* vol. 6, p. 357.

57. McFeely, *Frederick Douglass*, p. 234; Douglass to Theodore Tilton, October 15, 1864, in Foner, *Life and Writings*, p. 424.

58. On Civil War blacks and the meaning of American citizenship, see Eric Foner, "Rights and the Constitution in Black Life During the Civil War and Reconstruction," *Journal of American History* 74, no. 3 (December 1987): 863–883.

59. Elizabeth Cady Stanton, Susan B. Anthony, and Matilda Jocelyn Gage, *History of Woman Suffrage*, vol. 2 (New York: 1881), p. 44. James McPherson argues that Dickinson was second only to Wendell Phillips in her popularity as a speaker during the war. McPherson, *Struggle for Equality*, p. 128. Giraud Chester, *Embattled Maiden*, p. 37; *Springfield Weekly Republican*, January 23, 1864, cited in James Harvey Young, "Anna Elizabeth Dickinson and the Civil War" (Ph.D. dissertation, University of Illinois, Urbana, 1941), p. 165; *Connecticut Courant*, March 28, 1863.

60. Young, "Anna Elizabeth Dickinson," p. 3; Chester, *Embattled Maiden*, p. 12; Wendy Hamand Venet, *Neither Ballots Nor Bullets: Women Abolitionists and the Civil War* (Charlottesville, 1991), p. 2.

61. Venet, *Neither Ballots Nor Bullets*, pp. 39–40; Young, "Anna Elizabeth Dickinson," pp. 25–28.

62. Stanton, Anthony, and Gage, *History of Woman Suffrage*, vol. 2, pp. 43–44; Young, "Anna Elizabeth Dickinson," pp. 81–86.

63. Stanton, Anthony, and Gage, *History of Woman Suffrage*, vol. 2, pp. 44–45; Young, "Anna Elizabeth Dickinson," pp. 87–92, 95–112; *Springfield Republican*, n.d., cited in *Liberator*, May 8, 1863; Letter writer to a Hartford paper, cited in Chester, *Embattled Maiden*, p. 59. Wendell Phillips was quoted as saying, "And the Goliath of Connecticut Copperheads has been killed not by a stripling but by a girl." Phillips, cited in Joseph Ricketson to Anna Dickinson, May 30, 1863, cited in Young, "Anna Elizabeth Dickinson," p. 110.

64. Chester, *Embattled Maiden*, pp. 59–63; Wendell Phillips to Anna Dickinson, July 1863 and subsequent Phillips-Dickinson correspondence in *The Papers of Anna E. Dickinson*, Reel 13, Library of Congress. For the content of Dickinson's Speeches, see "The National Crisis," Dickinson Papers, Reel 17; *Philadelphia Inquirer*, March 12, 1862, May 5, 1863, May 27, 1863, October 1, 1863, January 28, 1864; *The Liberator*, May 2, 1862; *Chicago Tribune*, November 5, 1863; *Hartford Daily Courant*, April 5, 1863.

65. *New York World*, n.d., cited in *NASS*, February 13, 1864; Young, "Anna Elizabeth Dickinson," p. 22; Chester, *Embattled Maiden*, pp. 24, 47; Venet, *Neither Ballots Nor Bullets*, p. 41; Judith Anderson, "Anna Dickinson, Antislavery Radical," *Pennsylvania History* 3, no. 3 (July 1936): 147–163.

66. See, for example, *Chicago Tribune*, March 1, 1864; *Philadelphia Inquirer* January 28, 1864, and May 5, 1863. *Chicago Tribune*, November 5, 1863; *Chicago Tribune*, March 1, 1864. See also *Hartford Daily Courant*, April 6, 1863; *Liberator*, May 8, 1863; *NASS*, January 3, 1863.

67. *Chicago Tribune*, November 5, 1863; "Copy of letter to gentlemen in NY,

from chair, office Rep State Central Committee," *NASS*, April 25, 1863; see also *Connecticut Courant*, March 28, 1863.

68. *Philadelphia Inquirer*, May 5, 1863, and January 28, 1864. For attacks on Democrats, see also "The National Crisis," Dickinson Papers; *Hartford Courant*, April 6, 1863, and *Chicago Tribune*, November 5, 1863.

69. Dickinson in Chester, *Embattled Maiden*, pp. 28–29; *Philadelphia Inquirer*, May 5, 1863. For McClellan and the abolitionists, see McPherson, *Struggle for Equality*, p. 113; Phillips, *Speeches*, vol. 1, pp. 448–463.

70. *Philadelphia Inquirer*, May 5, 1863; see also *Philadelphia Inquirer*, March 12, 1864.

71. *Philadelphia Inquirer*, May 5, 1863; *Chicago Tribune*, November 5, 1863; for Dickinson's summer in a Philadelphia hospital, see Chester, *Embattled Maiden*, p. 40.

72. *Philadelphia Inquirer*, January 28, 1864. See also *Chicago Tribune*, November 5, 1863; *Philadelphia Inquirer*, May 27, 1863; *Chicago Tribune*, March 1, 1864.

73. *Philadelphia Inquirer*, January 28, 1864.

74. *Philadelphia Inquirer*, May 5, 1863; *Chicago Tribune*, March 1, 1864.

75. *Springfield Republican*, cited in the *Liberator*, May 8, 1863; *New York Times*, April 22, 1863; *Springfield Republican*, April 16, 1863, cited in *NASS*, April 25, 1863; *Hartford Daily Courant*, March 26, 1863.

76. *New York Journal of Commerce*, n.d., cited in *National Anti-Slavery Standard*, April 18, 1863; *New York World*, n.d., cited in *National Anti-Slavery Standard*, February 13, 1864; *New York World*, April 23, 1863, in Young, "Anna Elizabeth Dickinson," pp. 115–116. See also *Pennsylvania Termagent*, n.d., in *National Anti-Slavery Standard*, February 13, 1864; and *Hartford Times*, cited by Dickinson in *Hartford Daily Courant*, April 6, 1863.

77. *Independent Democrat*, March 26, 1863, in *Liberator*, May 8, 1863; *NASS* March 4, 1865; Venet, *Neither Ballots Nor Bullets*, pp. 43–44; Dickinson, cited in *Philadelphia Evening Bulletin*, n.d., cited in Young, "Anna Elizabeth Dickinson," p. 241; Dickinson, cited in Venet, *Neither Ballots Nor Bullets*, p. 44. For Dickinson's first speech, see Chester, *Embattled Maiden*, pp. 16–17.

78. Stanton, Anthony, and Gage, p. 42; Dickinson, cited in Chester, *Embattled Maiden*, p. 92; *Hartford Daily Courant*, April 6, 1863.

79. *Hartford Press*, in *Liberator*, May 8, 1863; *Springfield Republican*, cited in the *Liberator*, May 8, 1863. In 1863, Wendell Phillips wrote to Dickinson, "I traced your flashing tracks with most sheer delight." Wendell Phillips to Anna Dickinson, July 1863, Dickinson Papers, Reel 13.

80. McPherson, *Struggle for Equality*, pp. 301–307; Phillips, cited in McPherson, *Struggle for Equality*, p. 304.

81. Douglass, cited in McPherson, *Struggle for Equality*, p. 355. For the immediate postwar activities of Phillips, Douglass, and Dickinson, see Stewart, *Wendell Phillips*, pp. 270–295; Blight, *Frederick Douglass' Civil War*, pp. 189–218; McFeely, *Frederick Douglass*, pp. 238–273; Chester, *Embattled Maiden*, pp. 85–90; Anderson, "Anna Dickinson," pp. 162–163; and Stanton, Anthony,

and Gage, *History of Woman Suffrage,* vol. 2, pp. 327–329. For the Fourteenth Amendment, see Foner, *Reconstruction,* pp. 251–261.

82. McPherson, *Struggle for Equality,* pp. 360–363; Douglass, *Life and Times,* pp. 404–405; Stanton, Anthony, and Gage, *History of Woman Suffrage,* vol. 2, pp. 327–329. Frederick Douglass to Elizabeth Cady Stanton, February 6, 1882, cited in *History of Women Suffrage,* pp. 328–329.

83. McPherson, *Struggle for Equality,* pp. 424–427.

84. McPherson, *Struggle for Equality,* p. 426; Phillips, *NASS,* February 20, 1869, cited in ibid., p. 426.

85. Phillips to Charles Sumner, March 24, 1866, cited in Foner, *Reconstruction,* p. 239; Phillips, *NASS,* November 13, 1869, in Foner, *Reconstruction,* p. 449; McPherson, *Struggle for Equality,* p. 426.

86. Chester, *Embattled Maiden,* pp. 85–90; Anderson, "Anna Dickinson," pp. 162–163; Elisabeth Griffith, *In Her Own Right: The Life of Elizabeth Cady Stanton* (New York, 1984), pp. 136–137.

87. McFeely, *Frederick Douglass,* p. 359; Blight, *Frederick Douglass' Civil War,* pp. 210–211; Douglass, cited in Blight, *Frederick Douglass' Civil War,* p. 216; Douglass, "West India Emancipation," August 1, 1880, in *Life and Times,* p. 511; Douglass, cited in McFeely, *Frederick Douglass,* p. 381.

88. Phillips, cited in Stewart, *Wendell Phillips,* p. 295.

6. Lincoln and the Construction of National Patriotism

1. Potter, *The South and the Sectional Conflict,* p. 48.

2. Phillips Brooks, "The Character, Life, and Death of Abraham Lincoln: Sermon, Holy Trinity Episcopal Church Of Philadelphia, April 23, 1865," in *Building the Myth: Selected Speeches Memorializing Abraham Lincoln,* ed. Waldo W. Braden (Urbana, 1990), p. 52.

3. Basler, *Collected Works,* vol. 5, p. 537.

4. Basler, *Collected Works,* vol. 8, p. 394.

5. For the prosperity of the nation see Basler, *Collected Works,* vol. 5, pp. 47, 53; vol. 7, pp. 40–44. For the relationship between prosperity and a democratic free labor system see Basler, *Collected Works,* vol. 4, pp. 168–169, 437–441; G. S. Boritt, *Lincoln and the Economics of the American Dream* (Memphis, 1978); Gabor S. Boritt, "Lincoln and the Economics of the American Dream," in *The Historian's Lincoln: Pseudohistory, Psychohistory, and History,* Gabor Borett, ed. (Urbana, 1988), pp. 87–106. For Lincoln's prewar rhetoric and slavery's threat to the right to rise, see Don E. Fehrenbacher, ed., *Lincoln: Selected Speeches and Writings* (New York, 1992), pp. 49–51, 92–99, 108–114. For quotes see Basler, *Collected Works,* vol. 4, p. 438; vol. 5, p. 52.

6. Basler, *Collected Works,* vol. 4, pp. 434–436; Borritt, *Lincoln,* pp. 195–214, 243–244; Basler, *Collected Works,* vol. 5, p. 374.

7. Basler, *Collected Works,* vol. 8, pp. 260–261; vol. 6, p. 156.

8. Basler, *Collected Works,* vol. 5, p. 438; vol. 7, p. 395; vol. 8, p. 53; vol. 6, pp. 226–227. See also vol. 5, p. 450; vol. 6, pp. 114, 539; vol. 7, pp. 301, 334; vol. 8, p. 75.

9. Basler, *Collected Works,* vol. 7, pp. 334, 394–395; vol. 7, p. 24; vol. 5, pp. 370–371.

10. Basler, *Collected Works,* vol. 5, p. 223; vol. 6, pp. 261, 267–268. See also vol. 6, p. 406.

11. Mark E. Neely, Jr., *The Fate of Liberty: Abraham Lincoln and Civil Liberties* (New York, 1991), p. 131; Basler, *Collected Works,* vol. 6, p. 265. Neely sees the military response to Lincoln's August 8, 1862, suspension as an exception, but he attributes that to disorganization. Following that "disastrous" order, the procedures were modified.

12. For Lincoln and democratic leadership, see Bruce Miroff, *Icons of Democracy: American Leaders as Heroes, Aristocrats, Dissenters, and Democrats* (Lawrence, 2000), pp. 83–124, esp. 95. For Lincoln and patronage, see David Donald, *Lincoln Reconsidered* (New York, 1961), pp. 71–81. John H. Schaar, "The Case for Patriotism," in *Legitimacy in the Modern State,* ed. John H. Schaar (New Brunswick, 1981), pp. 285–311.

13. Wills, *Lincoln at Gettysburg,* p. 100; Fehrenbacher, *Selected Speeches,* pp. 94–99, esp. 96, and pp. 120–121; Basler, *Collected Works,* vol. 7, pp. 22–23.

14. Basler, *Collected Works,* vol. 4, p. 240; Fehrenbacher, *Selected Speeches,* pp. 145–146.

15. Basler, *Collected Works,* vol. 4, pp. 169, 235–236, 240.

16. Basler, *Collected Works,* vol. 4, p. 439; Basler, *Collected Works,* vol. 5, p. 537. My understanding of the relationship between Lincoln's notions of liberty, equality, and Union has been informed by Richard Current, "Lincoln, the Civil War, and the American Mission," in *The Public and Private Lincoln: Contemporary Perspectives,* ed. Cullom Davis (Carbondale, 1979), pp. 137–146; George M. Fredrickson, "The Search for Order and Community," in *The Public and Private Lincoln,* ed. Cullom Davis, pp. 86–98; Howe, *Political Culture of the American Whigs* (Chicago, 1979), pp. 263–298; James M. McPherson, "Abraham Lincoln and the Second American Revolution," *Abraham Lincoln and the Second American Revolution* (New York, 1990), pp. 23–42; McPherson, "Lincoln and Liberty," *Abraham Lincoln and the Second American Revolution,* pp. 43–64; Paludan, *Presidency of Abraham Lincoln;* and Wills, *Lincoln at Gettysburg.* For an emphasis on Lincoln as nationalist, see Edmund Wilson, *Patriotic Gore: Studies in the Literature of the American Civil War* (New York, 1962), pp. ix–xxxii, 99–130.

17. Fehrenbacher, *Selected Speeches,* pp. 93–99; Basler, *Collected Works,* vol. 5, pp. 388–389.

18. Basler, *Collected Works,* vol. 4, p. 439; vol. 7, p. 505.

19. Basler, *Collected Works,* vol. 5, pp. 388–389; Foner, *Life and Writings,* vol. 4, p. 312; Basler, *Collected Works,* vol. 5, pp. 370–374. See also Don E. Fehrenbacher, "Only His Stepchildren: Lincoln and the Negro," *Civil War History* 20

(December 1974): 293–310; George M. Fredrickson, "A Man but Not a Brother: Abraham Lincoln and Racial Equality," *Journal of Southern History* 41 (February 1975): 39–58.

20. Basler, *Collected Works*, vol. 5, p. 373. The emphasis is mine.

21. Basler, *Collected Works*, vol. 5, p. 423; vol. 6, p. 410, my emphasis.

22. Basler, *Collected Works*, vol. 7, p. 243; vol. 8, pp. 399–403; Foner, *Reconstruction*, p. 49. Whether or not Lincoln's ideas about and commitment to blacks changed over time is the topic of Fehrenbacher, "Only His Stepchildren," and Fredrickson, "A Man but Not a Brother."

23. Basler, *Collected Works*, vol. 5, pp. 420–424. Though he was unwilling publicly to embrace a providential view of the war at this moment, Lincoln was privately speculating on the Divine Will around the same time. See Basler, *Collected Works*, vol. 5, p. 403.

24. Don E. Fehrenbacher, "The Weight of Responsibility," in Fehrenbacher, *Lincoln in Text and Context: Collected Essays* (Stanford, 1987). See, for example, Basler, *Collected Works*, vol. 6, pp. 156, 535–536; vol. 7, pp. 22–23, 282–283, 368, 535; vol. 8, pp. 332–333.

25. Moorhead, *American Apocalypse*, pp. 1–22; Bloch, *Visionary Republic;* Foner, *Story of American Freedom*, pp. 57–58.

26. For the Northern clergy and the Civil War, see Moorhead, *American Apocalypse;* Phillip Shaw Paludan, "Religion and the American Civil War," in *Religion and the American Civil War*, ed. Randall M. Miller, Harry S. Stout, and Charles Reagan Wilson (New York, 1998), pp. 21–42; and George M. Fredrickson, "The Coming of the Lord: The Northern Protestant Clergy and the Civil War Crisis," in *Religion and the American Civil War*, ed. Miller, Stout, and Wilson, pp. 110–130.

27. Basler, *Collected Works*, vol. 7, pp. 22–23.

28. Basler, *Collected Works*, vol. 8, pp. 332–333, 356. For the relationship between American democratic identity and slavery, see Edmund P. Morgan, *American Slavery, American Freedom: The Ordeal of Colonial Virginia* (New York, 1975).

29. Stephen Oates, *With Malice Toward None: The Life of Abraham Lincoln* (New York, 1977), pp. 472–474; Merrill D. Peterson, *Lincoln in American Memory* (New York, 1994), p. 6; Strong, *Diary*, p. 585; Nevins, *War for the Union*, p. 335.

30. Brooks, in Braden, *Building the Myth*, pp. 58–60; Thomas Reed Turner, *Beware the People Weeping: Public Opinion and the Assassination of Abraham Lincoln* (Baton Rouge, 1982), pp. 43, 46–47.

31. Henry Ward Beecher, "A New Impulse of Patriotism for His Sake, Plymouth Church, Brooklyn, New York, April 23, 1865," in Braden, *Building the Myth*, p. 43; Brooks, in Braden, *Building the Myth*, p. 59. See also George Bancroft, "How Shall the Nation Show Its Sorrow? Union Square, New York City, April 25, 1865," in Braden, *Building the Myth*, p. 70.

32. Strong, *Diary*, p. 583; Eyal J. Naveh, *Crown of Thorns: Political Martyrdom in America from Abraham Lincoln to Martin Luther King, Jr.* (New York,

1990), p. 62; Bancroft, in Braden, *Building the Myth,* p. 69; *New York Times,* April 21, 1865, in Naveh, *Crown of Thorns,* p. 62; Beecher, in Braden, *Building the Myth,* p. 44.

33. Naveh, *Crown of Thorns,* pp. 51, 71–77; Beecher, in Braden, *Building the Myth,* p. 37; Matthew Simpson, "Under the Permissive Hand of God, Oak Ridge Cemetery, Springfield, Illinois, May 4, 1865," in Braden, *Building the Myth,* pp. 75–76.

34. Peterson, *Lincoln in American Memory,* p. 24; Naveh, *Crown of Thorns,* p. 67; Frederick De-Peyster Hitchcock, cited in Naveh, *Crown of Thorns,* p. 64.

35. For different interpretations of the relationship between Lincoln and the Radicals, see T. Harry Williams, *Lincoln and the Radicals,* and Trefousse, *Radical Republicans.* For Lincoln's "Quarrel-not" policy as one aspect of his leadership, see Miroff, *Icons of Democracy,* pp. 107–111.

One example of the ways in which Lincoln's charitable approach to statesmanship seemed at odds with an effective Reconstruction of the South is a letter he wrote in February 1864, in which he expressed his disapproval of an oath of office prescribed in Tennessee which required that the applicant swear he had "not sought nor accepted nor attempted to exercise the function of any office" in hostility to the United States: "On principle, I dislike an oath which requires a man to swear that he *has* not done wrong. It rejects the Christian principle of forgiveness on terms of repentance. I think it is enough if the man does no wrong hereafter." As Charles A. Dana informed the president, the oath to which he took objection was "verbally the same as that prescribed by Act of Congress approved July 2, 1862 to be taken by every person elected or appointed to any office or honor or profit under the government of the United States." Basler, *Collected Works,* vol. 7, p. 169.

36. Simpson, in Braden, *Building the Myth,* pp. 83–86.

37. Herman Melville, Hennig Cohen, ed., *Selected Poems of Herman Melville* (Carbondale, 1964), pp. 42–43; Melville, cited in Stanton Garner, *The Civil War World of Herman Melville* (Lawrence, 1993), p. 385; *Chicago Tribune,* April 17, 1865, cited in Turner, *Beware the People Weeping,* p. 23. For Melville's attitude toward Northern cries for vengeance, see also Aaron, *The Unwritten War.*

38. Naveh, *Crown of Thorns,* p. 66; Braden, *Building the Myth,* p. 62; Bancroft, in Braden, *Building the Myth,* p. 66; Beecher, in Braden, *Building the Myth,* pp. 45–46.

39. Peterson, *Lincoln in American Memory,* pp. 14, 21.

40. Peterson, *Lincoln in American Memory,* pp. 14–21; Braden, *Building the Myth,* pp. 25–26; Naveh, *Crown of Thorns,* p. 64. The train stopped for ceremonies and viewing in Baltimore, Harrisburg, Philadelphia, New York City, Albany, Buffalo, Cleveland, Columbus, Indianapolis, and Chicago.

41. Peterson, *Lincoln in American Memory,* pp. 18–19; Naveh, *Crown of Thorns,* p. 64; Lloyd Lewis, cited in Peterson, *Lincoln in American Memory,* p. 19.

42. Peterson, *Lincoln in American Memory*, pp. 14–21; Naveh, *Crown of Thorns*, p. 64.

43. Walt Whitman, "Death of Abraham Lincoln," Lecture delivered in New York, April 14, 1879, in *Walt Whitman: Complete Poetry and Selected Prose and Letters*, ed. Emory Holloway (London, 1938), p. 760.

44. Whitman, "Death of Abraham Lincoln," p. 761.

Conclusion

1. This description of the Grand Review is drawn from Stuart McConnell, *Glorious Contentment: The Grand Army of the Republic, 1865–1900* (Chapel Hill, 1992), pp. 1–17; Wilfred M. McClay, *The Masterless: Self and Society in Modern America* (Chapel Hill, 1994), pp. 9–39; David S. Reynolds, *Walt Whitman's America: A Cultural Biography* (New York, 1995), pp. 448–449; Thomas Fleming, "The Big Parade," *Civil War Chronicles: A Supplement to American Heritage* (New York, 1999), pp. 58–64; and Nevins, *War for the Union*, pp. 364–367.

2. Fleming, "The Big Parade," p. 61; Reynolds, *Walt Whitman*, p. 448.

3. McConnell, *Glorious Contentment*, pp. 2–4; McClay, *The Masterless*, pp. 10, 16; Fleming, "The Big Parade," p. 61.

4. *New York Herald*, cited in McClay, *The Masterless*, p. 10; Sherman, cited in McConnell, *Glorious Contentment*, p. 4; McClay, *The Masterless*, p. 14.

5. McConnell, *Glorious Contentment*, pp. 4, 5–17.

6. McConnell, *Glorious Contentment*, pp. 5–17.

7. McConnell, *Glorious Contentment*, p. 14.

8. Randolph S. Bourne, "The State," in *War and the Intellectuals: Collected Essays, 1915–1919*, ed. Carl Resek (New York, 1964), p. 69.

9. Foner, *Reconstruction*, pp. 243–261; Robert J. Kaczorowski, "To Begin the Nation Anew: Congress, Citizenship, and Civil Rights after the Civil War," *American Historical Review* 92 (February 1987): 45–68.

10. Foner, *Reconstruction*.

11. For various interpretations of the decline of the postwar state, see Bensel, *Yankee Leviathan*; Morton Keller, *Affairs of State: Public Life in Late Nineteenth-Century America* (London, 1977); and Stephen Skowronek, *Building a New American State: The Expansion of National Administrative Capacities, 1877–1920* (Cambridge, 1982).

12. David Blight, *Race and Reunion: The Civil War in American Memory* (Cambridge, 2001), esp. pp. 203–204; Amy Kinsel, "American Identity, National Reconciliation, and the Memory of the Civil War" (paper presented to the Organization of American Historians, Chicago, Illinois, 1996); Cecilia O'Leary, *To Die For: The Paradox of American Patriotism* (Princeton, 1999), pp. 49–69; 110–149, 245. For blacks' resistance to this redefinition, see Blight, *Race and Reunion*.

13. O'Leary, *To Die For,* pp. 91–109. The patriotic boom of the 1890s reinforced this trend toward a narrowed understanding of national loyalty. These years witnessed the rise of patriotic hereditary societies, a cultural obsession with the flag, and school military drills. Together, these phenomena provided, in Stuart McConnell's words, "an abstract national vision," one that offered to incorporate many of the particularisms of America, even as it worked to exclude non-whites, immigrants, and women. Thus, during the late nineteenth century, a resurgence of ascriptive notions of national identity overshadowed more egalitarian understandings. See McConnell, "Reading the Flag: A Reconsideration of the Patriotic Cults of the 1890s," in *Bonds of Affection: Americans Define Their Patriotism,* ed. John Bodnar (Princeton, 1996), pp. 102–119; Rogers M. Smith, *Civic Ideals: Conflicting Visions of Citizenship in U.S. History* (New Haven, 1997), pp. 347–409.

14. Curti, *Roots of American Loyalty,* pp. 173–199; Miroff, *Icons of Democracy,* pp. 158–199.

15. Curti, *Roots of American Loyalty,* pp. 199–222; O'Leary, *To Die For,* pp. 158–162.

16. Keller, *Affairs of State,* p. 600.

17. For more on the suggestion that the postwar national state was perceived differently from the antebellum state, see Richardson, *The Greatest Nation of the Earth;* and George Fletcher, *The Secret Constitution: How Lincoln Redefined American Democracy* (New York, 2001).

18. de Tocqueville, *Democracy in America,* vol. 1, pp. 250–251; Strong, *Diary,* vol. 2, November 8, 1854; Walt Whitman, "Death of Abraham Lincoln," Lecture delivered in New York, April 14, 1879, in Holloway, ed., *Walt Whitman,* p. 760.

For a discussion of the historical literature that either "maximizes" or "minimizes" the long-term impact of the Civil War, see George M. Fredrickson, "Nineteenth-Century American History," in *Imagined Histories: American Historians Interpret the Past,* ed. Anthony Molho and Gordon S. Wood (Princeton, 1998), pp. 164–184.

19. For the postwar growth of American museums see Paul Marshall Rea, *The Museum and the Community: A Study of Social Laws and Consequences* (Lancaster, 1932), pp. 6–9; Harris, *Humbug,* pp. 172–173; Coleman, *Museum in America,* p. 15; Gary Kulik, "Designing the Past: History Museum Exhibitions from Peale to the Present," in *History Museums,* ed. Leon and Rosenzweig, p. 27; Adam, *Museum and Popular Culture,* p. 27; Holloway, *Walt Whitman,* p. 139.

Robert Justice Goldstein, "This Flag Is Not for Burning," *Nation,* (July 18, 1994): 84–86. In testament to Hale's story's persistent influence and absorption into mainstream culture, a 1999 Captain America book boasts the subtitle, "Man Without a Country"; its plot involves the wrongful exile and subsequent suffering of Captain America. See Mark Waid, et al., *Captain America: Man Without a Country* (Marvel Books, 1998). For the fate of organic patriotism, see Curti, *Roots of American Loyalty,* pp. 173–199.

20. For Lincoln and the Gettysburg Address, see Wills, *Lincoln at Gettysburg.*

21. For the Civil War Amendments and American understandings of freedom, see Foner, *Story of American Freedom,* pp. 95–113. George Fletcher has pointed out that although the Supreme Court worked to reverse the Civil War's impact on the Constitution, the fourteen official amendments adopted between 1865 and 1993 suggest the continuing influence of Civil War ideals: each works to broaden the franchise, empower the federal government, or express compassion for the weak. Fletcher, *Our Secret Constitution,* pp. 7, 189–210.

22. *National Anti-Slavery Standard,* December 10, 1864.

Selected Bibliography

Manuscript Papers

Salmon Chase Papers, Library of Congress, Microfilm edition
Jay Cooke Papers, Baker Library, Harvard University
Jay Cooke Papers, Historical Society of Pennsylvania
Edward Carey Gardiner Papers, Historical Society of Pennsylvania
Anna Dickinson Papers, Library of Congress, Microfilm edition
Edward Everett Hale Papers, New York State Library
Francis Lieber Papers, Huntington Library
New England Loyal Publication Society Papers, Boston Public Library
George Templeton Strong Papers, Columbia University
Charles Sumner Papers, Houghton Library, Harvard University
Union League of Philadelphia Papers, Union League of Philadelphia
United States Sanitary Commission Papers, New York Public Library

Contemporary Publications and Published Documents

Basler, Roy P. *The Collected Works of Abraham Lincoln.* New Brunswick, N.J.: Rutgers University Press, 1953.

Bellows, Henry W. *Historical Sketch of the Union League Club of New York: Its Origin, Organization, and Work, 1863–1879.* New York: Press of G. P. Putnam's Sons, 1879.

Berlin, Ira, ed. *Freedom: A Documentary History of Emancipation,* ser. 2, *The Black Military Experience.* Cambridge: Cambridge University Press, 1982.

Blassingame, John W., ed. *The Frederick Douglass Papers,* series 1, vol. 3. New Haven: Yale University Press, 1985.

Boker, George. *A Memorial of the Union Club of Philadelphia.* Philadelphia: J. B. Lippincott and Co., 1871.

Braden, Waldo W., ed. *Building the Myth: Selected Speeches Memorializing Abraham Lincoln.* Urbana: University of Illinois Press, 1990.

Brockett, Linus Pierpont, and Mary C. Vaughn. *Women's Work in the Civil War: A Record of Heroism, Patriotism, and Patience.* Philadelphia: Zeigler, McCurdy, 1867.

Bullock, Alexander H. *The Relations of the Educated Man with American Nationality: Address of Alexander H. Bullock, before the Literary Societies of Williams College, August 1, 1864.* Boston: Wright and Potter, 1864.

Censer, Jane Turner, ed. *The Papers of Frederick Law Olmstead.* Vol. 4. Baltimore: Johns Hopkins University Press, 1986.

Cohen, Hennig, ed. *Selected Poems of Herman Melville.* Carbondale, Ill.: Southern Illinois University Press, 1964.

Daly, Maria Lydig. *Diary of a Union Lady, 1861–1865.* New York: Funk and Wagnalls, 1962.

The Days of Sixty-Three. Philadelphia: C. Sherman, Son and Co., 1864.

Dickson, Walter, ed. *St. Andrews Society of Albany Memorial of the Great Sanitary Fair, Held in the City of Albany, New York, February and March, 1864.* Albany: Van Benthuysen's Steam Print, 1864.

Douglass, Frederick. *Life and Times of Frederick Douglass.* Secaucus, N.J.: Citadel Press, 1983 reprint.

———. *My Bondage and My Freedom.* New York: Miller, Orton and Mulligan, 1855.

Fehrenbacher, Don E., ed. *Lincoln: Selected Speeches and Writings.* New York: Vintage Books, 1992.

Foner, Philip S. *The Life and Writings of Frederick Douglass,* vol. 3. New York: International Publishers, 1952.

Foot, Michael, and Isaac Kramnick, eds. *The Thomas Paine Reader.* New York: Penguin USA, 1987.

Freidel, Frank, ed. *Union Pamphlets of the Civil War, 1861–1865.* Cambridge: Belknap Press of Harvard University Press, 1967.

French, William M. *Life, Speeches, State Papers, and Public Services of Governor Oliver P. Morton.* Indianapolis: S. L. Marrow and Co., n.d.

Funk, Issac. *Copperheads Under the Heel of an Indiana Farmer: Speech of Mr. Funk in the Illinois State Legislature, February 28, 1863.* New York: G. P. Putnam, 1863.

Goodrich, Frank B. *The Tribute Book: A Record of the Munificence, Self-Sacrifice, and Patriotism of the American People During the War for the Union.* New York: Derby and Miller, 1865.

Hale, Edward Everett. "Introduction," *The Man Without a Country and Other Stories.* Boston: Little, Brown and Company, 1898.

———. *The Man Without a Country.* Boston: Roberts Brothers, 1893.

———. *Memories of a Hundred Years.* Vol. 2. New York: Macmillan Co., 1902.

Henshaw, Sarah Edwards. *Our Branch and Its Tributaries.* Chicago: A. L. Sewell, 1868.

History of the Brooklyn and Long Island Fair, February 22, 1864. Brooklyn: "The Union" Steam Presses, 1864.

History of the North-Western Soldiers' Fair, Held in Chicago, Last Week of October and First Week of November. Chicago: Dunlap, Sewell, and Spalding, n.d.

Hoge, Mrs. A. H. *The Boys in Blue, or Heroes of the Rank and File.* New York: E. B. Treat and Co., 1867.

Holloway, Emory, ed. *Walt Whitman: Complete Poetry and Selected Prose and Letters*. London: The Nonesuch Press, 1938.

Hughes, Sarah Forbes, ed. *Letters and Recollections of John Murray Forbes*. New York: Arno Press, 1981.

———, ed. *Reminiscences of John Murray Forbes*. Boston: George H. Ellis, 1902.

Julian, George W. *Speeches on Political Questions*. New York: Hurd and Houghton, 1872.

Lathrop, George Parsons. *History of the Union League of Philadelphia, from Its Origin and Foundation to the Year 1882*. Philadelphia: J. B. Lippincott and Co., 1884.

Lincoln, Charles Z., ed. *Messages from the Governors*. Albany: J. B. Lyon and Co., 1909.

Livermore, Mary A. *My Story of the War: A Woman's Narrative of Four Years Personal Experience*. New York: 1889; reprint, Arno Press, 1972.

McPherson, James M. *The Negro's Civil War: How American Blacks Felt and Acted During the War for the Union*. New York: Ballantine Books, 1991.

Nevins, Allan, and Milton Halsey Thomas, eds. *The Diary of George Templeton Strong*. New York: Macmillan, 1952.

New York Loyal Publication Society. *Pamphlets Issued by the Loyal Publication Society*. Vols. 1–3. New York: The Society, 1864–1866.

———. *Proceedings at the First Anniversary Meeting of the Loyal Publication Society*. New York: The Society, 1864.

Norton, Sara, and M. A. DeWolfe Howe, eds. *Letters of Charles Eliot Norton*. Boston: Houghton Mifflin, 1913.

Phillips, Wendell. *Speeches, Lectures, and Letters*. Vol. 1. Boston: Lee and Shepard, 1902.

———. *Speeches, Lectures, and Letters*. 2d ser. Boston: Arno Press, 1891.

Record of the Metropolitan Fair, Held in Aid of the United States Sanitary Commission. New York: Hurd and Houghton, 1867.

Report of the Duchess County and Poughkeepsie Sanitary Fair Held at Sanitary Hall in the City of Poughkeepsie, from March 15, 1864 to March 19, 1864. Poughkeepsie, N.Y.: Platt and Schram, 1864.

Stanton, Elizabeth Cady. *Eighty Years and More: Reminiscences, 1850–1897*. New York: Schocken Books, 1971.

Stanton, Elizabeth Cady, Susan B. Anthony, and Matilda Jocelyn Gage. *History of Woman Suffrage*. Vol. 2. New York: National American Woman Suffrage Association, 1881.

Stillé, Charles J. *The History of the United States Sanitary Commission*. New York: Hurd and Houghton, 1868.

———. *Memorial of the Great Central Fair for the U.S. Sanitary Commission, Held at Philadelphia, June 1864*. Philadelphia: U.S. Sanitary Commission, 1864.

Thorndike, S. Lothrop. *The Past Members of the Union Club of Boston*. Boston: Union Club of Boston, 1893.

————. *A Brief Sketch of the History of the Union Club of Boston*. Boston: Union Club of Boston, 1893.

Tocqueville, Alexis de. *Democracy in America*. Edited by Phillips Bradley. New York: Vintage Books, 1945.

Union League of Philadelphia. *Chronicle of the Union League of Philadelphia, 1862–1902*. Philadelphia: Fell, 1902.

United States Sanitary Commission, ed. *History of the Great Western Sanitary Fair*. Cincinnati: C. F. Vent, 1864.

United States Sanitary Commission, ed. *The Sanitary Reporter*. Louisville: U.S. Sanitary Commission, Western Dept., 1863–1864.

United States National Union Club. *KGC: An Authentic Exposition of the Origins, Objects, and Secret Work of the Organization Known as the Knights of the Golden Circle*. Louisville, Ky.: U.S. National Union Club, 1862.

Vallandigham, Clement L. *Speeches, Arguments, Addresses, and Letters of Clement L. Vallandigham*. New York: J. Walter and Co., 1864.

Books and Articles

Aaron, Daniel. *The Unwritten War: American Writers and the Civil War*. New York: Alfred A. Knopf, 1973.

Adam, Thomas Ritchie. *The Museum and Popular Culture*. New York: American Association for Adult Education, 1939.

Adams, John R. *Edward Everett Hale*. Boston: Twayne Publishers, 1977.

Anderson, Benedict. *Imagined Communities: Reflections on the Origins and Spread of Nationalism*. London: Verso, 1983.

Anderson, Judith. "Anna Dickinson, Antislavery Radical." *Pennsylvania History* 3 (July 1936): 147–163.

Appleby, Joyce. *Liberalism and Republicanism in the Historical Imagination*. Cambridge: Harvard University Press, 1992.

————. *Inheriting the Revolution: The First Generation of Americans*. Cambridge: Harvard University Press, 2000.

Arieli, Yehoshua. *Individualism and Nationalism in American Ideology*. Baltimore: Penguin Books, 1964.

Attie, Jeanie. *Patriotic Toil: Northern Women and the American Civil War*. Ithaca: Cornell University Press, 1998.

Attie, Jeanie. "Warwork and the Crisis of Domesticity in the North." In *Divided Houses: Gender and the Civil War*. Edited by Catherine Clinton and Nina Silber. New York: Oxford University Press, 1992.

Bailyn, Bernard. *The Origins of American Politics*. New York: Vintage Books, 1967.

Baker, Jean H. *Affairs of Party: The Political Culture of Northern Democrats in the Mid–Nineteenth Century*. Ithaca: Cornell University Press, 1983.

Baker, Paula. "The Domestication of American Politics: Women and American Political Society, 1780–1920." *American Historical Review* (1981): 620–647.

Barnes, Gilbert. *The Anti-Slavery Impulse.* New York: Harcourt, Brace and World, 1933.

Bartlett, Irving H. *Wendell Phillips: Brahmin Radical.* Boston: Beacon Press, 1961.

Baum, Dale. *The Civil War Party System: The Case of Massachusetts.* Chapel Hill: University of North Carolina Press, 1984.

Bender, Thomas. *New York Intellect: A History of Intellectual Life in New York City from 1750 to the Beginnings of Our Own Time.* New York: Alfred A. Knopf, 1987.

Bensel, Richard Franklin. *Yankee Leviathan: The Origins of Central State Authority in America, 1859–1877.* New York: Cambridge University Press, 1990.

Benson, Susan Porter, Stephen Brier, and Roy Rosenzweig, eds. *Presenting the Past: Essays on History and the Public.* Philadelphia: Temple University Press, 1986.

Bernstein, Iver. *The New York City Draft Riots: Their Significance for American Society and Politics in the Age of the Civil War.* New York: Oxford University Press, 1990.

Berry, Mary. *Military Necessity and Civil Rights Policy: Black Citizenship and the Constitution, 1861–1868.* Port Washington, N.Y.: Kennikatt Press, 1977.

Blight, David W. "No Desperate Hero: Manhood and Freedom in a Union Soldier's Experience." In *Divided Houses: Gender and the Civil War.* Edited by Catherine Clinton and Nina Silber. New York: Oxford University Press, 1992.

———. *Frederick Douglass' Civil War: Keeping Faith in Jubilee.* Baton Rouge: Louisiana State University Press, 1989.

———. *Race and Reunion: The Civil War in American Memory.* Cambridge: Belknap Press of Harvard University Press, 2001.

Bloch, Ruth H. *Visionary Republic: Millennial Themes in American Thought, 1756–1800.* New York: Cambridge University Press, 1985.

Blue, Frederick J. *Salmon P. Chase: A Life in Politics.* Kent, Ohio: Kent State University Press, 1987.

Blum, John Morton. *V Was for Victory: Politics and American Culture During World War II.* New York: Harcourt, Brace, Jovanovich, 1976.

Bode, Carl. *The American Lyceum: Town Meeting of the Mind.* New York: Oxford University Press, 1956.

Bodnar, John, ed. *Bonds of Affection: Americans Define Their Patriotism.* Princeton: Princeton University Press, 1996.

Boritt, Gabor S. *Lincoln and the Economics of the American Dream.* Memphis: Memphis State University Press, 1978.

———. "Lincoln and the Economics of the American Dream." In *The Historian's Lincoln: Pseudohistory, Psychohistory, and History.* Edited by Gabor S. Boritt. Urbana: University of Illinois Press, 1988.

———, ed. *Lincoln the War President: The Gettysburg Lectures.* New York: Oxford University Press, 1992.

Bourne, Randolph Silliman. *War and the Intellectuals: Collected Essays, 1915–1919.* Indianapolis: Hackett Publishing, 1999.

Bremmer, Robert Hawley. *The Public Good: Philanthropy and Welfare in the Civil War Era.* New York: Alfred A. Knopf, 1980.

Bridges, Amy. *A City in the Republic: Antebellum New York and the Origins of Machine Politics.* New York: Cambridge University Press, 1984.

Brown, Bernard Edward. *American Conservatives: The Political Thought of Francis Lieber and John W. Burgess.* New York: Columbia University Press, 1951.

Brummer, Sidney David. *Political History of New York State During the Period of the Civil War.* New York: AMS Press, 1967.

Carnes, Mark C. *Secret Ritual and Manhood in Victorian America.* New Haven: Yale University Press, 1989.

Chester, Giraud. *Embattled Maiden: The Life of Anna Dickinson.* New York: G. P. Putnam's Sons, 1951.

Church, Charles A. *The History of the Republican Party in Illinois, 1854–1912.* Rockford, Ill.: Press of Wilson Brothers Company, 1912.

Clark, Gregory, and S. Michael Halloran, eds. *Oratorical Culture in Nineteenth-Century America: Transformations in the Theory and Practice of Rhetoric.* Carbondale: Southern Illinois University Press, 1993.

Cochran, Thomas C. *Frontiers of Change: Early Industrialism in America.* New York: Oxford University Press, 1981.

———. *Railroad Leaders 1845–1890: The Business Mind in Action.* New York: Russell and Russell, 1965.

Coleman, Laurence Vail. *The Museum in America: A Critical Study.* Washington: American Association of Museums, 1939.

Colley, Linda. *Britons: Forging the Nation, 1707–1837.* New Haven: Yale University Press, 1992.

Cornish, Dudley Taylor. *The Sable Arm: Negro Troops in the Union Army, 1861–1865.* New York: W. W. Norton and Co., 1966.

Cott, Nancy F. *The Bonds of Womanhood: "Woman's Sphere" in New England.* New Haven: Yale University Press, 1977.

Cox, LaWanda. *Lincoln and Black Freedom: A Study in Presidential Leadership.* Urbana: University of Illinois Press, 1985.

Curti, Merle. *Roots of American Loyalty.* New York: Columbia University Press, 1946.

Dahl, Robert. *Who Governs? Democracy and Power in an American City.* New Haven: Yale University Press, 1961.

Davis, Cullom, ed. *The Public and Private Lincoln: Contemporary Perspectives.* Carbondale: Southern Illinois University Press, 1979.

Davis, Susan. *Parades and Power: Street Theatre in Nineteenth Century Philadelphia.* Philadelphia: Temple University Press, 1986.

Donald, David. *Lincoln.* New York: Simon and Schuster, 1995.

———. *Lincoln Reconsidered.* New York: Vintage Books, 1961.

DuBois, Carol Ellen. *Feminism and Suffrage: The Emergence of an Independent Women's Movement in America, 1848–1869*. Ithaca: Cornell University Press, 1978.

Duffy, Bernard K., and Halford R. Ryan, eds. *American Orators Before 1900: Critical Studies and Sources*. New York: Greenwood Press, 1987.

Dunning, William A. "The Second Birth of the Republican Party." *American Historical Review* 16 (October 1910): 56–63.

Dusinberre, William. *Civil War Issues in Philadelphia, 1856–1865*. Philadelphia: University of Pennsylvania Press, 1965.

Edelman, Murray. *Constructing the Political Spectacle*. Chicago: University of Chicago Press, 1988.

Faust, Drew Gilpin. *The Creation of Confederate Nationalism: Ideology and Identity in the Civil War South*. Baton Rouge: Louisiana State University Press, 1988.

Fehrenbacher, Don E. *Lincoln in Text and Context: Collected Essays*. Stanford: Stanford University Press, 1987.

———. "Only His Stepchildren: Lincoln and the Negro." *Civil War History* 20 (December 1974): 293–310.

Fletcher, George P. *Our Secret Constitution: How Lincoln Redefined American Democracy*. New York: Oxford University Press, 2001.

Foner, Eric. *Free Soil, Free Labor, Free Men: The Ideology of the Republican Party Before the Civil War*. New York: Oxford University Press, 1970.

———. "The Meaning of Freedom in the Age of Emancipation." *Journal of American History* (September 1994): 435–460.

———. *Politics and Ideology in the Age of the Civil War*. New York: Oxford University Press, 1980.

———. *Reconstruction: America's Unfinished Revolution,1863–1867*. New York: Harper and Row, 1988.

———. "Rights and the Constitution in Black Life During the Civil War and Reconstruction." *Journal of American History* 74 (December 1987): 863–883.

———. *The Story of American Freedom*. New York: W. W. Norton and Co., 1998.

———. *Tom Paine and Revolutionary America*. New York: Oxford University Press, 1976.

Foner, Philip S. *History of the Labor Movement in the United States*. Vol. 1. New York: International Publishers, 1947.

Formisano, Ronald, P. *The Birth of Mass Political Parties: Michigan, 1827–1861*. Princeton: Princeton University Press, 1971.

———. *The Transformation of Political Culture: Massachusetts Parties, 1790s–1840s*. New York: Oxford University Press, 1983.

Fredrickson, George M. *The Inner Civil War: Northern Intellectuals and the Crisis of the Union*. New York: Harper and Row, 1965.

———. "A Man but Not a Brother: Abraham Lincoln and Racial Equality." *Journal of Southern History* 41 (February 1975): 39–58.

———. "Nineteenth Century American History." In *Imagined Histories: American Historians Interpret the Past.* Edited by Anthony Molho and Gordon S. Wood. Princeton: Princeton University Press, 1998.

Freidel, Frank. *Francis Lieber: Nineteenth-Century Liberal.* Baton Rouge: Louisiana State University Press, 1947.

———. "The Loyal Publication Society: A Pro-Union Propaganda Agency." *Mississippi Valley Historical Review* 17 (December 1939).

Gallman, J. Matthew. "Voluntarism in Wartime: Philadelphia's Great Central Fair." In *Toward a Social History of the American Civil War: Exploratory Essays.* Edited by Maris A. Vinovskis. New York: Cambridge University Press, 1990.

———. *Mastering Wartime: A Social History of Philadelphia During the Civil War.* Philadelphia: University of Pennsylvania Press, 2000.

Garner, Stanton. *The Civil War World of Herman Melville.* Lawrence: University Press of Kansas, 1993.

Geertz, Clifford. *The Interpretation of Cultures.* New York: Basic Books, 1973.

Gellner, Ernest. *Nations and Nationalism.* Oxford: Blackwell, 1983.

George, Sister Mary Karl, R.S.M. *Zachariah Chandler: A Political Biography.* East Lansing: Michigan State University Press, 1969.

Gienapp, William E. *The Origins of the Republican Party, 1852–1856.* New York: Oxford University Press, 1987.

———. "Politics Seem to Enter into Everything." In *Essays on American Antebellum Politics, 1840–1860.* Edited by Stephen E. Maizlish and John J. Kushma. College Station: Texas A and M University Press, 1982.

Giesberg, Judith Ann. *Civil War Sisterhood: The U.S. Sanitary Commission and Women's Politics in Transition.* Boston: Northeastern University Press, 2000.

Ginzberg, Lori. *Women and the Work of Benevolence: Morality, Politics, and Class in the Nineteenth-Century United States.* New Haven: Yale University Press, 1990.

Glathaar, Joseph T. *Forged in Battle: The Civil War Alliance of Black Soldiers and White Officers.* New York: Free Press, 1990.

Goodwyn, Lawrence. *Democratic Promise: The Populist Moment in America.* New York: Oxford University Press, 1976.

Grant, Susan-Mary. *North Over South: Northern Nationalism and American Identity in the Antebellum Era.* Lawrence: University Press of Kansas, 2000.

Greenfeld, Liah. *Nationalism: Five Roads to Modernity.* Cambridge: Harvard University Press, 1992.

———. "The Modern Religion?" *Critical Review* 10, no. 2 (spring 1996): 169–191.

Griffith, Elisabeth. *In Her Own Right: The Life of Elizabeth Cady Stanton.* New York: Oxford University Press, 1984.

Gunn, L. Ray. *The Decline of Authority: Public Economic Policy and Political Development in New York, 1800–1860.* Ithaca: Cornell University Press, 1988.

Hall, Peter Dobkin. *The Organization of American Culture, 1700–1900.* New York: New York University Press, 1982.

Hammond, Bray. *Sovereignty and an Empty Purse: Banks and Politics in the Civil War.* Princeton: Princeton University Press, 1970.

Hammond, Jabez. *History of Political Parties in the State of New York.* Syracuse: Hall, Mills, and Company, 1852.

Handlin, Oscar. *Boston's Immigrants.* Cambridge: Belknap Press of Harvard University Press, 1959.

Hanson, Stephen L. *The Making of the Third Party System, Voters and Parties in Illinois, 1850–1876.* Ann Arbor: UMI Research Press, 1980.

Harding, Vincent. *There Is a River: The Black Struggle for Freedom in America.* 1981; reprint, New York: Vintage Books, 1983.

Harris, Neil. *The Artist in American Society: The Formative Years, 1790–1860.* New York: G. Braziller, 1966.

———. *Humbug: The Art of P. T. Barnum.* Boston: Little, Brown, 1973.

Hesseltine, William B. *Lincoln and the War Governors.* New York: Alfred A. Knopf, 1955.

Hewitt, Nancy A. *Women's Activism and Social Change: Rochester, New York, 1822–1872.* Ithaca: Cornell University Press, 1984.

Hobsbawm, E. J. *Nations and Nationalism Since 1780: Programme, Myth, Reality.* Cambridge: Cambridge University Press, 1990.

Hobsbawm, E. J., and Terence Ranger, eds. *The Invention of Tradition.* Cambridge: Cambridge University Press, 1983.

Hofstadter, Richard. *The American Political Tradition.* New York: Vintage Books, 1948.

———. *The Idea of a Party System: The Rise of Legitimate Opposition in the United States, 1780–1840.* Berkeley: University of California Press, 1969.

Holloway, Jean. *Edward Everett Hale.* Austin: University of Texas Press, 1956.

Holt, Michael F. *Political Parties and American Political Development: From the Age of Jackson to the Age of Lincoln.* Baton Rouge: Louisiana State University Press, 1992.

Howard, Robert P. *A History of the Prairie State.* Grand Rapids, Mich.: William B. Eederman's Publishing Company, 1972.

Howe, Daniel Walker. *The Political Culture of the American Whigs.* Chicago: University of Chicago Press, 1979.

———. *The Unitarian Conscience: Harvard Moral Philosophy, 1805–1861.* Cambridge: Harvard University Press, 1970.

Irwin, Will, Earl Chapin May, and Joseph Hotchkiss. *A History of the Union League Club of New York City.* New York: Dodd, Mead, 1952.

Jahar, Frederic Cople. *The Urban Establishment: Upper Strata in Boston, New York, Charleston, Chicago, and Los Angeles.* Urbana: University of Illinois Press, 1982.

Jentz, John. "The Anti-Slavery Constituency in Jacksonian New York City." *Civil War History* 27 (1981): 101–122.

Jimerson, Randall C. *The Private Civil War: Popular Thought During the Sectional Conflict*. Baton Rouge: Louisiana State University Press, 1988.

Jones, Howard Mumford, and Bessie Zaban Jones, eds. *The Many Voices of Boston: A Historical Anthology, 1630–1975*. Boston: Little, Brown, 1975.

Josephson, Matthew. *The Robber Barons: The Great American Capitalists, 1861–1901*. New York: Harcourt, Brace and Co., 1934.

Judd, Dennis R., and Todd Swanstrom. *City Politics: Private Power and Public Policy*. New York: Harper Collins College Publishers, 1994.

Kaczorowski, Robert J. "To Begin the Nation Anew: Congress, Citizenship, and Civil Rights after the Civil War." *American Historical Review* 92 (February 1987): 45–68.

Kammen, Michael. *Mystic Chords of Memory: The Transformation of Tradition in American Culture*. New York: Vintage Books, 1991.

Kantor, Alvin Robert, and Marjorie Sered Kantor. *Sanitary Fairs: A Philatelic and Historical Study of Civil War Benevolences*. Glencoe, Ill.: S. F. Publishing, 1992.

Kennedy, David M. *Over Here: The First World War and American Society*. New York: Oxford University Press, 1980.

Kennedy, William Sloane. "Edward Everett Hale." *Century Illustrated Monthly Magazine*, January 1885.

Kerber, Linda. *Women of the Republic: Intellect and Ideology in Revolutionary America*. Chapel Hill: University of North Carolina Press, 1980.

Klement, Frank. "Carrington and the Golden Circle Legend in Indiana During the Civil War," *Indiana Magazine of History* 61 (1965): 31–52.

———. "Copperhead Secret Societies in Illinois During the Civil War." *Journal of the Illinois State Historical Society* 68 (1955): 152–180.

———. *The Copperheads in the Middlewest*. Chicago: University of Chicago Press, 1960.

———. *Dark Lanterns: Secret Political Societies, Conspiracies, and Treason Trials in the Civil War*. Baton Rouge: Louisiana State University Press, 1984.

———. *The Limits of Dissent: Clement L. Vallandigham and the Civil War*. Lexington: University Press of Kentucky, 1970.

Kohn, Hans. *American Nationalism: An Interpretive Essay*. New York: The Macmillan Co., 1957.

———. *The Idea of Nationalism: A Study of Its Origins and Background*. New York: Macmillan Co., 1944.

Kraditor, Aileen. *Means and Ends in American Abolitionism, 1834–1850*. New York: Vintage Books, 1967.

Larson, Harriet. *Jay Cooke: Private Banker*. Cambridge: Harvard University Press, 1936.

Leon, Warren, and Roy Rosenzweig, eds. *History Museums in the United States: A Critical Assessment*. Urbana: University of Illinois Press, 1989.

Macpherson, C. B. *The Political Theory of Possessive Individualism: Hobbes to Locke*. New York: Clarendon Press, 1962.

Martin, Waldo E., Jr. *The Mind of Frederick Douglass*. Chapel Hill: University of North Carolina Press, 1984.

Massey, Mary Elizabeth. *Bonnet Brigades*. New York: Alfred A. Knopf, 1966.

Matthews, Glenna. *The Rise of Public Woman: Woman's Power and Woman's Place in the United States, 1630–1970*. New York: Oxford University Press, 1992.

Maxwell, William Quentin. *Lincoln's Fifth Wheel: The Political History of the United States Sanitary Commission*. New York: Longmans, Green, 1956.

McClay, Wifred M. *The Masterless: Self and Society in Modern America*. Chapel Hill: University of North Carolina Press, 1994.

McConnell, Stewart. *Glorious Contentment: The Grand Army of the Republic 1865–1900*. Chapel Hill: University of North Carolina Press, 1992.

McFeely, William S. *Frederick Douglass*. New York: W. W. Norton and Co., 1991.

McKitrick, Eric. "Party Politics and the Union and Confederate War Efforts." In *The American Party Systems*. Edited by Walter Dean Burnham and William Chambers. New York: Oxford University Press, 1967.

McPherson, James M. *Abraham Lincoln and the Second American Revolution*. New York: Oxford University Press, 1990.

———. *Battle Cry of Freedom: The Civil War Era*. New York: Oxford University Press, 1988.

———. *For Cause and Comrades: Why Men Fought in the Civil War*. New York: Oxford University Press, 1997.

———. *The Negro's Civil War: How American Blacks Felt and Acted During the War for the Union*. New York: Ballantine Books, 1991.

———. *The Struggle for Equality: Abolitionists and the Negro in the Civil War and Reconstruction*. Princeton: Princeton University Press, 1964.

Mendte, J. Robert. *The Union League of Philadelphia: 125 years*. Devon, Pa.: Union League of Philadelphia, 1987.

Meyers, Marvin. *The Jacksonian Persuasion*. Stanford, Calif.: Stanford University Press, 1957.

Miller, Randall M., Harry S. Stout, and Charles Reagan Wilson, eds. *Religion and the American Civil War*. New York: Oxford University Press, 1998.

Mills, C. Wright. *The Power Elite*. New York: Oxford University Press, 1956.

Miroff, Bruce. *Icons of Democracy: American Leaders as Heroes, Aristocrats, Dissenters, and Democrats*. Lawrence: University Press of Kansas, 2000.

Montgomery, David. *Beyond Equality: Labor and the Radical Republicans, 1862–1872*. Urbana: University of Illinois Press, 1981.

Moore, Barrington. *Social Origins of Dictatorship and Democracy: Lord and Peasant in the Making of the Modern World*. Boston: Beacon Press, 1966.

Moorhead, James H. *American Apocalypse: Yankee Protestants and the Civil War, 1860–1869*. New Haven: Yale University Press, 1978.

Moreland, Willis D., and Erwin H. Goldenstein. *Pioneers in Adult Education*. Chicago: Nelson Hall Publishers, 1985.

Morgan, Edmund P. *American Slavery, American Freedom: The Ordeal of Colonial Virginia*. New York: Norton, 1975.

Murdock, Eugene C. *One Million Men: The Civil War Draft in the North*. Madison: Historical Society of Wisconsin, 1971.

Nagel, Paul C. *One Nation Indivisible: The Union in American Thought*. New York: Oxford University Press, 1964.

———. *This Sacred Trust*. New York: Oxford University Press, 1971.

Naveh, Eyal J. *Crown of Thorns: Political Martyrdom in America from Abraham Lincoln to Martin Luther King, Jr*. New York: New York University Press, 1990.

Neely, Mark E., Jr. *The Fate of Liberty: Abraham Lincoln and Civil Liberties*. New York: Oxford University Press, 1991.

Nevins, Allan. "A Major Result of the Civil War." *Civil War History* 5 (September 1959): 237–250.

———. *The War for the Union*, vols. 1–4. New York: Charles Scribner's Sons, 1959–1971.

Norton, Mary Beth. *Liberty's Daughters: The Revolutionary Experience of American Women, 1750–1800*. Boston: Little, Brown, 1980.

Oates, Stephen B. *Abraham Lincoln: The Man Behind the Myth*. New York: Harper and Row, 1984.

———. *With Malice Toward None: The Life of Abraham Lincoln*. New York: Mentor Books, 1977.

Oberholtzer, Ellis Paxson. *Jay Cooke: Financier of the Civil War*. Philadelphia: G. W. Jacobs and Co., 1907.

O'Leary, Cecilia. *To Die For: The Paradox of American Patriotism*. Princeton: Princeton University Press, 1999.

Palladino, Grace. *Another Civil War: Labor, Capital, and the State in the Anthracite Regions of Pennsylvania, 1840–1868*. Urbana: University of Illinois Press, 1990.

Paludan, Phillip Shaw. *"A People's Contest": The Union and the Civil War, 1861–1865*. New York: Harper and Row, 1988.

———. *The Presidency of Abraham Lincoln*. Lawrence: University Press of Kansas, 1994.

Parish, Peter J. *The American Civil War*. New York: Holmes and Meier Publishers, 1975.

Patterson, Robert T. "Government Finance on the Eve of the Civil War." *Journal of Economic History* 12 (1952): 35–44.

Pearson, Henry Greenleaf. *An American Railroad Builder: John Murray Forbes*. New York: Houghton Mifflin, 1911.

Peterson, Merrill D. *The Great Triumvirate: Webster, Clay, and Calhoun*. New York: Oxford University Press, 1987.

———. *Lincoln in American Memory*. New York: Oxford University Press, 1994.

Pierson, William Whatley. "The Committee on the Conduct of the Civil War." *American Historical Review* 23 (April 1918): 550–576.

Porter, George H. *Ohio Politics During the Civil War Period*. New York: AMS Press, 1911.

Potter, David. *The Impending Crisis: 1848–1861*. New York: Harper Torchbooks, 1976.

———. *The South and the Sectional Conflict*. Baton Rouge: Louisiana State University Press, 1968.

Quarles, Benjamin. *The Negro in the Civil War*. Boston: Little, Brown, 1953.

———. *Lincoln and the Negro*. New York: Oxford University Press, 1962.

Reynolds, David S. *Walt Whitman's America: A Cultural Biography*. New York: Alfred A. Knopf, 1995.

Richardson, Heather. *The Greatest Nation of the Earth: Republican Economic Policies During the Civil War*. Cambridge: Harvard University Press, 1997.

Rogin, Michael Paul. *Subversive Genealogy: The Politics and Art of Herman Melville*. New York: Alfred A. Knopf, 1983.

Rosenzweig, Roy, and Elizabeth Blackmar. *The Park and the People: A History of Central Park*. New York: Cornell University Press, 1992.

Ross, Kristie. "Arranging a Doll's House: Refined Women as Union Nurses." In *Divided Houses: Gender and the Civil War*. Edited by Catherine Clinton and Nina Silber. New York: Oxford University Press, 1992.

Ryan, Mary P. *Cradle of the Middle Class: The Family in Oneida County, New York, 1790–1865*. New York: Cambridge University Press, 1981.

Samuel, Raphael, ed. *Patriotism: The Making and Unmaking of British National Identity*. Vols. 1 and 2. London: Routledge, 1989.

Saum, Lewis O. *The Popular Mood of Pre–Civil War America*. Westport, Conn.: Greenwood Press, 1980.

Schaar, John H. "The Case for Patriotism." In *Legitimacy in the Modern State*. New Brunswick, N.J.: Transaction Books, 1981.

Schlesinger, Arthur M., Jr., ed. *History of U.S. Political Parties*. Vol. 2. New York: Chelsea House Publishers, 1973.

Sellers, Charles. *The Market Revolution: Jacksonian America, 1815–1846*. New York: Oxford University Press, 1991.

Shalhope, Robert E. "Toward a Republican Synthesis: The Emergence of an Understanding of Republicanism in American Historiography." *William and Mary Quarterly* 29 (1972): 49–80.

Shankman, Arnold M. *The Pennsylvania Antiwar Movement, 1861–1865*. Rutherford, N.J.: Fairleigh Dickinson University Press, 1980.

Sherwin, Oscar. *Prophet of Liberty: The Life and Times of Wendell Phillips*. New York: Bookman Associates, 1958.

Silbey, Joel H. *The American Political Nation, 1838–1893*. Stanford: Stanford University Press, 1991.

———. *A Respectable Minority: The Democratic Party in the Civil War Era, 1860–1868*. New York: W. W. Norton and Co., 1977.

Skowronek, Stephen. *Building a New American State: The Expansion of National Administrative Capacities, 1877–1920*. New York: Cambridge University Press, 1982.

Smith, Elbert B. *Francis Preston Blair*. New York: Free Press, 1980.

Smith, George Winston. "Broadsides for Freedom: Civil War Propaganda in New England." *New England Quarterly* (September 1948): 292.

Smith, Rogers. *Civic Ideals: Conflicting Visions of Citizenship in U.S. History.* New Haven: Yale University Press, 1997.

Stampp, Kenneth M. *And the War Came: The North and the Secession Crisis.* Baton Rouge: Louisiana State University Press, 1950.

———. *Indiana Politics During the Civil War.* Bloomington: Indiana University Press, 1949.

Stewart, James Brewer. *Holy Warriors: The Abolitionists and American Slavery.* New York: Hill and Wang, 1976.

———. *Wendell Phillips: Liberty's Hero.* Baton Rouge: Louisiana State University Press, 1986.

Stillinger, Elizabeth. *The Antiquers.* New York: Alfred A. Knopf, 1980.

Studenski, Paul, and Herman E. Kroos. *Financial History of the United States.* New York: McGraw-Hill, 1952.

Tambini, Damian. "Explaining Monoculturalism: Beyond Gellner's Theory of Nationalism." *Critical Review* 10, no. 2 (spring 1996): 251–270.

Tap, Bruce. *Over Lincoln's Shoulder: The Committee on the Conduct of the War.* Lawrence: University Press of Kansas, 1998.

Thompson, William Y. "Sanitary Fairs of the Civil War." *Civil War History* 4 (March 1958): 51–67.

Thurow, Glen E. "Abraham Lincoln and American Political Religion." In *The Historian's Lincoln: Pseudohistory, Psychohistory, and History.* Edited by Gabor S. Boritt. Urbana: University of Illinois Press, 1988.

Tilly, Charles, ed. *The Formation of National States in Western Europe.* Princeton: Princeton University Press, 1975.

Trefousse, Hans L. *Benjamin Wade Franklin: Radical Republican from Ohio.* New York: Twayne Publishers, 1963.

———. "The Joint Committee on the Conduct of the War: A Reassessment." *Civil War History* 10 (1964): 5–19.

———. *The Radical Republicans: Lincoln's Vanguard for Racial Justice.* New York: Alfred A. Knopf, 1969.

———. "The Republican Party, 1854–1864." In *History of U.S. Political Parties.* Vol. 2. Edited by Arthur M. Schlesinger, Jr. New York: R. R. Bowker, 1973.

Turner, Thomas Reed. *Beware the People Weeping: Public Opinion and the Assassination of Abraham Lincoln.* Baton Rouge: Louisiana State University Press, 1982.

———. "Beware the People Weeping." In *The Historian's Lincoln: Pseudohistory, Psychohistory, and History.* Edited by Gabor S. Boritt. Urbana: University of Illinois Press, 1988.

Tyrrell, Martin. "Nation-States and States of Mind: Nationalism as Psychology." *Critical Review* 10, no. 2 (spring 1996): 233–250.

Vanderbilt, Kermit. *Charles Eliot Norton: Apostle of Culture in a Democracy.* Cambridge: Belknap Press of Harvard University Press, 1959.

Venet, Wendy Hamand. *Neither Ballots Nor Bullets: Women Abolitionists and the Civil War.* Charlottesville: University Press of Virginia, 1991.

Vinovskis, Maris A. "Have Social Historians Lost the Civil War? Some Preliminary Demographic Speculations." In *Toward a Social History of the American Civil War: Exploratory Essays.* Edited by Maris A. Vinovskis. New York: Cambridge University Press, 1990, pp. 1–30.

Viroli, Maurizio. *For Love of Country: An Essay on Patriotism and Nationalism.* New York: Oxford University Press, 1995.

Wade, Richard C. *The Urban Frontier: The Rise of the Western Cities, 1790–1830.* Cambridge: Harvard University Press, 1959.

Wald, Priscilla. *Constituting Americans: Cultural Anxiety and Narrative Form.* Durham, N.C.: Duke University Press, 1995.

Wallace, Michael. "Changing Concepts of Party in the United States: New York in 1815–1828." *American Historical Review* 74 (December 1968): 471–474.

Walters, Ronald G. *The Anti-Slavery Appeal: American Abolitionism After 1830.* Baltimore: Johns Hopkins University Press, 1976.

Ware, Edith E. "Committees of Public Information, 1863–1866." *Historical Outlook* 10 (February 1919): 65–66.

Warner, Sam Bass. *The Private City: Philadelphia in Three Periods of Its Growth.* Philadelphia: University of Pennsylvania Press, 1968.

Watson, Harry L. *Jacksonian Politics and Community Conflict: The Emergence of the Second Party System in Cumberland County, North Carolina.* Baton Rouge: Louisiana State University Press, 1981.

———. *Liberty and Power: The Politics of Jacksonian America.* New York: The Noonday Press, 1990.

Welter, Rush. *The Mind of America, 1820–1860.* New York: Columbia University Press, 1975.

West, Patricia. *Domesticating History: The Political Origins of America's House Museums.* Washington, D.C.: Smithsonian Institution Press, 1999.

Westbrook, Robert. "'I Want a Girl, Just Like the Girl That Married Harry James': American Women and the Problem of Political Obligation in World War II." *American Quarterly* 42, no. 4 (December 1990): 587–614.

Whiteman, Maxwell. *Gentlemen in Crisis: The First Century of the Union League of Philadelphia, 1862–1962.* Philadelphia: Union League of Philadelphia, 1975.

Whites, Leeann. "The Civil War as a Crisis in Gender." In *Divided Houses: Gender and the Civil War.* Edited by Catherine Clinton and Nina Silber. New York: Oxford University Press, 1992.

Widmer, Edward L. *Young America: The Flowering of Democracy in New York City.* New York: Oxford University Press, 1999.

Wiebe, Robert H. *The Opening of American Society: From the Adoption of the Constitution to the Eve of Disunion.* New York: Alfred A. Knopf, 1984.

———. *Self-Rule: A Cultural History of American Democracy.* Chicago: University of Chicago Press, 1995.

Williams, T. Harry. *Lincoln and His Generals*. New York: Vintage Books, 1952.
———. *Lincoln and the Radicals*. Madison: University of Wisconsin Press, 1960.
Wills, Garry. *Lincoln at Gettysburg: The Words That Remade America*. New York: Simon and Schuster, 1992.
Wilson, Edmund. *Patriotic Gore: Studies in the Literature of the American Civil War*. New York: Farrar, Straus and Giroux, 1977.
Wilson, Major. *Space, Time, and Freedom: The Quest for American Nationality*. Westport, Conn.: Greenwood Press, 1974.
Wood, Gordon S. *The Creation of the American Republic*. Chapel Hill: University of North Carolina, 1969.
———. *The Radicalism of the American Revolution*. New York: Alfred A. Knopf, 1992.
Xenos, Nicholas. "Civic Nationalism: Oxymoron?" *Critical Review* 10, no. 2 (spring 1996): 213–231.
Yack, Bernard. "The Myth of the Civic Nation." *Critical Review* 10, no. 2 (spring 1996): 193–211.
Zelinsky, Wilbur. *Nation into State: The Shifting Symbolic Foundations of American Nationalism*. Chapel Hill: University of North Carolina Press, 1988.
Ziff, Larzer. *Literary Democracy: The Declaration of Cultural Independence in America*. New York: Penguin Books, 1982.

Dissertations

Beckert, Sven. "The Making of New York City's Bourgeoisie, 1850–1886." Columbia University, 1995.
Cardwell, Gary Lee. "The Rise of the Stalwarts and the Transformation of Illinois Republican Politics, 1860–1880." University of Virginia, 1976.
Gibson, Guy. "Lincoln's League: The Union League Movement During the Civil War." University of Illinois, 1957.
James, Nancy Esther. "Realism in Romance: A Critical Study of the Short Stories of Edward Everett Hale." Pennsylvania State University, 1969.
Silvestro, Clement. "None But Patriots: The Union Leagues in the Civil War and Reconstruction." University of Wisconsin, 1959.
Smith, George Winston. "Generative Forces of Union Propaganda: A Study of Civil War Pressure Groups." University of Wisconsin, 1940.
West, Patricia. "Clio at Home: Historic House Museums and the History of Women." State University of New York at Binghamton, 1988.
Young, James Harvey. "Anna Elizabeth Dickinson and the Civil War." University of Illinois, 1941.

Index

Page references in *italic type* indicate illustrations.